Hooray for Momfidence!

"Finally! A mom who parents from her gut, not her guilt! Paula Spencer dares to trust her instincts and her common sense, while humorously inspiring readers to do the same. Advice as sensible as it is entertaining."

—JOHN ROSEMOND, syndicated parenting columnist and author

"Paula Spencer leads by example and does so hysterically. I only wish I had a copy of this book when my children were younger. *Momfidence!* is a book every mother should keep close by for those inevitable 'have I totally screwed up' moments. A great gift for every mom who needs some perspective. I love this book."

—MIMI DOE, author of *Busy but Balanced* and founder of SpiritualParenting.com

"Toss away *all* your parental insecurities along with dust-gathering parent-advice books as Paula Spencer provides you with both wondrous comic relief and the 'Momfidence' to trust your own good sense!"

—STACY DEBROFF, founder, www.momcentral.com

"Smart, sassy, and . . . right on target! *Momfidence!* is *momderful!*"

—HARVEY KARP, M.D., pediatrician and author of *The Happiest Baby on the Block*

"Being informed is one thing. Being overwhelmed is another. Written with warmth, humor, and real-world wisdom, *Momfidence!* reminds parents to keep the advice that works, leave what doesn't, and cue-in to those all-important instincts that help families grow, thrive, and enjoy the ride."

—DEBBIE GLASSER, PH.D., past chair of Parenting Education Network

"*Momfidence!* is perfect mom food—good for you and a real treat. It's smart, inspiring, and makes you proud to be a mother."

—JANET CHAN, editorial director, *Parenting* and *Baby Talk*

Momfidence!

An Oreo Never Killed Anybody and
Other Secrets of Happier Parenting

PAULA SPENCER

 THREE RIVERS PRESS • NEW YORK

Published in the United States by Three Rivers Press, an imprint of the
Crown Publishing Group, a division of Random House, Inc., New York.
www.crownpublishing.com

Three Rivers Press and the Tugboat design are registered trademarks
of Random House, Inc.

Library of Congress Cataloging-in-Publication Data
Spencer, Paula.
    Momfidence! : an Oreo never killed anybody and other secrets
of happier parenting / Paula Spencer.—1st ed.
    Based on author's columns published in *Woman's Day*.
    1. Motherhood. 2. Mothers—Psychology. 3. Mother and
child. 4. Child rearing. 5. Parenting. 6. Homemakers—
Time management. I. Title.
HQ759.S652   2006
306.874'3—dc22   2006002464

ISBN-13: 978-0307-33742-9
ISBN-10: 0-307-33742-1

Printed in the United States of America

Design by Barbara Sturman

10 9 8 7 6 5 4 3 2 1

First Edition

For the main characters in my life,

with love,

George Moseley Spencer

and our Henry, Eleanor, Margaret, and Page

Contents

Momfidence!

Make Way for Momfidence!
Opening Pep Talk

You can call me crazy.

Call me a traitor.

Call me barking mad. (Four kids ages ten and under and a dachshund puppy will do that to a woman.)

Certain preschoolers have been known to call me a party-pooping Mrs. Tomato Head, while certain bigger kids prefer "so old fashioned." And you can call me those things, too.

But I just don't dog-pile on to this notion that motherhood has to be so hard.

This, from someone who makes a living by perpetuating the popular wisdom about how to raise healthy, happy kids.

I've studied the art of parenting at the feet of the masters—both the tall and the small. As a longtime magazine writer, I've interviewed scores of experts for hundreds of articles. I've read all their books. I've even authored a few myself. And did I mention giving birth four times in seven years? That's ten years—an entire decade of my life—of continuous diaper changing. If there were a frequent-changer club, I'd be lounging on a tropical beach right now, courtesy of my accumulated diaper points.

And I've come to the conclusion that moms are being sorely misled about the whole business.

I'll be the first to agree that we do lots of things that aren't fun—like having to mop up assorted bodily fluids, cork whines, and answer such questions at midnight as "Why do you get to sleep with Dad but I have to sleep alone?" Pesky, perhaps, but not *hard*.

We do perform a lot of hard labor. Hoisting the dead weight of a sleeping child from sofa to bed comes to mind. As does scaling mountains of laundry. And running marathons of errands (with miles to go before you sleep). All physical jobs, but not exactly grueling.

Momming is surely not as hard as other work I've tried—less monotonous than telephone soliciting, easier on the eyes than proofreading, and, well, not too different from my stints as a cafeteria dishwasher or a resident assistant in the wildest freshman dorm on campus. And I certainly had fun applying for parenthood.

My memories of the day I finally got the job are fond, too. Giving birth is a great way to get flowers, and there's nothing like that first sip of Diet Coke after nine months of deprivation (though labor, I grant you, does qualify as excruciatingly hard).

It's the prevailing expectations about motherhood that wear a body out. Today's diligent mom can't just do the weekly marketing and drop food down hungry gullets. She must buy fresh and whole and often, scanning labels for lethal trans fats and the many disguises of "white poison" (the staple formerly known as sugar) in order to prevent diabetes and heart attacks in her children forty years down the road. She must maintain 24/7 vigilance against random toxins and schools with lousy test scores. She can't holler or swat an errant bottom for fear of bruising a tender psyche (or of being arrested). She certainly shouldn't be letting Jimmy Neutron and Master Chief in the front door.

And lucky are the 98.9 percent of moms who have a child gifted in music, sports, dance, acting, mathematics, robotics, chess, emotional intelligence, and/or cancer research—or who just want their kid to get into Harvard. Those good moms also get to arrange carpools to practices six nights a week and take out third or fourth home mortgages to pay for the requisite specialty camps and international competitions. All while staying supermodel fit, thin, stylin', and "balanced" herself, of course, in order to be a positive role model.

The very verbs of modern motherhood—scheduling, stimulating, supporting, enriching, enrolling, enhancing, empowering, expanding, coaching, advocating—make me want to call everyone together for a big family nap.

Toiling in a Siberian labor camp is hard. Running for president is hard. Landing on Mars is hard. Trying to lose those last ten pounds is hard—especially once you can no longer legitimately call it "baby weight" because said baby has just started kindergarten.

But shepherding a child from helpless infancy to independent adulthood? I'd call that really important, time-consuming, exasperating, surprising, depressingly expensive, and occasionally nerve-racking—as well as a host of more positive adjectives. But hard? *It's only as hard as you make it.*

You can more or less wing it through parenthood and your child will still soar. *Winging it,* according to my *Cambridge International Dictionary of Idioms,* means "to do the best you can in a situation you're not prepared for," which pretty well defines my freefall into parenthood. It's not like whole generations of our species haven't been raised without the benefit of Baby Einstein or Drs. Spock and Phil.

Five little ingredients are missing from most motherhood messages, and it's time they became part of our lives again.

1. Instinct
. . . .

"Are you an attachment parent?" a woman asks me, conspiratorially, at a party. We're sitting off to one side, breast-feeding our newborns.

"Well, she's attached now."

"So how does your husband like the family bed?" she asks next, warming to the subject. "Sam complains he can't sleep. I can't either because I'm worried we'll squash the baby."

"Have you tried a crib?"

She looks at me as though I've just suggested giving her baby a cocktail of Similac and Sominex. "But that would mess up our bonding. I couldn't leave her all by herself. She's used to me."

"But you're not sleeping."

"Oh, it's just a few years until she's weaned."

Too late, I see where this conversation is heading. *Co-sleeping. Baby wearing. Gentle discipline. Child-led weaning.* Mommying by the numbers. My new friend does not want to hear that my tot sleeps alone down the hall without even a baby monitor because we needed to borrow its batteries for an ailing Game Boy six months ago. I love my Snugli, but it has less to do with building secure attachment than with keeping two hands free to load the dishwasher. I'm breast-feeding in the middle of this party not as an act of "lactivism"—although I have discreetly opened my shirt in stores, in planes, on trains, and probably in the rain and while reading Dr. Seuss aloud—but to stop my other three kids from slipping half-eaten canapés back onto the trays. I certainly don't plan to keep at it until my daughter can walk up and ask for "Mommy juice" when she's perfectly capable of holding her own Hi-C box. By the time each of my kids' first teeth came in, I figured they had leached from my milk enough protective antibodies (whatever those are) to tide them over until they were old enough to learn how to wash their hands and use a Kleenex.

Plain old parenting is exhausting enough. Now we're supposed to pick a "style": attachment parenting, mindful parenting, playful parenting, proactive parenting, unconditional parenting, scream-free parenting.

Okay, fine. Mine is parenting by the seat of my black stretch pants.

2. Reality

Being an enlightened, forward-thinking, *People*-magazine-reading American consumer, I'm as drawn to what's new as the next sucker. I follow the hottest child development theories. I scan the headlines for the latest controlled double-blind study. (Even if they never seem to probe the sorts of things I *really* want to know, like why oh why won't kids lick around the base of the ice-cream cone?)

Before I change the way I mom, however, I want to know a few salient facts that the *Journal of Advanced Child Navel Gazing* never reports.

- How many of the MDs, PhDs, and EDs who author the studies behind all the Latest Advice actually live with kids who snarf Scooby-Doo Fruit Roll-Rups with Tongue Tattoos and whine for electronics so cool and new that no adult in the house has heard of them yet?
- When was the last time the reporters who spread the word about the Latest Advice played Beat the Late-for-School Clock or Find the Missing Shin Guard (or even more realistically, both games simultaneously)?

- Have America's favorite telegenic authority figurines—whose eye-opening TV segments finally codify the Latest Advice into All the Rage as of This Millisecond—faced off lately against a naked toddler calling them a "poopy doopy snortypants who wees in your butt"?

Parenting instructions that aren't smudged with peanut butter and underscored in red crayon risk sounding like so much momfoolery.

3. Common Sense

What makes a happy child? Chocolate cake for breakfast! A ban on homework! Christmas every day! Or so my kids tell me anyway. No mom in her right mind would give all those things. And yet we all find ourselves doing other things that are just as irrational.

Why worry whether to teach your baby sign language when you speak English? Why buy dolls called Bratz and play clothes emblazoned with the brand name B.U.M. when you'd slug a mom who used such words to describe your own child?

Why fear letting your kids walk two blocks to school by themselves down a quiet lane if you don't think twice about strapping them into two tons of steel and dialing Dad on the cell from behind the wheel while you're hollering at them to quit pinching one another and sipping a caffe latte grande no foam to go?

Why drive three hours to watch a pack of fourth-graders chase a ball around a field, when all the local playgrounds are empty? Why contort myself into an empathetic pretzel to respect my child's feelings when she's not respecting mine—and besides, we're late?

Why does everybody keep repeating platitudes that can't possibly be true? Babies must never cry. Sugar makes kids hyper. "No" damages a budding psyche. There is such a thing as siblings without rivalry.

I used to think nonsense was the province of kids. But all around I see evidence that this assumption is, well, nonsense.

4. Fun
....

Another underreported aspect of momming is the fun. Over the years, editors have deleted many surprising things from the parenting articles I write. One editor said I couldn't recommend that children burn off energy on a rainy day by jumping on an old sofa, for example. (They could get hurt!) Another said no dice to thinly spreading peanut butter on a toddler's sandwich. (Under age three they might develop allergies and die, don't you know!) Yet another edited out a seemingly innocuous reference to the fact that my kids played with squirt guns in summer. (One word: Columbine.)

No squirt guns! No jumping! No PBJ! What kind of childhood is that?

Raising kids has become such a dreary business. Spending eighteen years cutting the lawn with baby nail clippers sounds more enjoyable than the endless safety proofing, neural-pathway stimulating, self-esteem buffing, and college application plotting that modern motherhood now demands. And that's just the prekindergarten plan.

Ever notice how the good-mothering messages always focus on the dark side? We're alerted to lists of warning signs so long that every toddler on the planet proves a candidate for ADHD and every teen is ripe for suicide. We know more about dreadful, if rare, conditions than we do about the perfectly normal disgusting realities of life with kids (which no doubt explains why the average mother is better prepared to deal with radiation sickness than poop jokes). We're given cautionary scripts for how to talk and how to listen that imply just barking out a simple command would be ruinous. We're coached with a zillion tips for raising an eager learner, a curious mind, an active body—as if those things didn't come naturally to a child. We're soberly urged to shield our kids from diseases that may have started well before our own DNA was strung or that may not show up in them until long after we're in the grave ourselves.

All of which is pretty ironic, considering that the kids themselves are a riot. They're cute. They say funny things. They act goofy. They make you laugh.

And here's the best part: You don't have to do anything extraordinary to achieve these magical effects. You don't have to tumble on the floor if you don't want to, or sign up for Mommy and Me music appreciation class or cruise the Caribbean on the Big Red Boat. You don't even have to buy stuff to unleash the fun (not even that mind-numbing tot favorite Candyland, unless you have a built-in sibling to sit there and roll the dice over and over until the board is upended in a tantrum).

You just have to let them be kids. Which, I realize, is an increasingly difficult proposition in a land where six-month-olds need lapware for their own PCs, six-year-olds wear pro-quality team uniforms, preteens use makeup, and liposuction and steroids are seen as boons to teen self-esteem. These things would be comical if they weren't so sad. But they're not fun.

5. Parents

. . . .

More than anything, though, what's missing in most of the dreary canon on child rearing today is . . . parents!

It's always about the child. How to make the child smarter, healthier, happier, sleepier. How to support one who's "spirited" or "sensitive" or has "high needs." How to discipline without diluting your child's essence. (As if!) How to track his every move with sleep logs, potty logs, growth charts, and chore charts. How to rear a child who's more secure, more confident, more obedient, more motivated, more likely to make it to the Ivy League so he or she, too, can join the rat race and raise hypercompetitive kids who will make it to the Ivy League and . . . wait a minute!

Don't we parents count for something? Sure, raising kids demands a certain amount of sacrifice—new Manolo knockoffs can be hard to justify when lots of little feet are outgrowing their Wal-Mart specials every six weeks, to name just one example. A certain (huge!) amount of sleeplessness, mind-numbing repetitiveness, and plain old "being there" simply go with the territory, and most parents semicheerfully supply it. But must all the directives for "good" moms and dads require infinite patience and selflessness?

Can't we ever lose our tempers? Or play the music *we* like in the car? When did everybody else's unending happiness and success become our sole responsibility?

When do we get to send ourselves to time out?

Enough, already! It's time to hear how we *parents* get to be smarter, healthier, happier, and saner.

Instinct. Reality. Common sense. Fun. Parents. These five little ideas are the building blocks of something I call Momfidence.

Momfidence is an attitude. It's the confidence that comes from parenting by your gut, not your guilt. Tuning out the oughta-woulda-shouldas and trusting your own good sense. Being more mellow on the outside, less marshmallow on the inside. Doing what works for you—experts, headlines, playgroup pals, neighbor ladies, grandmas, and the long shadows of TV Land perfectamoms be danged. Worrying about the next ten minutes, not ten years, down the road. Skimming the latest child-rearing advice and tossing out two-thirds. Realizing that most issues mothers face can't be neatly condensed into a handy checklist of bulleted, boldfaced tips. Winging it. It's a lot harder than you'd think to scar a kid for life.

Momfidence is a lost art. It's daring to be laid-back in a tensed-up world. It's reality parenting for surreal times.

Having Momfidence won't make your children happy all the time. (But that's not your job.) You might earn some raised eyebrows on your cul de sac. (You'll live.) You'll surely have to forfeit a spot in the PC Hall of Fame. (A dubious distinction in any case.) And Momfidence won't prevent you from making some mistakes along the way. (You'd make them anyway.)

You will, however, sleep better at night! You will destress and obsess less. You'll enjoy your kids more—and, perhaps, vice versa. You'll probably save money and certainly save sanity. Think of it—sleep!

Works for me.

I began this book by writing a considerably more defensive take on my contrarian ideas. My eight-year-old spotted a draft lying on my desk. She pointed to the title: "How You, Too, Can Be the Worst Mom on Earth." "What's that?"

"Oh, it's a book I might write."

"Why is it called that?"

"It's a joke."

"Well, I don't think it's very funny!" she cried indignantly. "You're the best mom I ever had!"

Good mothering, ultimately, is in the eye of the beneficiary. Too often we play to a crowd that doesn't count: to the advice-mongers in the media, to future college admissions officers, to the imagined stares of perfect strangers, to the darting eyes of other insecure mommies. Worst of all, we play to the perfect mother of all mothers who exists exclusively in our heads.

The reassuring truth: The only audience that matters is the one we tuck in at night. Knowing that is one thing. But will we let ourselves believe it?

Make way for Momfidence.

Why Not *Dad*fidence?

Because guilt is a girl thing. Moms pretty much have the monopoly on it. Even the very best fathers—a prime specimen of which I am blessed to have in my own home—just don't get all our child-related stressing, obsessing, self blame, and tears.

Maybe they're inoculated by virtue of never having experienced hormonal fireworks or fetal kicks from the inside out. Or maybe it's that fathers simply get exposed to fewer feverish conversations with other mothers and fewer episodes of *A Baby Story* on TLC. Possible exception: I'm willing to wager that some at-home dads experience guilt in direct proportion to how many lap hours they log.

Truth is, most guys—even the postmodern hands-on, diaper-handy variety—don't care much what someone else thinks they're "supposed" to be doing. They don't take hints very well, much less flat-out suggestions. They didn't grow up reading catchy lists of dos and don'ts. They're genetically predisposed not to ask for directions.

Thus, they manage to elude much of the Advice Mafia. Undistracted by the information overload, they're able to zero in on what's important: The kid.

Is he and/or she alive? Check.

Loved? Check.

Secure? Check.

Happy (more or less)? Check.

Well fed? Well educated? Well mannered (more or less)? Check, check, check.

Everything's fine, dear. Turn off the damn baby monitor and come here, you hot mama.

(Come to think of it, my own kids' Daddyo is the most Momfident person I know.)

Don't Cry Over Spilt Guilt
On the Oughta-Woulda-Shouldas

Oughta *be playing Candyland instead of sitting here logged on to eBay with a glass of merlot. Woulda signed up to chaperone the class party— if only I'd remembered to check the backpack and find the call for help in the first place. Coulda avoided that cavity, if only I'd started rubbing my baby's gums spotless with sterile gauze back when he was toothless. Shoulda—really shoulda—deleted that expletive before it came out in the car on the way to Brownies.*

But didn't.

There go the Good Mommy points I racked up making Rice Krispies treats from scratch. Scout troop leader, 10 points. PTA dodger, −10. Snuggling, 5 points. Itching to flip through fat new catalog that slid out of lap while snuggling, −5. All-nighter of projectile vomiting and fever, 25 points. Failure to schedule haircut or even brush child's hair before school picture day, −100.

On the mother of all scoreboards—the one in my head—I'm forever behind. Working. Not working. Forgetting snack day. Pretending not to notice that we've entered the fifth straight hour of Cartoon Network. Nuking Chef Boyardee for dinner. (Again.) Losing my cool. Losing my daughter at Disney World. (Hey, it was only for ten minutes. Each time.)

Not that anybody's keeping score but me.

Still! This is no game! I'm supposed to be molding their hearts and minds! Keeping them free from all germs and toxins! Launching well-adjusted, productive members of society who will look after me when I'm a dotty old dame, not sit around in therapy blaming me!

Oughta, woulda, coulda, shoulda, expletive deleted.

All mothers hear voices. Actually just one voice, as insistent as it is irksome. That would be your momologue, your internal running commentary on how it's going as a mom.

But it's never saying, "Good job, Mom! Brilliant navigation of that sibling rivalry incident! How fine and upstanding your children are! Pats on the back for that quick save of the ice cream cone!"

No. These momologues are not about praise and positive reinforcement. They hector and nag. They cluck at you. They fret. The voice in your head recites an endless to-do list. It whispers comparisons to everybody else's kids. It tallies up your shortcomings with the precision of the IRS. It's never satisfied.

Oughta cleverly conceal more spinach in their casseroles. Oughta scrub out the bathtub every time with Clorox before I send them into it. Shoulda signed them up for after-school Chinese lessons so they can compete in the new economy. Shoulda taken more home movies last vacation. Shoulda taken more home movies ever since the youngest was born.

Woulda helped organize the school fund-raiser, if only I had more time, inclination, and tolerance for inane meetings. Woulda slathered the kids in sunscreen, if I'd remembered to buy any. Coulda found a more respectful way to nip today's bickering than "Keep that up and I might tell Santa to cancel Christmas!"

Never mind that my kids still kiss me voluntarily and make me funny hats for Mother's Day. Or that they're happy, healthy, and reasonably responsive to the word *no*. No matter what I do, or don't do, this annoying sense that it's never enough follows me like a phantom limb waggling an accusing finger. A perfect score on the mom-o-meter remains forever out of reach. "Oughta, woulda, coulda, shoulda" is the sound track of my life, more annoying and repetitive than a Raffi refrain.

Oughta buy elbow pads and knee pads for the skateboarders. Oughta make sure they actually use them. Shoulda counted to ten before going ballistic when the girls used the commode as a Barbie whirlpool. Woulda pulled the plug on that noisy, addictive video game system—if it didn't seem to make the house so quiet and happy.

Coulda stayed home cherishing their presence and running them through vocabulary flash cards instead of hiring that babysitter in order to enjoy a meal during which I had to cut up no one's meat but my own. Shoulda, oh lordy shoulda, showed that sitter where we keep the first-aid kit before we left the house.

But didn't.

Didn't!

Like I say fifty times a day around here to everybody else, "Enough already!"

There's no stopping the pesky momologues looping through your brain. They're as much a part of the condition of motherhood as sleep deprivation and uterine muscle flop. You can, however, quit paying attention to them.

How? By instead tuning in to the louder real-life noises right under your feet.

Both kinds of voices are constant. Both are insistent. But only one—"Mo-om!" "MOM!" "Moooooom!" "Maaaaaaaaaaaaaaaaaaaaa-aaaaaaaaaaa!"—is real and worth living by.

No Experience Necessary!
On Winging It

Trust yourself. You know more than you think you do.
> —*first lines of* Baby and Child Care *by Dr. Benjamin Spock*

Zinc stearate powder, warning against.
> —*last entry in index of* Baby and Child Care, 647 *pages later*

Sometimes—while standing naked in the nursery at 3 a.m. with a crying baby who has just gotten sick all over my nightgown, or while interviewing some bigwig pediatrician and frantically motioning for a barking toddler in a dog costume to quit eating Goldfish crackers off the floor as her three older siblings use them to cajole her into fetching, begging, and rolling over—a question pops into my head. *How did I get here?*

How does a woman once afraid of babies become "expert" enough at motherhood to write about it for a living? More to the point, proficient enough to keep her own four children alive and swell?

It's easier than you'd think.

Reassuring Tale 1: My Maternal Instincts Backfire

I am eight months pregnant, taking my evening stroll, when I spy the tiny, squirming ball of fur, so fresh from the womb that his eyes are still fused shut. It looks like a squirrel without a tail, or a puppy with paddles for paws. I think of Mole, the main rodent from *The Wind in the Willows,* only smaller and cuter, as if drawn by Beatrix Potter. A baby mole!

How a baby mole wound up in the middle of my suburban street, I'll never know. I pick him up, wrap him in a Kleenex fished out of my pocket, and carry him home.

Deep inside, I begin to sense a strange, reassuring glow. I feel . . . *nurturing!* Maybe this means I'll wind up being a good mother after all.

Growing up, see, I'd seldom played house. Never babysat. Held a baby only once, for twenty polite and panicky seconds, before returning it to its rightful owner, my boss's wife. I called kids "rugrats," and not in the cute Nickelodeon sense of the word. I was a workaholic with a dry-clean-only wardrobe, the sort of person friends might vote Least Likely to Wear a Snugli. My only pets were a pair of newts and an albino African water frog named Hugo, the product of a Grow-a-Frog kit bought as a joke, who all lived in a glass aquarium and did not require much in the way of maternal attention.

Then I turned thirty. Walking down my driveway after retrieving birthday cards from the mailbox, I heard someone say, "I want to have a baby." I looked around. Nobody there but me. And since it couldn't have been me saying those words, I am pretty sure it was my hormones talking. Thanks to my husband, a man of action and enthusiasm, I was pregnant within a month.

Naturally, I was thrilled. When I wasn't petrified. Mothers, after all, are mysterious creatures with supernatural powers, from the wisdom of Solomon to eyes in the back of their heads. How this transformation was going to happen to me, of all people, mystified me even more than where my waistline had gone overnight. Solomon? I was the girl who couldn't even decide between two different sweater colors. (I'd end up buying both.) And as for paranormal vision, I often have trouble seeing the truth when it's staring me right in the face. What kind of mother would I make?

The Mother of My Dreams played catch and handcrafted prize-winning Halloween costumes. She served hot, balanced meals three times a day. She always knew the right answer. Her clean, obedient children slept through the night and never talked back. She had the carefree glow, European superstroller, and instant washboard abs as seen on the latest celebramom. My idyllic vision was a selfless soufflé whipped up from equal parts *InStyle,* June Cleaver, Betty Crocker, Mary Poppins, highly selective memories of my own mom, and thin air.

The Mother of My Fears, on the other hand, was the one who achieved none of these descriptions.

How could I know that she'd be the one closer to my eventual reality? And that she would be a-okay?

If an unpromising specimen like me can cheerfully navigate motherhood, anybody can. This is how it went.

"Hey, little baby," I begin to croon to the baby mole in the same primordial singsong I sometimes use on the creature growing within me. "It's okay, little baby."

A few minutes earlier, I'd been lumbering along preoccupied by an overdue work project and the embarrassing problem of which of my maternity shirts still stretched across my midsection so I could wear it tomorrow. Then in an instant, everything changes. All my focus lasers onto the helpless bitty thing in my hands. Forget blazers that wouldn't button. Deadlines, who cares? All that matters now is that I help and protect this tiny fellow. I haven't held a tissue so tenderly since I was eight years old and using one to tuck in my Liddle Kiddle dolls at night.

Crossing my front lawn back to my house, I try to figure out what to do with Baby M. That's when I see all the holes in the grass. *Mole holes!*

"Welcome home, little guy," I whisper as I unwrap the critter and kneel down (the hardest part, since my center of gravity has relocated several inches out from the rest of my body). Even if this particular mole hole doesn't lead to his nest, I figure some tunneling distant relative might take him in. Or send a message to his mother. I vaguely remember hearing that moles cover a lot of territory in a day. I try to calculate how many houses I've passed since I picked him up. Then I lurch upright and go inside happy. Not only have I done a good deed, but I am a natural at nurturing! *Whew!*

"Hey! Guess what happened?" I call to my husband, Daddyo-to-be, who is preparing for parenthood in his own way, by sorting through many long pieces of white wood and short silver screws that don't look anything like the picture of the gleaming Bellini baby crib on the box they'd come in.

"What?"

"I found a baby mole!"

"A what?"

"A baby mole, with his eyes still shut, and he was so cute and helpless, and I think it was like a sign or something!"

"A sign of wha—Ah dang!" A silver screw skitters across the wood floor and two crib slats clatter after it. He sets down the screwdriver and repeats, "You found a baby mole. And it was a sign." Only he makes both sentences sound like questions. "Where is it?"

"I put it in a mole hole so its mother, or somebody's mother, could find it."

Daddyo doesn't say anything. But his telltale right dimple deepens. It always does that when he's telling a joke—or finds something hilarious but is trying to keep a straight face.

"What?" I demand.

"Um, snakes use those old tunnels to look for food."

"You mean—?"

Oh.

Great.

My first maternal stirrings led me to deliver my innocent young charge to a copperhead for breakfast.

Reassuring Tale 2: I Have No Apparent Child-Care Skill

Next thing I know, I am dropping babies on their heads. Not real babies, let me hasten to add. Plastic practice ones. Even so, another unpromising omen.

My own mom didn't know Lamaze from La Bamba. I'd been born while she was under "twilight sleep," the prettiest euphemism for heavy drugs I've ever heard, with my dad down the hall in the waiting room, missing his General Motors League bowling night. But I am determined to be prepared. I'd learned photography, step aerobics, yoga, and algebra by taking classes, hadn't I? So why not childbearing? For good measure I sign up for courses on breast-feeding and parenting preparation, too.

I mean, I sign up both of us.

"Why do I have to go?" Daddyo wants to know.

"As my backup," I say. "In case I forget anything."

What I don't admit is that I don't want to go either. I simply feel propelled along. My belly grows bigger, I go to the doctor every two weeks, my friends make noises about showers, I begin turning my old home office (and spare bedroom) into a nursery, I take Lamaze. It all unfolds matter-of-factly and practically without me, the great conveyor belt of expectant motherhood. At the same time, I am at that point in my pregnancy where the baby is no longer an abstraction. It is big, and active, and like the title of a seriously bad 1950s movie, *It Had to Come Out.* I figure I may as well face up to learning how.

During the first few Lamaze sessions I discover that I am best at the academics of the whole business. When we learn about the signs of labor and the stages of labor, I take copious notes. I memorize assorted breathing patterns as earnestly as if I were a third-grader learning times tables before a big test. Just as I begin to think I might "pass" after all, we get to the relaxation exercises. I am pretty much hopeless.

"Relax," my husband croons in his best labor supporter tone as I am supposed to be letting the tension float away from my legs, my calves, my ankles, my toes. But the more I concentrate on letting go, the more self-conscious I become.

"Relax!" (More urgently now.)

"I am!"

"Stop tensing up!"

"Stop saying that—it's making me more tense!"

"I wish I was the one who got to lay there," he complains, stifling a yawn.

I wish you were, too, I think grimly.

Then comes newborn-care night.

"Tonight," the instructor, Sharon, smiles warmly, "we'll move from the abstract to the hands-on." We gather around a big table piled with newborn baby dolls. "I want each couple to take a baby," she instructs. Eager hands dart out. The dolls come in slightly different models and colors, so people begin reaching over one another to make a selection. You'd think we were prospective adoptive parents in an orphanage rather than clueless students in a church basement awaiting a short lesson in Pampers application. Some of the women begin to coo and talk to their "newborns" as if they were real.

Daddyo grabs the doll nearest to us. It is distressingly lifelike, right down to the scrunched-up fists and chubby crooked legs.

Sharon begins handing out tiny triangles of white. "Now, you want to have all your supplies handy before you get started: diaper, wipe, ointment, cornstarch. Never take your hand off the baby, not even for a second." She shows how to unfold the disposable triangle, position the baby's bottom in the center, and then deftly open the sticky tabs on the sides and refasten them around the baby's legs. Changing a dirty diaper proves a little trickier, since you have to add a more thorough swipe before whisking the old one away while putting the replacement in position.

The couples get to work. My husband goes first. He's a natural, once I point out that the diaper has a back and a front (distinguished by the notch cut out to accommodate the umbilical stump, which I feel mighty smug to have noticed). He whips the diaper on and off a few times.

Okay, check, I think as I watch. *I get it. Not too difficult.*

"Now switch and let your partner have a turn," Sharon calls over the happy chatter of pretending moms and dads. That's when I realize that in all the other couples, the mom-to-be had gone first.

How hard could it be, really?

Now, maybe the diaper tabs aren't meant to be reused over and over. Maybe the baby doll was slick from too much practice powder. Maybe I just needed a bit more practice centering a plump baby's bottom in a taco-sized diaper that refused to unfold.

All I know is that suddenly there is a loud smack, as plastic newborn skull strikes church basement linoleum. Then a sick instant of absolute silence. "Remember you have to keep one hand on the baby at all times," Sharon says evenly, addressing the whole group with a thin smile but looking right at me.

When it happens a second time, she skips the smile. Daddyo looks a little worried.

Reassuring Tale 3: I Just Don't Seem Like the Motherly Type

A few days after the last class, one of the secretaries at work, Michelle, brings her new baby in for a visit. A new mom's first return to the office with her tot in tow triggers all the excitement and fuss of a triumphant war hero's homecoming. Her Purple Heart—the newborn, swaddled in pink or blue—draws the mommies like a magnet. One minute they were serious androgynous executives sending memos and backstabbing colleagues. Now they're tapioca.

"Paula! Come see the baby!"

I am sitting in my office, two doors from the group ogle. *Why hadn't I headed to the restroom five minutes earlier? Why oh why didn't my phone ring?* They drag me over.

In the past I always flat-out ignored these clusters of baby admirers, and nobody paid me any attention. The mommies seemed far outside my realm of reality, like retirees or marathon runners. I was content leaving them to themselves. But now my protruding belly makes me a target. In everyone's eyes, I am already One of Them. And so like Elizabeth Bennet caught off guard by the objectionable Mr. Darcy's application for her hand at a ball, I find myself on the dance floor with a partner I do not want, in this case a fat, drooly four-week-old.

Four female colleagues have been taking turns with baby Chandler. As they pass him around, their hips sway with the unconscious mama-cuddle rhythms of time eternal. "So sweet!" they coo. "Oh, look how he puckers his lips!" Chandler's mother, rarely the center of attention like this on a normal workday unless some crisis is at hand requiring her to FedEx out twenty urgent documents, beams.

I watch quietly from the outer edge of the cluster. I try to paste on the beatific expression I'd studied on the corny pastel woman rocking calmly on the cover of *What to Expect When You're Expecting*. But inside I feel like I am back in my tenth grade Drama Club's production of *Rebel Without a Cause*. I'd joined only because some of my friends said it would be fun. Unlike the stories I'd always heard about famous actors who described going onstage for the first time and feeling instantly, safely at home, however, I had felt only awkward, self-conscious, and bored. Here in my office with baby Chandler, I feel even worse: awkward, self-conscious, bored—and petrified.

Now the mommies compare notes with gusto. The talk turns from pacifiers to labor.

"When I got to seven it really hurt . . ."

"I felt her slice me because the epidural hadn't taken yet."

Once a foreign language, their words—*effaced, Stadol, lactation consultant*—had grown familiar, thanks to Lamaze class. Yet I didn't truly understand the depth of their meanings. Baby talk for me had all the substance of cotton candy or false-front Western buildings. No there there. I had to escape before they made me hold the creature.

"Oh, you'll be next!" someone trilled. That was my cue.

In *Rebel Without a Cause,* some of my performances had been rotated with my understudy, so we'd both get a chance in the spotlight. Opening night, I went on. The next night, a Friday, was the understudy's turn. Relieved to be free, I fled to the big football game with all my nontheatrical friends. When I turned up for Saturday night's performance—the one I'd told my parents to attend, so they'd miss my opening night jitters—the flamboyant theater club adviser was furious. "Where were you last night? Don't you realize you violated the code of cast camaraderie by choosing football over our show? Don't you know *we* are a team?" she declared, waving her hands. "What if your understudy had been sick? Just as she stands by to support you, you must be here to support her!" I shrugged. She canned me. Imagine my parents' surprise as I sat down next to them in the audience before the curtain rose and asked for a ride home. "You know, I hate acting," I told them. Still do.

So I stand there uncomfortably among my colleagues. Then I remember that a pregnant woman has the handiest of exit lines: "Excuse me, I've got to pee again."

I escape to the ladies' room, latch the stall door behind me, and begin heaving silent cries. What's wrong with me? That baby Chandler was floppy and horrible. He kept making little noises. He looked so needy. I found him even less compelling than the plastic practice baby in childbirth class. What's wrong with me?

Unfortunately I can't quit this drama. Opening night is coming fast.

The Happy Ending: Nothing Ventured, Nothing Gained

Before I enter motherhood, stage left, let me make a quick reassuring return to the present. Four children and one solid decade of bottom wiping after the Mole Incident, I've turned out nothing like that mythical mom I once envisioned. But neither am I as truly inept as I'd feared.

Turns out that motherhood is all improvisation. Without another class or a single script, I muddle through. *Everybody* muddles through.

Fortunately, kids start out very small, with low expectations and short memories. And they grow just one day at a time.

So far, knock wood, not one of mine has been devoured by a snake.

Momfidence...

. . . is the bungee jump, the sky dive, the step off the cliff, the leap of faith—whose only real risk is not death but temporary insanity.

. . . is using "perfect" only to describe such wonders as a ripe peach, a cloudless day at the beach, a husband who does diapers and dinner. Its use in describing children is limited to how they look and how they hug, which are always perfect. It has no application whatsoever in describing motherhood.

. . . is Dr. Spock's famous opener: "Trust yourself. You know more than you think you do." But it's also just skimming—or skipping—the 647 pages that follow.

Too Much Advice Spoils the Confidence

On Experts

You'll learn, and put into play, skills in example-setting, discipline, negotiation, communications, intelligence-building, strengthening self worth and self confidence, behavior control and family lifestyle management, useful not only in raising your children but also in structuring the content of your family life so that it supports and uplifts your efforts. Get these skills right and the rest of your life as a parent will be easy.

— *Dr. Phil McGraw (aka Dr. Phil),* Family First

I can't be in each of your homes, but if you have my handy little acronyms in your head, maybe it will seem like I'm standing next to you, reminding you what to do.

— *Tracy Hogg,* The Baby Whisperer Solves All Your Problems

Had I known that the thrill of counting newborn fingers and toes would be followed so quickly by jaundice, engorgement, an unhealed umbilical stump, projectile vomiting, and a nightly horror cheerfully described in upbeat magazine spin as "the crankies," I might well have stuffed my beloved newborn into a snake hole, crossed my fingers, and fished him out again eighteen years later.

But I kept thinking, *Any day now.* Soon I would master

motherhood. Instead, astonishing new experiences I'd never heard of before just kept coming at me. I'd no sooner figure out how to swaddle my son without needing Scotch tape or rope to keep him inside the blanket than I'd have to wrassle a so-called collapsible stroller into a car trunk with one hand. Meanwhile my own body leaked startling amounts of blood, milk, and tears.

So I did what any educated, modern mother does. I freaked.

I fired up the computer, hit the bookstore, cased the newsstand, and grabbed every brochure I could off the pediatrician's racks. I also quizzed every friend who had procreated before me. Drs. Spock, Sears, Brazelton, Leach, Stern, and all the rest of the hottest media baby docs formed a very private practice in a tower of guides at my bedside table.

Then I called my mom.

"Mom! When will these crankies end?"

"Cranky? Try having a beer. It might calm you both down."

"Mom! How many diapers should he be going through a day so I can tell if he's eating enough?"

"Oh, I have no idea. If he's hungry, he'll eat."

"Mom! His head circumference only grew one eighth of an inch—what did mine measure at the four-week checkup?"

"Oh, nobody keeps track of that. Don't worry so much. You're doing fine."

We're talking about the most seismic, enormous event of life! How could she not remember, especially since it had happened to her five times? Granted, almost three decades had passed since she'd last powdered a bottom, back before baby powder became baby *cornstarch,* back when disposables, which she never used anyway, were still so newfangled they had to be fastened with a pin. Little did I know that the day would soon come when I wouldn't have the foggiest idea when I'd last bathed my child, much less myself, or the day's diaper tally, much less anybody's vital statistics.

But if I was unable to see the wisdom in Mom's answers it was because they sounded overly simple to someone who had been conditioned by nine months of obsessive pregnancy dos and don'ts. Hadn't I diligently panicked over the white-wine sauce atop the mercury-laden fish I happened to eat on the likely day that sperm met egg? Hadn't I fretted over my microwave, nail polish, cell phone, hair dye, favorite sleeping position, high heels, morning coffee, and ten thousand other life essentials that had morphed overnight into mortal threats?

Guilt over an abstract, unseen, unborn creature is one thing. Guilt over a helpless screeching creature who is totally dependent on you to survive in this vast, scary world is enough to make you assume the fetal position yourself.

No wonder I braced for motherhood to be not only longer than pregnancy but even more complicated.

Here, for example, is how my very first day as a mom went:

Daddyo's thrilled words—"It's a boy!"—reach my ears the instant before our slippery, salmon-skinned little guy is placed on my chest. My heart swells with a symphony of new emotions: Awe. Pride. Protectiveness. Fierce, raging love.

And then, exhaustion. I'd been awake for thirty-odd hours, the first half spent going *hee-hee-hee-ho* and the other half going *Ohmy-Godwehaveababy!*

"Why don't we keep Henry in the nursery so you can sleep, and we'll bring him to you for feedings?" the nurse suggests.

Now I'd picked the hospital in part because it allowed newborns to room in with their mothers. I'd read on a checklist somewhere that this was not merely a cozy option but a necessary feature of successful breast-feeding and mother-infant bonding—nothing less than the cornerstone of our entire future together. I did not yet realize, of course, that this advice was just the first in a lifetime of momfooleries—things that sound important until applied to a real situation involving your real child. When I was reading up on the merits of rooming in, I hadn't stayed up all night being squeezed by the python of labor. Banish him to the nursery so I can do something so pedestrian as sleep?

"Sure," I say.

But sleep won't come. Another strange feeling courses through my newly maternal veins. *Should I have kept the baby with me? What if they forget to wake me up? Will he miss me? Feel abandoned from the get-go? What if they feed him a bottle of sugar water? What if his ID bracelet falls off and they bring me some other baby but I can't tell because I forgot what Henry looked like and he winds up raised in a commune full of illiterate tattooed Hells Angels who run a meth lab across town, all because I can't even recognize my own flesh and blood? What kind of mother am I anyway? We haven't been apart for nine months. Aren't I supposed to be unable to take my eyes off him?*

Less than twenty-four hours into the job and I'm a wreck. Henry makes much better use of his time. He sleeps. I still had to learn: *Tune out the pesky whispers. Tune in to what's real.*

But not yet.

I spend the first year scrutinizing Henry for the developmental milestones described in a popular baby guide: "By the end of this month your baby should be able to respond to a bell . . . pay attention to a raisin . . . say 'ah goo' . . ." What does a baby need bells and raisins for? To make his poor mother believe he's either a genius or a dunce, obviously.

I get maternal whiplash from the conflicting opinions on how to take care of the boy. Cloth or disposables? Pacifier or no pacifier? Day care or nanny? Sun hat or sunblock? Every hour brings a new multiple-choice exam. I feel as if I'm living that recurring high school dream where you're taking a test on material you've never seen before. Only I never wake up. (Which is ironic considering that in real life, the opposite is true. I never sleep.)

Time-outs or no time-outs? To spank or not to spank? What's the "right" age for computers? Lip gloss? Football? Staying home alone? Who can say?

Everybody!

One prominent pediatrician claims to have never let her children cry. *Not ever?* I think of colic, tantrums over candy in the check-out lane, and just-don't-want-to-go-to-bed nights. *Wow!* An equally respected baby doc is famous for letting babies of a certain age "cry it out" to learn to sleep. How could they both be right?

They can the same way that my mom (who fed me Pablum at three weeks), my pediatrician (who put Henry on solids at three months), and the American Academy of Pediatrics (which now recommends holding off the Gerber for *half a year*) are all right. There are as many ways to raise a baby as there are, well, babies. The AAP isn't "more right" than my own mom just because it's the AAP.

The biggest myth in parenting, perpetuated by the reality of all this ready-made advice, is that if you consume enough information on the subject, you'll find all the answers. There's no calculus that lets a hapless mom ever catch up! Look at me. Ten years (since that first baby was born) divided by four kids @ 3,559 diapers, six dozen tantrums, and ten billion snack servings apiece, multiplied by five parenting book collaborations, 452 magazine articles, and umpteen interviews with MDs and PhDs, plus incalculable hours of girlfriend note-comparing and mother-in-law "suggestions"— and I still don't know what the heck I'm doing half the time.

I've yet to meet the mother who does.

I try to limit my input to a handful of favorite sources. Not that I agree with every opinion they issue. One acclaimed parent educator—who likes to point out that his advice is based on decades of extensive in-home observations of parents and children—gets one of my votes of confidence for his firm but rational ideas about things like spoiling and discipline. But I've completely disregarded his oft-quoted recommendation about spacing kids three years apart to minimize rivalry. Three times now, in fact.

And why not? Three of his own kids were all under age three at one point!

"But if I'd been privy to my own research, I would have done things differently," he once told me. We'll never know, though, whether that would have really made his household a calmer or happier one, will we?

Having my kids closely spaced (twenty-two, thirty-three, and twenty-seven months apart) is, as this expert cautions, exhausting, messy, loud, and expensive. It's also efficient, enthralling, and basket-o-puppies cuddly. Not to mention necessary, given my tardy start.

The real trouble with depending too much on the "experts" is that we start thinking of ourselves as the "amateurs." How else to explain the trend toward $295 a day infant sleep consultants and $125 an hour "parent coaches" who hire themselves out to manage tantrums and set limits for the real parents? Or the popular quest for a nanny who has a degree in child development or child psychology, as if this will make her love your child better, or who is a certain height, so that she will project an image of authority? And what else but rampant amateur-itis could account for the fact that TV programs starring brat-wrangling nannies have captured the fancy of a nation that once flopped in front of the tube as a respite from a hard day of disciplining its own?

Across the land parents are outsourcing the most basic activities of the job; you can hire a consultant to get your tot to eat her veggies, learn to ride a bike without training wheels, or find a mutually acceptable prom dress. But even if my pockets were even deeper than my insecurity, I think I'd rather face the broccoli sneers and dressing room hissy fits myself, and then blow what I'd save on consultant fees on my own shopping spree. Or on college tuition.

I'll never forget the first time I began to see through the emperor's clothes. It was not long after my writing life and my real life began to merge.

Having one baby had been so much fun, Daddyo and I think, *Again! Again!* And before you can say Tinky Winky, Dipsy, Laa Laa, and Po—indeed, when Henry was barely a year old—I am pregnant again. (And again and again, but that's getting ahead of the story.) I worked in an office as a magazine editor during my first pregnancy. But things are different this time. Rumors of the imminent demise of our company leads my colleagues to network furiously and take days off for job interviews. I go on maternity leave. Three weeks after I return, the company is kaput. Daddyo is in graduate school. I am concerned but not alarmed. I have a plan.

I will become a freelance writer.

I don't think about what it will be like to interview Famous Doctor of the Week about his breakthrough *JAMA* article while hiding in the pantry and tossing out cheese doodles with my free hand to keep a pesky toddler sated. I don't stop to factor in the unlikelihood of writing thousands of words on an iMac on deadline when I haven't strung together three coherent sentences to my husband in months.

I see only the advantages. No more dry cleaning; I can work in graham-cracker-smeared sweatpants. No more attaching myself to a pump like a moo-cow before heading to the office. I can breastfeed while typing—a handy hold, incidentally, described in no breastfeeding guide I've read. Best of all, no more reading the advice of America's foremost baby authorities. Now I can quiz them over the phone!

"Write what you *don't* know" becomes my motto.

One of my first assignments, from one of the big national parenting magazines, is a subject near and dear to my heart: toilet training. What luck! What timing! Henry's pediatrician has mentioned at his eighteen-month checkup that I might want to get a potty chair so he'll grow accustomed to seeing it. And now my paid mission is to present the latest, best thinking on how to get him to actually use it.

So eager am I to train Henry perfectly—I mean, to impress my editors with my diligence—that I make a list of the noblest names in the toddler business. Then I proceed to track them down, one by one.

First, of course, must be Dr. Benjamin Spock himself. A reprint of his 1946 guide had been the first of the ten thousand volumes in my parenting library (it was a shower gift). Now in his nineties, Dr. Spock is still dispensing advice to the grandchildren of his first clients. (He would die a few years later, at age ninety-four; whether I achieved the coup of snaring his last recorded words on the critical subject of potties, I do not know.)

Brand-name nonagenarian that he is, Dr. Spock works with his wife and an assistant in his sunny San Diego home. The Oracle can't come to the phone, though. I must submit my questions via e-mail. I imagine him, Oz green and all-knowing beneath his shock of white hair, on the other side of my computer screen.

"What do you seek?"

"The answer to the mysteries of potty training, O Great and Powerful One!"

"Introduce the potty in a casual way! The goal is to let the child feel that he's in charge, that he can use the seat however he wishes!"

Oh.

My own pediatrician had said pretty much the same thing.

But coming from the Wizard himself, I quit procrastinating. I rush out that day to buy Henry a spiffy blue and white plastic potty chair. I leave it in the bathroom next to the big commode. I try to act cool.

"Hey Mommy, what's that?'

"Oh, it's a potty."

"What for?"

"For you. To sit on. And for your wee and poop to go in." Afraid I'm rushing things, I lamely add, "For someday. Soon. Later. Then you won't need diapers anymore."

Henry loves it. First the potty is a toy—a giant 3-D puzzle to take apart and reassemble. Then it becomes a step stool. Funny, Spock didn't mention that he wouldn't even know what the thing was for.

After Spock, I approach Dr. T. Berry Brazelton, the smiling Texan who is arguably the second-most-famous pediatrician in America. He won't talk to me voice to voice either. His excuse is financial. He has a contract with a rival magazine, he explains; he may only pass his pearls of wisdom directly unto them. He kindly refers me instead to his long paper trail on the topic. Brazelton's big theme is readiness. Does the child wake up dry from a nap? Follow basic directions? Imitate your behavior? Have words for urine and bowel movements? Yes, yes, yes, yes! The potty-training window is indeed wide open for me! (How am I to know that Henry will never again exhibit one of these signs, "an interest in cleanliness and orderliness"?)

I have better luck talking live with Penelope Leach, a crisp British psychologist then at her peak popularity in the United States because she is starring in her own American TV show. I still can't get over the miraculous job perk of watching someone on cable in the morning and then being able to pepper her with thinly disguised personal questions by phone to England that same after-noon: "Say, for example, Dr. Leach, that a mom had a twenty-two-month-old named, oh, let's call him Henry, who would rather wear his potty seat as a pith helmet than sit down on it . . ."

Eventually he does sit. In fact, it becomes his favorite reading chair. He sits there (clothed) for hours poring over his prized Richard Scarry books. Sometimes I crouch next to him rereading *Cars and Trucks and Things That Go*—note the subliminally hopeful title—until I get a crick in my back.

After a few weeks, the boy consents to sit bare-bottomed. *I* feel ready to wet my pants; I haven't felt this excited about child devel-opment since I brought him into my office during my maternity leave so that my colleagues could watch him roll from tummy to back. (So much for my carefully cultivated professional cool.)

Sure enough, one momentous day soon after the bare-bottom breakthrough, he jumps up triumphantly to utter the words I'll never forget: "Hey! I made a wee wee!"

I applaud. I ceremoniously pour the waste into the big toilet and—his favorite part—he flushes. "What's the big deal about toi-let training?" I wonder smugly.

In the interests of thorough journalism, though, I also consult every other luminary I can find in the potty-training firmament. The toilet-training-in-less-than-a-day guru offers a complicated plan involving a Betsy Wetsy–type doll, M&M's, and a kinky mili-taristic step called dry-pants inspections. Henry shows zero interest in the doll and raids the M&M's when I'm not looking. I am too busy (or is it lazy?) to remember to inspect his pants every hour.

Dr. William Sears—a prolific and cheerful California pediatri-cian who has collaborated with his nurse-wife on as many books as offspring (about three hundred)—finds BM charts and tinkle tar-gets helpful. Henry uses the last of the M&M's as targets but his aim isn't so hot. And since I can't even remember to write down all my checks in the checkbook, I am a disaster at keeping poop charts.

In between cleaning up near-misses and accidents, I find Marianne "Dr. Mom" Neifert, another pediatrician with a large family. She mentions a children's book on the subject that has separate editions for girls and for boys. I had no idea toileting was a literary genre. I promptly buy every title in it. Henry, however, is partial to a video that comes with one of them. It features dozens of ecstatic toddlers clad only in diapers, dancing. "Yes, I'm going to the potty, potty!" goes the calypso-beat theme song. Soon I can't get the tune out of my head. I sing along while he watches. I sing while I'm changing him. I sing while rocking him to sleep. I sing at my computer. The day I begin singing in the freezer aisle at the grocery, we put the video away for a while.

One source objects to my use of the word *training*. It's potty *teaching* now, I'm advised. So I'm careful to use this kindler, gentler phrase with my next expert—who finds the emphasis all wrong. She prefers toilet *learning*, please.

Yet for all my research, I seem to be the only one learning anything. Weeks go by. Henry holds fast to his Huggies.

I confess to my next source that I'm getting a little anxious.

"Oh, everybody thinks that if you misstep in toilet training, you'll have a child with indelible psychological bruises," poohpoohs John Rosemond, a popular syndicated family psychologist who is my last interview. He doesn't believe in waiting around until the child decides. *Just do it.* Take away the diapers, slap on the undies, and pretty soon that sopping feeling will have your child running to the potty (or ruining your rug). A few years later, when jumbo pull-ups for kindergartners and small elephants are introduced, Rosemond will duke it out with Dr. Brazelton on this subject in the lofty arena of the front page of the *New York Times.*

Brazelton, naturally, is all for these supersized diapers because not every child is ready at the same time. (He's also a paid consultant to Huggies.) Rosemond is appalled. Claiming that in the 1960s 90 percent of all toddlers were toilet-trained by age two and a half, compared with just 20 percent today, he begins touting the "naked and $75" approach, a phrase he hadn't yet coined when I wrote my article: Let your two-year-old run around nekkid and in a few days, voila! The $75 is to clean all those carpets afterward.

I think both men are right—readiness is important and obsessing is ridiculous—though Rosemond also maintains that puppies can be housebroken in a matter of days, which I will long remember while cleaning dog poo off future playroom carpets. Mostly I find it funny that the headliner voices on the topic are of the gender not usually associated with wiping bottoms.

Years later I will look back in relief that the toilet-train-your-newborn movement had not yet caught fire. I'm all for laborsaving conveniences. (How did moms function without the microwave oven?) But a method that involves watching your diaperless baby 24/7 for his signs of "elimination communication" and signaling reminders by hissing "psspsspss"—not to mention cleaning the mess up should you miss one another's hints—hardly sounds laborsaving. Besides, the latest diaper bags are too fab to lug around only for a few short months.

At last my article "The Essential Potty Training Guide" is published. It's the cover story. A close reader can find a few phrases like "the right way is whatever works," but the piece is mostly notable for its thorough dissection of all the finer points, under such subheads as "Little Potty or Big?" and "The Watch-Me Way."

The story wins a big national award for consumer magazine feature writing.

Henry remains in diapers until the day before he turns four.

His three younger sisters, on the other hand, somehow all make it into their Disney Princess undies when they are two. (Again without the elimination communication, the all-in-one-day tactics, the charts, et al.) The only difference, near as I can figure, is that by the time I was learning them, I'd begun to ignore the inside poop.

Over the years I've evolved from your basic don't-know-nothin'-'bout-birthin'-babies American woman to the Mom Who Knew Too Much. Not that I recommend either extreme.

But I no longer yearn to be the Perfect Mom of my advice-stoked imagination when there's a Perfectly Adequate Mom wiping up my kitchen floor. The two have collided countless times since the toilet-training episode, and guess who comes up the victor every time?

At last I can accept that I don't have to put everything I know into practice. Better still, that I don't even have to know everything. A page of this, a kernel of that, a tip picked up on the playground crossed with a few dollops of intuition and common sense, along with plenty of trial-and-error—and there you have it.

No pacifiers. *They're ugly.*

Yes to snacks in the living room. *Messy but harmless.*

Bedtime at 8 p.m. sharp. *I need my downtime!*

My list might appall some people. As theirs, in turn, may rankle me. The point is not to dictate more how-tos. It's that every mother works up her own crib sheet. No matter how many tax dollars are being spent in order to finance the careers of America's MD-PhD-alphabet soup of researchers dissecting the minds, bodies, and stomachs of our kids, raising a child will always be an art form, not a science. It's like piecing together a crazy quilt, stitching together random bits of silk, velvet, and wool in ways that look right to you. I'm always on the lookout for scraps that might work. But I've learned to toss plenty aside, too.

Or here's another homemaking analogy. (Admittedly strange coming from a woman who will never be described by the words *domestic* and *goddess* in the same sentence, but what is motherhood if not strange?) Think of the universe of parenting advice as so many recipes. Most of us know how to throw a meal together without ever looking in a cookbook. We check what's in the fridge, ask our husband what he thinks, consider what the kids will actually swallow, and use our basic knowledge of how to work a stove and a knife to produce something moderately edible or at least nourishing enough to keep us alive another day. It's nice to know that if we need to, we can look up specific directions to a special dish in Mom's old *Fannie Farmer*. But few of us run to the cookbook shelf, let alone to one almighty chef, for instructions on every morsel we consume. Fewer still pay for somebody else to show us how.

It should be the same with parenting. If you're really in the dark over colic or stuttering or ear infections, there's no quicker route to peace of mind and answers than "looking up the recipe" by consulting an expert. Just remember that Nigella, Martha, Julia, Emeril, Betty C., Rachael Ray, and the *Southern Living* kitchens all have different ideas about what to do with a chicken breast. And they're just ideas. Pick one recipe (or like me, simultaneously flip between a few) and cross your fingers. Use the experts as a reference, not as your conscience.

Anyway, the best cooks just improvise.

Momfidence...

. . . is raising your child freehand, rather than with a paint-by-numbers kit. To paraphrase Lucy van Pelt of *Peanuts:* The expert is Within.

. . . is taking one look at your child lying listlessly on the sofa—not clambering over its cushions, not pinching his sisters, not filching Fritos from the cupboard—and knowing he's really sick, even before you rest your palm over his burning forehead to check for fever.

. . . is the confidence that comes from knowing everybody else is pretty much winging it, too.

You Can Lead a Child to Carrots, but You Can't Make Him Crunch

On Control

Who are these people and where did they come from?

— *Me, to Daddyo*

Let's press fast-forward for a few years.

"And what would Henry like to eat?" Bett asks. We're at her house for a cookout and she knows he's a little, um, finicky.

"Oh, don't worry about him," I say. "He ate four chicken nuggets before we left home." I omit that he'd eaten four chicken nuggets for lunch as well, just as he had for lunch and dinner the previous day, and frankly, every day as far back as I can remember.

Bett brightens. "We've got chicken nuggets."

That's when I have to explain that not just any microwaved frozen chicken nuggets will do, only Tyson Southern Fried Chick 'n Chunks chicken nuggets. The bite-sized type, not the fillets.

"That's exactly what Hannah eats!" Bett says of her own six-year-old as she takes a box from the freezer. Before we can marvel at this wonderful coincidence, though, I see that the box is the wrong color. Her bite-sized chicken chunks are made by Banquet. Wrong brand. Henry won't touch them.

If only I'd known from the start about Craig Flatman of Stow-market, Suffolk, England. Craig Flatman makes my heart sing. He is fifteen, six feet tall, and perfectly healthy, according to his doctor. He recently made international headlines for having subsisted exclusively on jam sandwiches, milk, cereal, and chocolate cake. For his whole life. Fifteen years. The news reports did not say how many sleepless nights his mum spent wondering where she'd gone wrong and what must the neighbors think.

At least my son has added a protein source to this regimen.

Mrs. Flatman did not purposely limit her son to a lifetime of jam and cake. Nor is this diet a Suffolkian cultural quirk. Young Craig apparently has been like this since he was a small baby. Even if he one day starts snarfing fish 'n chips, the boy's essential self— tenacious, consistent, impervious to threats and bribes, and a little monomaniacal—isn't likely to change. And he's fine.

Children are born more fully formed than we give them credit for.

Once upon a time I naively expected a baby. That's what I told everybody. "Guess what? We're having a baby." That's what everyone played back to me: "Wow! I hear you're going to have a baby!" Then life slithered out from between my legs, slippery red-blue and as startling as a glimpse of a shooting star, and Daddyo and I murmured in disbelief, "Oh God! We have a baby!" Soon my colleagues were clustering around me at the office and shrieking, "I can't believe *you* had a baby!"

This is a misleading turn of phrase. Mothers don't have mere babies. We have *people.* One-of-a-kind, hard-wired, absolutely distinct individuals. Who expects this? In utero, our children are blank canvasses onto which we embroider our dreams. You imagine Futurebaby adorably gurgling her appreciation as she takes in her themed and color-coordinated Pottery Barn Kids nursery with the hand-painted wall mural featuring her name. You see her drifting placidly to sleep—right at bedtime—in her pristine smocked gown. Life with baby is dreamed as a soft-focus montage of sunny meadows and white wicker rockers.

Note that these fantasies always have the sound turned down.

My own imaginary cherub-to-be had been a bald, big-eyed smiler—which incredibly, Henry turned out to be. Somehow, though, I never fleshed out that Gerber jar sketch to include such adjectives as demanding, mercurial, athletic, and energetically sociable, which also happen to define the baby I got.

I shouldn't have been so surprised. Babies confound their parents' expectations all the time. Extroverts give birth to cling-ons. Math professors beget artists. PhDs must hire tutors. Moms want girls and get boys, or vice versa. And you can bet that at least one indigo-auraed offspring of a hemp-wearing, flax-chewing conscientious objector will change his name from Zen to Buzz and go ROTC. Reality happens.

Sometimes your child is so alien to your own mind-set that it feels like she was teleported from Zorax, even though you swear you were right there in the delivery room when she was handed over. It can take a while to figure out who this creature is and what makes her tick. Although neither of his parents are athletes, for example (we toss the Sports section before bringing the newspaper into the house), Henry's very first sentence was "Play ball, Daddy!" Avid readers, we plied him with all the juvenile classics as well as books on any topic he showed an interest in. He spent five solid years rereading dog-eared *Calvin and Hobbes* collections (although anything featuring World War II weaponry or zombies was also a hit). And we tried—Lord knows we tried—to expand his palate beyond a particular brand of fatty brown microwavable pseudo-proteins.

At first, I misunderstood these idiosyncrasies. I just figured, *So. This is what babies are like.* Then when number two, a daughter, came along, I thought, *Well, he is what boys are like and she is what girls are like.* Wrong twice, of course. By the time another sister arrived, and then another, it became clear that all I knew was what *this particular child* is like.

Try as you will to mold them, shape them, control them, tidy them up, and make them eat their carrots, you keep coming up against one unalterable fact: Kids are born as rugged individuals.

Sometimes you make headway. Sometimes you just butt heads.

Not that I'm complaining. One of my favorite things about having children—I confess, a big part of the reason I kept on having them—is watching their individuality unfold, like one of those long-exposure films of a flower unfurling its leaves and bursting into bloom.

Let me introduce the specimens growing in my hothouse:

Henry (aka Hardway, when he's out of earshot) has thrived for ten years on a diet of chicken nuggets, Jif, popcorn, and Cocoa Puffs. (No, no vegetables. Not even ketchup. Unless popcorn counts?) Whether the subject is food, homework, chores, or getting along with the other humans in the house, there is the easy way and then there is Henry's way. He's like an ice cutter on a northern sea, breaking in his novice parents and making a smooth path for the sisters who follow in his mighty wake.

Henry has the intelligence, prowess, and feisty gumption of the giants who made this country great. Probably not coincidentally, he spent his preschool years wearing fringed buckskin, moccasins, and a "skoonskin" cap. Grandma had made the getup for

Halloween in honor of his Davy Crockett obsession. (Typical bed-time prayer at age three: "Thank you for bedtime, Richard Scarry, Old Betsy, and sharks." Old Betsy being Davy's famous Kentucky long rifle, of course.) If we lived in pioneer days, Henry would probably have lit out for the Territories by now to seek his fame and fortune, Ol' Bess slung over his shoulder and a jar of PB in his saddlebag. And I'd be blubbering on the front porch, knowing in my broken Ma heart that an iconoclast's gotta do what an iconoclast's gotta do.

Next-in-line Eleanor is only a grade younger. Almost nine, she's a Swell-a-nor for writing her daddy and I mash notes telling us what wonderful parents we are and how much she loves us. She reads all my favorite old books. Her bedroom is spotless (if you don't open the closet). For her birthday last year, she wanted only a doll and sponge rollers. It's almost enough to make you overlook the way she bosses around her sisters and tattles on her brother.

Eleanor was born with a better sense of fashion, design, and what colors "look gooder" on me than I had accumulated in thirty-four years. As soon as she had the dexterity to fasten her own dia-pers, she was turning herself out in boho-chic getups the likes of which Mary Kate and Ashley wouldn't discover until they hit college. You might cringe at the idea of a yellow floral dress over a lime-green turtleneck, candy-cane striped leggings, leftover Mardi Gras beads, and bright purple Keds—all topped off by an inside-out Easter bonnet—but on Eleanor, such looks come off with the fashionista assurance of a lilliputian Stella McCartney. (Or so I could appreci-ate them, once I finally gave up coaxing her into the mix-'n-match Gymboree playsets I'd thought were so sweet. Mornings went a lot more smoothly when I butted out, too.)

Because she arrived so close on Henry's heels, she's his loyal sidekick, whether it's snitching Ring Dings from the pantry for him or allowing his little green army men to make camp in her dollhouse. That first year Henry went trick-or-treating as Davy Crockett, Eleanor called herself Davy's trusty sidekick Georgie Russel—in a fluffy white tutu. For an archetypal boy and an archetypal girl, they get along remarkably well. When they're not beating on one another anyway.

And then there's Marge in Charge—er, Margaret. Our kindergartner wants to rule the world, or at least the playroom. But because she is third in line, her prodigious mental energies are often spent fending off her unimpressed elder sibs. Even as a baby she had little time for snuggling or other niceties. She'd sit at her high chair like a pasha pointing to each spot on the tray where she expected her lunch to appear: "Nyuk!" (*Milk!*) "Poon!" (*Spoon!*) And my personal favorite, the elegant "La Goat!" (*Yogurt!*).

You can't put much past Margaret. "Dad! Turn left!" she screeched from her baby car seat when we once took an alternate route home. Her questions keep me on my toes: "What's magic made of?" "How do they cry in Spanish?" "Why would they make a Barbie with a beautiful dress but no underwear?"

Unlike her siblings, who are all blue-eyed blondes, Margaret is a brunette like me, but with eyes so alluringly dark and deep her daddy tells her he could get lost inside them and never come out. "Oh Dad," she sighs, ever practical. "I would throw you a ladder." Once I scooped her up on my lap. "You sweet thing, I am going to eat you up," I said, as mommies are wont to do. "You can't eat me up," she matter-of-factly replied, "because I am one hard Margaret."

Last but no way least is Page, the baby. Page thinks she is a puppy. When we brought home our dog, Brownie, from the miniature dachshund puppy farm in Siler City, North Carolina, Page developed such a bad case of sibling rivalry that she began crawling around on all fours in a floppy-eared dog costume left over from Halloween. "My name is Teeny," she says. "I am zero days old."

At first we patted her on the head and smiled, but I think a different tactic is in order now that she's begun barking on the preschool playground.

Four children with the same gene pool, the same household rules, the same two parents watching their every move. Yet four completely different sets of preferences, opinions, habits, and taste buds—all of which are slowly, slyly sucking the life from the loving DNA donors who brought them here. The smarter they get, the dumber we feel.

Silly me, I thought I was just bringing home flannel-wrapped blank slates from the hospital.

That's not to say parents don't have any influence over who their children turn out to be. I like to think that our insistence on "please" and "thank you" will rub off. Someday. And though I don't expect Henry, Eleanor, Margaret, and Page to mime our values or our politics as they hit adulthood, I do hope they'll follow our general example on such scores as honesty, integrity, self-discipline, and all the rest (not to mention finally quit barking in public).

But I've grown a lot less anxious about transmitting all this character. I used to think they needed to be handled and molded like so many lumps of Play-Doh. Now I realize pie dough is more like it. Handle that too much and it turns out awful.

I've heard that great artists, from Michelangelo facing a block of marble to folk artist Bessie Harvey looking at a gnarled tree branch, felt that they saw the final work in the raw material; their job was just to help it come forward.

Kids, too, are who they are. We parents simply provide the finishing touches.

Which pretty much explains why I don't worry anymore about my son and his chicken nuggets.

Henry's first taste of those lip-smacking hydrogenated oils came the day he became a big brother. Daddyo had treated him to his first Happy Meal on that happy day. "Hi baby! Would you like a french fry?" he said in his high, sweet, twenty-one-month-old voice as he tried to insert one between Eleanor's pursed newborn lips. That he was more excited about the McDonald's food and my bed crank than his new sister I registered only with relief. It was a big day of change for the little guy after all.

Just how life-changing, I had no idea.

Hints of his persnickety palate had come earlier. As he made the transition from jars of mush, which he downed without protest, to solids, I had trouble finding anything agreeable to him. This was about the time all the tags in his clothes and the seams in his socks were "too scratchy," and he hated to get his hands dirty (kind of useful in self-feeding). If only I'd had him properly evaluated and enrolled in intervention therapy for borderline sensory disorder, he might be downing pepperoni pizza today. And I might have been, well, just a teeny tiny bit paranoid about choking. I obsessed over what was safe to feed him. Corn kernels? Boiled carrots? Diced turkey? I chopped them all to bits. No wonder Henry steadfastly refused them.

One fateful day I hit on cottage cheese. Nutritious, soft, and easy to pick up, so long as I remembered to buy the large curd kind. Soon Henry clamored greedily for it—meal after meal after meal. Gerber meat sticks, yogurt, and Tater Tots fell away. In a pathetic attempt to vary this menu, I sometimes topped the curds with a dusting of wheat germ. We called them "sprinkles" and I congratulated myself on my wholesome invention. Oh, I kept trying alternatives. But he kept spitting them out.

We had spent several months stuck at cottage cheese with sprinkles by the time Eleanor was born, and then, thanks to that introductory Happy Meal, the chicken nugget jag took off. By the time Margaret came along two years later, he'd gotten stuck on peanut butter. On saltine crackers, six, please, open faced. After a year he consented to our slathering it between two slices of wheat bread.

And that's where we've stayed. Among the foods that have never touched my ten-year-old's lips in their nonpureed form: pizza, hamburger, spaghetti, *any* vegetables, *any* pasta, *any* fish, *any* meat (other than chicken nuggets).

Sometimes his stubborn refusal to try anything new is funny, like when he politely informed a waitress who asked if he, too, wanted scrambled eggs, "No thanks, I'm a crackertarian." More often, it's been a source of worry. Will he starve? Stunt his growth? Set a bad example for his three sisters (all fine eaters)? Horrify dates and prospective employers when he orders a PBJ—hold the J—at a swanky restaurant? Okay, the angst is personal, too: Obviously, I'm a failure at this aspect of motherhood.

Everyone is obsessed with Henry's dietary monotony. My mother-in-law once insisted he had a tapeworm. My dad fears the boy won't grow strong without all-American beef coursing through his veins. Daddyo, who loves baba ghanoush, Szechuan pork, and Japanese squid, is merely disappointed.

I'm concerned, too—nutrition and all that. But I have more than a little empathy for my son. I know fussy. I was the child who refused to eat ketchup or spare ribs or bagels, unlike my four siblings, who gobbled them. My culinary passion was a folded-over cheese sandwich: one slice of orange American cradled in one slice of white bread. In restaurants, I'd concede to grilled cheese, but even that could lead to disaster. Case in point: age seven, Pennsylvania

Dutch country vacation, roadside diner, grilled cheese on the menu. I can still see the rubber-cement-like goo oozing from the sandwich on the plate I was presented—*white* American cheese! I had never dreamed such a horrible deviation from my comforting expectations could be possible. Nobody in my family talks about the barns or battlefields we saw on that trip, but they all remember the tantrum I threw when they tried to force me to eat grilled cheese that was not orange.

Not that most of the advice on picky eaters is framed as a personality issue:

"It's a bad habit. You have to nip it in the bud early." (Probably. But if you miss that window of opportunity, then what?)

"Keep offering a variety of foods, and eventually he'll grow out of it." (Although *eventually* is a word with no exact time frame. Eventually he'll go to college, too.)

"Make him taste one bite before he gets anything else." (And ruin your own supper while he ignores said bite and revels in the attention.)

"Starve him out. He'll cave in." (Oh yeah?)

Nothing we read told us to leave him alone and focus on his sweet nature and unmistakable growth.

He's still a crackertarian.

Our doctor says that like Craig Flatman of the jam sandwiches, Henry's growing just fine. With six-pack abs a lifeguard would envy and a hand-crushing grip, the boy was one of only two kids in his class to earn the elite Presidential Physical Fitness Award. He runs like a colt, especially if he's running toward his sisters or away from his parents.

Those sisters—who have not a single dietary quirk among them—ignore his diet. I expect he'll outgrow his pickiness, or at least its excessiveness, Though, like me, he'll probably never gobble baba ghanoush.

The other day the boy nonchalantly mentioned he'd tried a hot dog at a school picnic. Didn't like it, or the mustard, or the bun. But he tried it. My heart soared—his future was saved!

But all I said out loud, just as casually, was "That's nice. I don't like mustard either."

Momfidence...

. . . is recognizing that you are mothering a moving target. By the time you get one stage down pat, your child is already ten steps ahead of you. Being a quick study beats being an exhaustively thorough one.

. . . is buying cups, straws, washcloths, and toothbrushes in a different color for every kid because, of course, no rugged individual wants red if her sister already has it.

. . . is loving the one you're with.

You Can Run, but They Will Find You

On Work–Family Balance

> Set aside a specific amount of time—at least 30 minutes a day—simply to be together . . . No fair keeping one eye on the newspaper—the idea is to give your child your undivided attention . . . floor time shows your child that you can get on his level and stay interested in him. This gives him a tremendous feeling of being understood and cherished.
>
> — *Dr. Stanley Greenspan, "Floor Time for the Normal Child,"* Child *magazine*

I am hiding from my children. Not hide-and-seek hiding. It's more like *please-please-please-leave-me-alone* hiding. Please don't tell me the Looney Tunes DVD ended. Please no tattletaleing. Please not even any climbing aboard my lap to tell me how beautiful and wondersweet my hair is today and can I—cue the fluttering toddler eyelashes—have some Oreos?

The door to my home office, with its lovely view of the driveway and unpainted privacy fence and its convenient location right off the kitchen, is shut. The shades are drawn. It's a glorious Monday afternoon. I'm still wearing the fifteen-year-old baggy-kneed sweatpants and faded University of Iowa sweatshirt I threw on when I let the dog out at dawn. I've been squirreled away here for eighty-six minutes since the DVD began. Then again, I'm here pretty much any time I'm not sleeping, dispensing snacks, punching microwave or DVD buttons, emptying or loading the dishwasher, finding lost shin guards, converting fractions into decimals, picking up or dropping off, reading a story or urging someone to read a story, refereeing, investigating really loud thumps, or answering questions like "Mom, did you used to have a penis?"

I am working. Just a few more minutes and I'll be done with my penetrating probe of the most mysterious, life-altering issue facing America's future adults today. No, not global warming. Colic. It's a magazine article on crying that's due tomorrow. Now if I could just think a little faster . . .

"Let's play work," I hear Eleanor say right outside my door.

"Sure," agrees Margaret.

"Rrrrr—yip! Woof! Woof!" adds Page, apparently still playing the Teach-the-Zero-Year-Old-Puppy game that ended an eon of thirty seconds ago.

Outside, the real dog scratches at the screen door. "Awooooooo!" he whines as he widens the mosquito entrance he's already torn there.

Let's play work? Maybe there's a silver lining to the way my guilty heart blackens whenever I'm trying to earn a living and be a mom at the same time (which, as previously indicated, is every waking hour and every other sleeping one). Could it be that my children see me as a positive role model? They want to imitate me? I am secretly flattered. And relieved that they've found something to do that doesn't involve invoking older brother Henry's loud retaliatory wrath.

Then my door blams open. Found! And they don't just want to say hi or that they are going outside. They want *me*, in the eager, greedy way zombies want the flesh of the not-yet-undead. I try to sigh silently, so nobody notices.

"Mom? Mom? Canwehavesomeboxes? Canwecanwe? Canwe-havesome? Doweevenhaveany?"

"What for?" I reply with well-honed suspicion. As a parent you learn all too quickly that the most angelic of children can make the most innocent of requests for, say, crayons or cotton balls or string. Only later do you learn the true diabolical intention: The crayons wind up melted on the driveway like patternless mosaic tile. The cotton balls are Elmer's-glued to the heirloom dining-room table (something you don't notice until five months later at Thanksgiving, the only day of the year that you actually use the room). The string has been tied to every bush, tree, and stick of patio furniture in the backyard—incredible to behold but forget about trying to mow the grass.

"We need boxes. We're making computers," they claim.

Sounds enterprising enough. And refreshingly wholesome, too. I hit SAVE and shuffle into the kitchen. I fish around in the trash for Cookie Crisp and Froot Loops cartons that they'd emptied at breakfast.

A minute later, back at my desk, trying to "play work" myself, I hear, "Mom?" Actually what I hear is more like the rapid firing of a machine gun: "Mom?Mom?Mom?Mom?Mom?" in all manner of pitches, tones, and emotional states, as though the child is experimenting with every possible way to utter this syllable, as a degenerate gambler might try one hundred different methods of pulling a slot-machine handle in the hope of winning favor from the casino gods.

No one lets up until I say the magic word. "What?"

"Where are the scissors?"

Back to the kitchen. I fish some out of the all-purpose junk drawer (sippy cup lids, shoelaces, dachshund-shaped corn holders, leftover baby chew toys). Then I notice the sticky pinkness of the scissor ends. Someone's been using them to snip open Go-GURT tubes again. Well, better than using their teeth, right? I wipe off the encrustations and hand the scissors over with the reminder that they are for paper only (lest everyone's bangs soon resemble the uneven bars of a wireless reception indicator). Back to work. For three minutes.

"Mom?Mom?Mom? Where is the paper?"

"Mom?Mom?Mom? Where are the markers?"

"Rrrrrr! Yip! Yip!" yaps Page as she runs in circles around the kitchen island on hands and knees. She's no longer wearing her usual dog costume. Or much of anything else.

"Scritch scritch scritch" goes the real dog, destroying another wire-mesh panel.

"Don't do that," I say halfheartedly to both pups. "And please put your underwear back on." I know full well that Brownie will pay me no mind. But with the children I am delusional, still hoping they can be trained.

Finally the children have everything they need to manufacture two cardboard iMacs. I grab a Diet A&W and slink back to my office. They say it takes 2.9 minutes to get your concentration back on track after being interrupted. At this rate I will meet my deadline when the puppy goes to college.

Making computers keeps them busy for a long time. Five minutes. I don't even mind too much when they make several furtive runs behind me to check to see how the letters on my keyboard are arranged.

"Page!" I hear Margaret finally yell. "Do you want to play work?"

"Yip!"

"You can only play if we can use Ratty," says Eleanor in her most imperial big-sister voice.

Ratty is Page's lovey. I wish I could say it were a cute stuffed animal. But by no, er, stretch of the imagination is that true. Ratty is a foot-long ash gray rubber rat, made of the softest, squishiest, and yes, stretchiest Chinese rubber. The toy is disgustingly realistic down to its long droopy whiskers and even longer tail which, when pulled, elongates Ratty to a yard or more in length (outdistancing Brownie, himself no slouch in the length department, considering he's the longest miniature dachshund ever seen outside of a cartoon).

Daddyo, aka my loving and generous husband known to periodically take leave of his senses, bought Ratty for Page at the supermarket. It's not as though the child were begging for it. He saw the rat hanging, inexplicably, alongside a rubber lobster and a rubber squid in the store's soda aisle like some surrealist's butcher shop. He let Page choose one. She picked rat. On her first day at her new 100 percent organic, put-on-your-slippers-to-save-the-earth Montessori preschool, she howled when she accidentally (though to my secret relief) left it in our dust-and-vomit-encrusted Chevy minivan. "Ratty! Ratty! I want my Ratty!" She never forgot him again. Unfortunately her classmates had only the usual allergies, to wheat, nuts, eggs, and dust—not a latex allergy in the bunch. All that money spent on adorable flannel blankies and Corolle baby dolls, and my daughter carries a goo-rat everywhere.

Now Eleanor and Margaret have decided it will make the perfect mouse for their computers. They start to play.

I start to work. Again.

"I am Mommy. Typetypetytpetype," begins Margaret.

"Hey! Be quiet out there!" Eleanor hollers in her nastiest Mommy voice to a swarm of pretend children. Or maybe to Page.

I have a sinking feeling that imitation is not the sincerest form of flattery after all.

I peer around the corner to watch. They are all staring at an inside-out cereal box that's been taped together with half a mile of Scotch tape. Margaret's fingers dance above a construction paper keyboard while Page gnaws on the edge of the table, her fingers creeping toward Ratty, who has been tied to the cereal box with Brownie's leash.

"Typetypetypetypetype."

"This is booo-ring," Eleanor finally complains.

"I know," agrees Margaret. "But Mommy can't help it. It's her job."

Yes, it's a glamorous life cranking out glossy magazine articles. Or so I've heard. I wouldn't know. I'm too busy writing "Everything You Need to Know About Diapers" and "Will We Ever Have Sex Again?"

People tend to have predictable reactions when they find out I am a mother who is a writer:

Reaction 1: "How nice that you can work at home!" say Grayhead Mothers with Grown Children or Busy Moms with Panty Hose-Wearing-Traffic-Fighting Jobs.

Reaction 2: "How *do* you find the time?" say Busy Playgroup Book-Group Moms Whose Houses, Children, and Family Photo Albums All Put Mine to Shame.

Reaction 3: "I suppose there is a market for that sort of thing," say Most Men before ignoring me for the rest of the evening so they can talk over Iron City beers with Daddyo about the merits of the Black & Decker GH 600 14-inch Grass Hog with Automatic Feed Trimmer/Edger.

(Then there is his reaction: "When do we get to be famous? When do they make a sitcom out of us? And when are you going to iron my ^%@^#! shirts?")

All of these responses, except my husband's, are perfectly legitimate observations. I still have them myself. Working at home makes me feel like a spy who splits her time in two worlds, belonging to neither but sympathetic to both. What makes me squirm is when people think that because I talk to the parenting gurus all the time and I am a mother of four, I must be a parenting guru, too.

"My child won't eat/sleep/stop biting the cat/use the potty/ apply himself in school so he can get the AP credits he needs eight years from now in high school," they begin. "What do you think I should do?"

I am always torn. Do they want me to tell them what famous Dr. X just quoted in *USA Today* recommended when I interviewed him for a feature story on that very topic? Or do they want to know what *I* think? The two are rarely the same.

My usual solution to many burning child development issues is to settle into the soft embrace of an easy chair with a glass of merlot. Most garden-variety, middle-class child-rearing problems solve themselves. Few are worth obsession, much less adult intervention. As for the genuine knuckle biters, that's why we have schools, the police, and organized religion.

I might have access to all the supposed answers, but when it comes to my own family, I tend to make it up as I go along.

Shhh, don't tell the kids!

"Mom?"

"Hmmm?"

"Mom, how do you make a baby?"

The girls' work game busted up half an hour ago when Page unplugged Ratty and fled. But somehow I missed the transition from rodents to birds and bees.

Obviously those gentle bedtime books about hatching chicks and how kittens are born were too subtle. I like to think I am an honest, forthcoming kind of mom. But the question freezes me. In the first place, it's not what most people expect to hear when they're sitting at their desk minding their own business. I know I should be used to it—interruptions by kids are for me the time-sucking equivalent of office water-cooler chitchat. But questions about reproduction tend to be a little more startling than, say, "Can you drive me to Erin's house?"

And then there is the delicate matter of how much information to pass along. More than cabbage patches, obviously. But how much detail can a kindergartner need? There's nothing like being Mommy-on-the-spot to make a writer really eloquent.

"Well . . ." I begin.

Margaret's big coffee-black eyes bore into me, waiting.

"Uh, well," I begin again.

"I mean, do you make them from being married or from going to the hospital?"

"Oh!" This gives me a new starting point. "Well . . ."

"Neither!" Eleanor bursts in behind her younger sister. "They come from sperms and eggs!"

"Do not!"

"Do, too!"

"Do not!"

They run off.

I'm alone again.

Nobody waits for my answer. Nobody wants to know any facts of life. I wonder vaguely if I should follow them, and take advantage of this "teachable moment." I could gently explain that they're both on the right track, sketch out the basics. I picture a pastel Modess pamphlet mother–daughter moment, in duplicate.

Nah.

And I'm not just saying that because I'm racing a deadline. I watch them out the window, chasing one another. Rivalry, not biology, was apparently behind Margaret's question this time. If she were really wondering she'd not be so easily deterred. Or she'll ask again when Eleanor's not around. On this occasion I was merely a walk-on referee in a fencing match. I reach for my root beer and squint at my computer screen.

Now Henry pokes his head in. I thought he'd been upstairs in a ten-year-old's Xbox trance, but he'd clearly heard everything. "Yo, Mom," he says. "Do you *have* to be married to have a baby?"

A thousand tiny soda bubbles explode in my nose. In a house with kids, there's no getting off the hook. "Um, well, you see, as a matter of fact, no, you don't," I say with clinically neutral sex-ed accuracy—before adding, "but it's the best way."

I'm impressed that he's putting it all together. I brace myself for follow-ups about premarital sex and what exactly is wrong with out-of-wedlock babies.

Instead, he bolts from the room triumphantly shouting, "Yeeeeessss! I knew it!" A second later the screen door bangs. "Hey! Eleanor! You're right! That sperm thing is true!"

Ah, yes, that sperm thing. That's what brought me to this happy point in my life, and who would have thunk it?

Ask my four kids what they want to be when they grow up and they will tell you: a casino owner, a ballerina, the solver of the mystery of why people hiccup, a puppy.

Or that's what they say today. Last month their answers were a millionaire, Queen of the Earth, the solver of the unknown math problems, and a baby.

"I want to be what you are, Mom," Margaret recently decided. "A write-ist."

"That's not what you call it," snorted Eleanor. "You mean a bookmaker!"

I'm not placing any bets on either of their destinies. Most people follow a serpentine path to their eventual careers. I am one of those odd ducks, though, who's always had the only job I ever wanted. It says so in the diary I began keeping when I was nine (and have written in every day in the decades since):

February 7: "Read *Henry Huggins* by Beverly Cleary. Thick."

May 30: "Patti spilled red pop all over her white Communion dress at the beginning of the party."

September 16: "Pam read my beloved secret-full diary. Oh! The pain of it!"

December 1: "Wrote a rough draft of My Career for the bulletin board in the classroom. I wish to be an Authorist."

By age ten, I was making money from my scribbles, selling copies of my self-produced newspaper, *The Thursday Journal,* to my large and generous family. (Typical headlines: "Fad Alert: Smiley Faces Are Everywhere!" and "Squirrel Disrupts Nine O'Clock Mass!") Then it was a predictable track from editing my school yearbook and newspaper to journalism degree to New York City and magazine career to full-time writer.

All of which is to say I'd been preparing forever for the life I have now—except for one little detail. Make that four little aforementioned details: Henry, Eleanor, Margaret, and Page. Five, if you count Brownie, whom I certainly never counted on myself until I was lured over the cliff of rationality by the siren mosquito whine of "Canwehaveadogpleasepleasecanwehaveadogwe'llfeeditwe-promise!"

Authorist? Just as I'd hoped.

Mom? Shock of my life.

Yes, my family is an embarrassment of riches (excepting the moments when one or more of them is merely an embarrassment). Dinner came at 5 p.m. sharp and ended at 5:07. The first two minutes were consumed with arguments over whose turn it was to say "the blesser." Eleanor is named. We link hands. "Thank you for—ewww! Mom! Page was playing with the applesauce again!" A napkin is procured. Sticky fingers are wiped. "ThankyouforSpaghettiOs-amen." (We're having chicken, but never mind.)

Tonight's meal was relatively calm and civilized. It featured five "Stop rocking your chair"s, three "Keep your hands to yourself"s, one "Do not lick your plate," and a lively debate between Margaret and Page over who had more *a*s in her name.

At 5:09 I leave the table, having sat two minutes longer than everyone else for my evening meditation. I don't have the patience to actually meditate. I just zone there fantasizing about white tablecloths, attentive waiters, espresso, and lively after-dinner conversation. None of these things remotely resemble a Spencer family dinner, save the last item. Daddyo and I do have after-dinner conversation, and it invariably goes like this:

"Do you want to do the dishes?"

"I dunno. Do you want to do the dishes?"

"No."

"No, I'll do it."

"Are you sure?"

"Okay. I'm going to try to get something done."

"Okay. But will you first see what they're screaming about?"

It doesn't matter who said what. Depending on the evening, and what crises are at hand, we're pretty much interchangeable (except that I have the softer lap and he has the longer fuse).

You'd think that being the mother of four and writing about being a mother of four would be perfect complements, the green eggs and ham of vocation and career. Some of the time, it is. The commute, for example, consists of about ten paces from the breakfast table to my office off the kitchen. Another work-at-home plus: I don't have to pretend my family is secondary in my life to the corporate gods and masters by hiding the many crayon portraits, wobbly clay pots of construction paper flowers, and the sculpture of Brownie constructed entirely of Kleenex and tape. I can come to work with graham-cracker smears on both shoulders, and nobody's there to make a snide remark.

And then there are the hours. I work, more or less, from 9 a.m. to 3 p.m. when most everyone is at school, and another post-bedtime shift in the event of a hideous deadline or a day peppered with doctor's appointments, school plays, splitting headaches, or several hundred interruptions.

Chief among the snags in this idyllic arrangement, on the other hand, are the aforementioned kids. Stephen King said that what one needs most in a writing space is a door you are willing to shut. I'm willing. I'm just not sure why, since it's never given anybody else around here a moment's pause.

At last I am deep in that second shift. Twenty-second shift, if you count all the times my concentration has been snapped by interruptions and restarted. This is the final shift, the one that starts after the bath-pj's-toothbrushing-story-story-story-story-story routine has ended.

Tip, tap, tip, tap on my keyboard. My back is to the door to the kitchen. The house—dark. The only light—glowing Macintosh screen. Quiet. Very. Finally.

Suddenly, I'm aware of a presence behind my shoulder. It's too tall to be Brownie. Something's looming, coming closer, something big, possible knife, possible crackhead intruder. *Oh-no-rapist-psycho-killer-eveningnews-funeral-orphans-ohnoohno!* Hairs on back of neck stand tall.

"Boooo!"

"Aiiiieee!" I thrash in my chair.

Much giggling. It's Page, who was tucked in over an hour ago, wearing her blankie over her head for ghostly effect, and dragging Ratty by his string-thin tail.

"Oh God! Don't! Do! That!"

Much crying.

Okay. Never mind. Quitting time. I log out and put my lumpling on my lap. "I forgot to tell you how beautiful your shirt is," she says, caressing the stained gray cotton.

"Really," I say.

A moment later Margaret traipses in. "Can't sleep. Need a bednight snack."

"Me, too," echoes the night stalker.

I give them each a Fig Newton fished from a desk drawer where I stashed it in an attempt to wean myself from deadline-coping chocolate.

"Mom?" says Margaret, suddenly remembering. "Tell Page I have two *a*s and she has only one."

Mild panic flash. A's? Was it report card day? I never saw Henry and Eleanor's—but wait, Page is only in preschool. And in Margaret's kindergarten they only give check marks, not A's and B's. They're back to competing over the vowels in their names.

"*A* is my letter," Page says stubbornly.

"So it is," I agree. "You both have *a*s. You're both A-plus."

The praise momentarily distracts Margaret, nibbling her cookie as she studies a photograph tacked to the bulletin board near my desk. It's a family portrait taken for a magazine article I wrote while I was pregnant with her. One of my few glamour perks is that sometimes publications I write for send a photographer my way to make images of me imitating my real life, minus the messy hair on the kids and the dark circles on me. In this photo I'm wearing a swingy black dress, surrounded by my husband and two blond moppets, Henry at four and Eleanor, two, who chewed the leg of a stuffed white bear throughout most of the shoot. Aside from the rare cosmic occurrence—never since repeated—of all of us looking directly into the camera with nothing in anyone's mouth, I like this picture because even though I am great with child, I still have the midpregnancy glow one gets in the weeks before you look like you're impersonating yourself in an inflatable fat suit. Even if this glow is just the professional makeup.

"Is that me?" asks Page, pointing to Eleanor in the picture.

"No, that's Eleanor." Eleanor and Page look like identical twins born five years apart. Not even I can always tell them apart in photos, unless there is another sibling around to use as a chronological yardstick, or a telltale stuffed animal. Fluffy bear, Eleanor. Rubber rat, Page.

"Where am I?" Margaret asks.

"You're in my tummy," I say. "This picture was taken just before you were born."

Margaret turns on her sister to gloat. "Ha, ha, Page! I'm in the picture, and you're not!"

"I am, too!" Page replies. "I am a twinkie in Dad's eye."

Now who told her that?

"You are both my twinkies," I say, kissing them on their foreheads. "A-plus twinkies."

That's the silver lining of trying to string sentences together in a noisy house where doors don't work. My kids give me great material. You can't make this stuff up.

Momfidence...

. . . is making a list of all the things that *aren't* your job: Keeper of Everybody's Happiness. Chief Entertainment Programmer. Homework Corrector. Homework Doer. First Responder to Every Call for Help at School or Place of Worship. Science Night Participant (that would be your child; you are the supply purchaser and project transporter).

. . . is displaying a clay stegosaurus and many drawings of happy, heart-festooned stick people in your workspace—no matter what your profession or level.

. . . is venting about how "doing it all" is one of the dopier cliché goals leftover from the 1980s. Doing the best you can while trying to do as much as you really truly need to is the best anybody can hope for.

An Ounce of Prevention, Not a Ton

On Safety

DO watch your child at all times while she's playing . . . DON'T allow her to eat there.

> — *"Playground Do's and Don'ts,"* Parents *magazine*

Fifty-six.

> —*number of products in the "Bathroom Safety" category of babyproofingplus.com*

On to the primal truths about keeping children alive. You'd think that the instinct to protect one's offspring would have relaxed a bit now that the threat of saber-toothed tigers and open fire pits have been eliminated. But no. No exhaling yet. Now we have cyberstalkers and mad cow threatening our young. *E. coli!* Lyme disease! Avian flu! Tainted vaccines! Arsenic-infested play structure wood! Mercury-laced tunafish sandwiches! Pesticides! Lead! It's all out there, lurking in the bushes, in your kitchen, just waiting for you . . . to . . . turn . . . your . . . back . . .

And you don't even get to wait until you have an actual child in hand to worry over. Protection paranoia infects while you're still gestating.

The scene: My first baby shower. The tension level: About to rise rapidly.

PREGNANT OBLIVIOUS ME: Gee, what's this?

EAGER GIFT GIVER: A toilet lock!

ME (*struggling for proper facial expression, somewhere between polite gratitude and crestfallen disbelief*): A what?

EAGER GIFT GIVER: To prevent drowning!

I put the device on the pile with the three tub seats (also to prevent drowning), two monitors (to hear any distress call that the child's ordinary lungs cannot make), blind winder (to prevent dangling blind cords from strangling your tot), wipes warmer (to avoid shocking tot's filthy tush with cold), and—my favorite mystery object—a firm foam wedge. This last item, I was told, would prevent my careless newborn from fatally rolling onto his stomach in his sleep.

Historical sidenote: This shower took place back when it was still encouraged to lay your baby to sleep on his side, a position now forbidden by the Gold Standard of Good Mothering and the American Academy of Pediatrics. You used to be able to roll a blanket—or place a pricey foam wedge—behind the newborn's back and thus prop him into a comfy curl. By sheer good luck, all four of my side sleepers survived this perilous care. Perhaps more incredibly, so did my husband, my four siblings, and I, who had all been placed in our cribs not on our sides or our backs, but in the Position of Doom, on our tummies. Try that today and your neighbor might call protective services.

At least I can be grateful that when I was expecting Henry, the under-mattress sensor pad had not yet been invented. This newer device helpfully signals if your baby is "absolutely still for twenty seconds." Funny, I thought stillness was the goal, only for more like eight hours.

What happened to the bibs and rattles I was expecting?

If ever an event warranted stiff drinks, it's a baby shower—the one occasion where the guest of honor is sure to be offered none. It was a party designed to give me a warm welcome to the sorority of motherhood and celebrate new life, and there I sat, unwrapping harbingers of death.

I came home wondering how the human race has managed to keep going lo these many years.

"You can't give a child too much safety," a mom once told me by way of explaining her addiction to product recall updates on a certain Web site. (Of course she doesn't need a lab technician to tell her the toys she bought are potential death traps; she just needs to tell her kids to keep them off the stairs!)

My friend's rationale, though, explains why twenty-first-century boys and girls must by law wear helmets when they roller-skate in some neighborhoods. Why parents insist they report every move by cell phone (while simultaneously freaking out about the latest headline linking kids' mobiles to brain tumors). Why doctors order them to pull book bags on wheels to protect their backs across the parking lots into schools where they walk through metal detectors to get to class. At day care, they're Web-cammed. At home, it's spyware in the teddy bears to keep an eye on the sitter. We slather tots with sunblock before driving them to padded, jungle-gym-free "play systems"—where we don't dare take our hovering eyes off them, lest . . . what? A childnapper pluck them from the plastic slide the minute we look down to fetch the hand sanitizer? They splat off the monkey bars because the Superglue beam of our watchful gaze wasn't there to keep them up?

We're way past flirting with disaster. We're lovestruck.

Which is why I like to remind myself of the four safety tips that nobody tells you about.

Safety Reality 1: "Every firstborn is a guinea pig."

And every first-time parent is a sucker. I mean that in the kindest way. After all I was one once.

Not long after we'd brought Henry home, as I sat in the nursery rocking him, my gaze fell on the window. Did I watch the rustling leaves and count my blessings for the healthy baby in my arms? No. All I saw were the venetian blind cords. The way they hung there. Ominously.

Henry wasn't even sitting up yet. The windows were quite out of his reach. Well actually he wasn't reaching yet either. Still, guilt pricked my very soul. Hadn't this danger been clearly listed on every baby-proofing list I'd studied? Hadn't some baby in Topeka met an untimely demise by getting tangled in long cords? I shuddered and held Henry more tightly. How could I have missed this? *What kind of mother was I?*

I rocked. The cords dangled. I didn't exactly fathom how this particular danger worked; all that mattered was that *they could get him.*

I made Daddyo install the blind-winder thingies that very day.

Soon after, he walked in on me crawling around on my hands and my knees in the living room. "Lose a contact lens again?"

"No. I'm safety-proofing."

"The floor?"

"I'm looking for hazards that are invisible to us but are right at Henry's level."

"Henry's level is carpet-fuzz high," he pointed out. "He can't even scoot." Then he rolled his eyes and walked away. Just like that. If I'd lost a contact he'd be right down there with me, but with his son's life in the balance, he's off!

Like I said, he came by his Momfidence more naturally than I did.

When Henry did begin crawling—all outlets having long been plugged and all long tablecloths whisked away—I realized we'd overlooked the brick fireplace hearth. It suddenly looked so hard, and his round, bald head, so soft. Even Daddyo understood this peril, perhaps because the solution involved the manly application of duct tape. He promptly taped leftover foam carpet pad all around the hearth. We lived in plain view of those hideous home-made bumpers for the next several years. Incredibly, not one guest who was a veteran parent, bless their hearts and bitten tongues, managed to laugh in our faces at the lunacy.

We meant well. We really did. When every safety precaution is presented with equal gravity and you don't know any better, you readily fork out the money and sacrifice your decor. *Of course* you believe you need a hippo-shaped faucet cover, every bit as much as you need an infant car seat. Only over time do you realize that the faucet cover looks silly and the odds of your tot's head colliding with the metal are about as remote as the odds of a crash, though in the unlikely event of a faucet-noggin collision, your baby would probably only be bruised, whereas a car crash could be fatal without the seat.

The house that Henry was a baby in looked a lot different by the time Page came along seven years later. She knew no plastic locks on the drawers, no doorknob covers, no corner protectors. No hearth bumpers. Half these safety devices had been destroyed by siblings over the years. The other half proved too much hassle for their small fingers (or our big ones). There's nothing like a toilet lock to slow the progress of a potty trainee, so there weren't any of those either.

Page's tender face went unshielded from harmful rays by a sun-shade in the window of our minivan because nobody else sitting back there could resist yanking it off its suction cups. We even pretty much gave up on baby gates. Although they kept her from the stairs, they also restricted the movements of Henry, Eleanor, and Margaret, who couldn't maneuver the gate lock. They had more accidents try-ing to vault or climb over the gate than Page would have had she been let loose. Besides, I had a built-in warning system: "MOOOOOM! The baby's on the stairs again!" When nobody could keep an eye on her, she went in the playpen. Pardon me, play *yard.* That's the pre-ferred humane term nowadays, as if a baby cared about the seman-tic difference between a plastic cage and an expanse of lawn.

I should point out that newbie zeal is not limited to safety con-cerns. We never bothered to stimulate Page with black and white pictures propped in her line of vision in the car, either. We did not keep an art book open on the floor near her swing, so she could take in Matisse and Picasso while nodding off rather than gazing dopily at the bare wood. We did not take her to tour museums while she was still Snugli-sized (though of course, with Henry, our sweet little guinea pig, we did all these things and more).

Near as I can figure, our later-life laxity led to no obvious dif-ference in their brain potentials, although who can be sure? Maybe being kept in a pen and not exposed to fine art are the reasons my youngest child now thinks she is a puppy.

Safety Reality 2: "Children are so durable!"—My friend Julia

Durable. I savor that word like a chocolate drop. I first heard it from a mom with much older children who had just watched one of my babies careen off her porch unscathed. It is the perfect adjective to describe a child, though most of us tend to think of the fruits of our loins in far more *fragile* terms. After all a child has a soft skull, small bones, and the irresistible big-eyed delicacy of a Keane painting.

Don't let appearances fool you. Kids are tough. They trip and fall off skateboards, they fly over bicycle handles—and they bounce back up. They scrape their skin weekly and find it highly entertaining, not to mention educational, to watch the rapid progress of the ensuing scab. Their bones are even softer than ours, so they're more likely to bend than break. Though they *will* break, rest assured. And then they, too, will swiftly heal.

In other words, children are not only built to last, they are built to fall apart. One who makes it through childhood without a scratch is either extremely lucky (maybe with an advanced sense of balance) or excessively cautious. Or else the unscathed child has simply been deprived of the normal childhood opportunities to ride a scooter, scramble over a woodpile, walk barefoot, fling himself around the room in a wild fit, or perform feats of daredevilry that seem utterly senseless to anyone but another child.

When they do fall, I've learned the following surefire responses.

- Resist the natural impulse to exclaim and cluck. If you do, their cries will get louder. If you look over surreptitiously and, upon seeing no blood or broken bones, look quickly away, the cries will stop.
- Feel relieved, not horrified, if a big bruised lump pops up. It's the dents, not the bumps, that signal more serious injury. Usually the scarier the mishap looks, the milder it turns out to be.
- Dispense Band-Aids with Popsicles, no matter the hour of the day or season of the year. They work more effectively this way.
- Spring for the Band-Aids with cartoon characters and bright colors. They have been proven to heal 50 percent faster.
- Never discount the curative power of the lap.

Safety Reality 3: "If the thunder don't get you, then the lightning will."—Robert Hunter

You can buy all the water wings, walkie-talkies, global positioning system monitors, child leashes—er, *harnesses*—and antibacterial everything that your nerves desire. You can latch away poisons, knives, matches, and guns. You can invest in color video baby monitors with "night vision for viewing in total darkness" and then, when your baby gets more mobile, a "child distance monitor," which sounds an alarm when your tot strays more than a few feet away from you. (I am not, for the record, making these products up.) And then your child will wind up in the emergency room anyway. That's what "fluke" means.

Although even in my more paranoid days I never went so far as GPS systems and knee pads for crawlers, I did spray Skin So Soft to repel mosquitoes and keep a semi-hawkish eye on toddlers and preschoolers outside. I never neglected to chant "Be careful!" whenever they climbed a slide ladder or careened down the driveway in a large plastic wagon with a broken door.

Not good enough.

ER visit 1: Henry, age two, throws a wild tantrum upon being told it's bedtime while vacationing at his grandmother's house. His skull flails into a bookcase. Four stitches. Should I have let him stay up until midnight to avoid the tantrum? Or rearranged Mima's furniture?

ER visit 2: Two years later. Daddyo heads out of town. "Drive carefully!" I call after him as Henry, Eleanor, and I blow kisses from the driveway.

Our neighbor, Horace, sees us and ambles over with his six-year-old grandson, Tyler. Henry runs to the boy as if pulled by a magnet. Nothing is quite so exciting to a little boy than a bigger one. They start kicking around a soccer ball while Horace and I discuss important neighborhood issues like how to kill moles, which are still tearing up my front lawn with holes. In addition to looking like hell, they present a danger to running children, albeit a whole new hobby for my husband, who has so far variously tried traps, poison, kerosene, water, and smoke to eradicate the beasts. Horace is extolling the virtues of chewing gum, of all things, to get the job done.

Out of the corner of my eye, I see Eleanor, who is across the yard, tumble. Nothing too unusual there. Even without the mole holes, she's still a little wobbly on her feet.

"And then the moles eat the Juicy Fruit—make sure it's Juicy Fruit—and—"

She's still down. Not crying, just sitting there.

"And it binds them up inside, you see—"

"Juicy Fruit. Right. Just a sec," I interrupt. I walk toward Eleanor, more curious than alarmed. I'm about to call out, "Are you tired, Swellie?" when I see that she is so covered by angry, swarming yellow jackets that she looks like a beekeeper without the protective netting. They're everywhere—in her clothes, her baby-fine hair, even her mouth. So that's why she couldn't holler.

I'm terrified of bees. I'll do almost anything to avoid them. But one of the marvels of motherhood is how danger turns a chickenshit into a Mother Teresa hen. I plunge into the cloud of bees like a nun rescuing the unwashed, like a firefighter storming a burning building. Lifting my daughter up from the underground nest that she'd stumbled into, I sprint away, yellow jackets in hot pursuit. I tear off her clothes as I go—first to a spot a few yards away, then to the garage, and finally into the house. They still seem everywhere.

It all happens so fast Horace and the boys have no idea I'm playing the heroine in Attack of the Killer Bees. Finally Eleanor's screams (or mine?) alert them and they follow us inside. Horace tells me that half an onion is just the thing for bee stings, though his wife, Myrna, favors a mud poultice, while the boys have a blast clambering on furniture to swat the last of the swarm with rolled-up newspapers.

I frantically dial the pediatrician.

Eleanor looks like a porcupine having an acupuncture treatment. Red welts and tiny protruding stingers have transformed her into a dazed, whimpering doll. Through the yellow tufts of hair that stick straight up where the bees got tangled and could not escape, I see more red spots.

It's only when the ER doctor has removed all the stingers and pronounced her okay, no anaphylactic shock, no lasting damage, that I notice my own legs are welted, too. And it's not until after I've collected Henry from Horace and Myrna's house and am tucking him into bed that I realize how terrifying the whole episode was. And how guilty I feel. George hadn't been gone for ten minutes when the evening calm exploded.

Henry is full of questions: "When the bees stung Eleanor, did it hurt? What did the doctor do? How did he get the stingers out? Did she cry?"

I explain it all. "You were a brave boy to wait and wonder about her," I say. He'd never had an impromptu babysitting session like that before.

"I didn't wait and wonder! I played with Tyler's *squort* guns!"

Okay, then, *some* of us were terrified.

Should I have prevented this mishap by scouring our whole two acres for nests every day? Sprayed the kids with DEET before turning them out to play? Shadowed Eleanor's every step so I might have spotted the winged stingers before she stepped near? No, no, and no. Reality just stings sometimes.

I'm not saying we shouldn't be careful. As much as anybody, I try to enforce the buddy system, teach bike safety, give swim lessons (after age three), nag about helmets, meet their friends' parents, and issue reminders about not helping strangers look for lost puppies. I even buy the occasional safety device (water wings being a personal favorite). But the oceans of information and products designed to help ward off every peril obscure a key message: If you're a mom, you ought to *count on* a certain amount of disaster.

You can:
- Expect to see blood.
- Expect to visit the ER at least once per childhood.
- Expect to feel like a bad mother because your child spilled blood and/or visited the ER.
- Say "Be careful!" as much as you want. Nobody will listen but it always makes you feel proactive.

You cannot:
- Protect your child from everything. Swaddling should end around four months.
- Quit worrying. You think pioneer moms weren't the slightest bit anxious when their sons went out to shoot supper? You wouldn't be a mother if you didn't fret about something. No safety device has yet been invented to prevent it.
- Score any Mommy points for worrying harder or being more aggressively vigilant than anybody else. Nobody will care, though they may feel a little sorry for your child.

Which brings me to the next key point.

Safety Reality 4: "There is such a thing as too much safety."

There is one way to keep a child perfectly safe: Hold him on your lap in a padded room for eighteen years. Unfortunately, aside from being highly impractical, you'd cause as much damage as you were trying to prevent.

There's a line we all have to find between vigilance and nutcase.

I once saw a boy's pride deflated when his mother began screeching at him from an upstairs window, in the middle of a party, because he wasn't wearing his bike helmet. He was tooling around on the backyard lawn. On a tricycle. Another time I spent an hour at the beach watching a family shelling along the surf—you know, the part of the ocean where there are more seashells than water—the kids' progress slowed by full flotation suits. A 1951 Brownie scout handbook I picked up at a garage sale shows girls "how to use a pocket knife." A useful skill—but if I tried to teach my troop that today, I'd probably be sued if someone got nicked.

Life is full of risks. Still, you go to the beach even though, in theory, a tsunami could sweep you to sea. You buy a house in California even though the earth might split open and swallow you whole. An asteroid might crash into the earth tomorrow, for that matter. But you keep inhabiting it anyway because along with the risks come certain rewards—like life. And adventure! New skills! Growing independence!

Or that's what I tell myself when my ten-year-old utters those fateful words, "Can I ride my bike to Isaac's?"

It's a simple enough request. Henry wants to play with his buddy, and I don't even have to drive him over. So what's with the slight anxiety in the pit of my stomach even as I appear to grant him a cheery okay?

I'm torn between giving my children the measure of freedom

they crave and deserve—the freedom they need—and battling all the "what ifs" a modern imagination can dream up. It's wrenching. Yet slightly melodramatic, too. American parents are suffering from a collectively overactive imagination.

Statistics show that more kids are killed riding in cars than on bikes, for example. But we drive them everywhere without a thought while not letting them coast freely around the neighborhood. What's the point of stocking up on junior-sized gas masks if you drive them to soccer every day while working your BlackBerry? And there's not much consolation in a school having metal detectors if its textbooks aren't up-to-date and the teacher salaries are indecent. There's nothing like paranoia to skew priorities.

For all our melodramatic fretting, the numbers are on our side. The death rate is down for this cocooned generation! Horrible diseases, down or vanquished! Even school crime and violence have been steadily dropping for years! And unless you've got problems with your spouse or an unsavory relative, you probably don't have too much to fear from that biggest modern bogeyman, "stranger danger." Most abuse and kidnapping occurs at the hands of relatives, not strangers or caregivers, statistics show. I don't know the ratio of children who visit playgrounds in most neighborhoods to children who are snatched away from them, but I have to think it's pretty infinitesimal. The odds of, say, drowning are far higher.

And then there are the scares that pop up like Halloween decorations for a few weeks of fright, only to fade into the next news cycle. (Anybody remember the Alar apple panic? Toxic crayons made in China? Electric blankets and their currents of death?) For a few scary weeks, nightlights, of all things, were the villain du jour. Something about causing nearsightedness—or leukemia. Then, whoops! Never mind, bad data, bad interpretation. Lights on. Whew!

So we're left weighing the risks, which are usually lower than we think, with the benefits, which are usually higher than we give them credit for. After all, the whole point of parenting is to feed your hatchlings, make them strong, and let them flap their wings—so that one day you push them out of the nest and watch them fly away.

The empty nest is a goal, not a syndrome (only 5,475 more days for Daddyo and me!)

Admittedly it's easier to be cavalier on paper than in my own kitchen. I'm struggling to build up to this snipped-apron-strings thing—a walk to a friend's today, a solo movie tomorrow—so that I can get used to the growing amounts of independence they'll need as they get ever bigger. (The mall? Driving a car? College!)

The phone rings. "I'm here at Isaac's, Mom."

Oh sweet relief!

"We're gonna ride over to the drugstore, okay?"

Momfidence...

. . . means knowing the difference between a nonnegotiable precaution (seat belts, vaccinations, constant pool supervision) and a laughable one (Thudguard, the stylish new hat made for "toddling on hard surfaces").

. . . is worrying that your child will crack his femur in two on his skateboard—but letting him go to the new skate park anyway.

. . . is sticking to cute cotton pj's not only because the flame-retardant kind is stiff and scratchy, but because you feel perfectly confident that your little ones will not smoke in bed.

. . . is having a little faith in numbers. Number of kidnap victims abducted by family members: more than 75 percent. Number of children kidnapped in 1997 by nonfamily members, including friends, acquaintances, neighbors, and creepy uncles: 115. Number of children under age eighteen in the United States: *more than 72 million.*

Number of tots who drown in toilets each year: 30. Total number of toilets: ????

An Oreo Never Killed Anybody

On Feeding

Subversive elements are everywhere . . . play dates at homes where junk food is the snack of choice . . . kids at pre-school whose lunch boxes flaunt white-bread sandwiches, chocolate cookies, and sugar-sweetened fruit punch . . ."

—*Arlene Eisenberg, Heidi E. Murkoff, and Sandee E. Hathaway,* What to Expect in the Toddler Years

I'm cruising the Costco aisles in our weekly quest for seven gallons of milk (nonorganic, reduced fat, from a cow) and other family-of-six staples. Five pounds of hamburger, check. Trix–Lucky Charms–Cocoa Puffs econo-box, check. Fruit by the Foot by the crate, check. Vat of lemon–lime Gatorade Instant Mix ("makes 9 gallons!"), check.

"Oreo, Mommy!"

I turn to reply, until I realize that, for a change, the little voice doesn't belong to one of mine. It's coming from the cart just ahead. A three-year-old with auburn ringlets, a sequinned cashmere hoodie, and what I swear look like a very shrunken pair of True Religion jeans rises from the quilted seat liner placed to protect her from the germ-infested seat, and lunges ecstatically. The mere sight of those flying black discs with the creamy iced centers will do that to a kid.

"I want Oreo! I want Oreo!"

"No, Willow," says a tall woman in yoga pants and a tight T-shirt that says "Co-exist."

"Oreo! Oreo!"

"Oreo yuck!" Mommy replies. "Icky!"

"Not icky!" the toddler insists. "Oreo my best!"

"Oh, I know, Willi! Let's play I Spy. I spy something green! Is it broccoli? Is it edamame?"

"Oreoooooooooooooooo!"

"I spy the green apples in our cart! Apples rock! We'll have shiny apple moons when we get home! Yay!"

"OREOOOOOOOOOOO!"

Mommy shoots me an embarrassed look. "Honestly, I don't know how they find out about these things," she murmurs as she rolls Willi away toward greener aisles.

My hand freezes in midair. I was just about to reach for a gleaming royal blue three-pound ten-pack myself. For a second, a full-grown Willow glides across my consciousness, lean and apple-cheeked, while my own four darlings galumph around their future like choco-toxicated Boohbahs.

It occurs to me that I am about to commit an act so vile that it's banned at the two groceries nearest to my house. Neither Whole Foods nor Earth Fare—their very names signaling their priorities as clearly as Costco's—stock Oreos. Nor do they carry Diet Coke, Campbell's soup, Toastchee crackers, Velveeta Shells & Cheese, or most of the brand names we live on. Of course they do carry pricey all-natural imitations that nobody around here will touch, as well as picture-perfect produce with twice the price tag and exactly the same nutritional value of Costco's "conventional" greens. I don't know what's more annoying about these organic superstores (four in my town of forty-five thousand!): the sanctimonious exclusivity of the stock, the prices, or the magazines at the checkout aisle. *Breathe. Natural Health & Garden. Vegetarian Times. Spirituality and Health.* Wouldn't it be more "holistic" to offer a mix of alternative items *and* normal ones—I mean mainstream—I mean ordinary—I mean the stuff we all grew up on? At least the magazines sold in the parallel universe of regular grocery stores, the ones featuring glossy chocolate cakes next to the words "Walk Off Weight!" reflect the cheerfully incongruous lives of most people I know.

"Am I in here?" Margaret once asked, leafing through one of the colorful issues positioned near the conveyor belt at Whole Foods the way she does at our usual Harris Teeter. She likes to hunt for the articles I write, which sometimes feature a photo of me with the kids.

"Let's see," I replied with a glance at the title. It's *Living Without.* Nope, not us.

Now I picture another future for the organically grown Willow. This time she's secretly gorging herself on forbidden chocolate and ice cream every time she gets a chance while Henry, Eleanor, Margaret, and Page do what they do most afternoons: dunk a few Oreos in a glass of after-school milk and move on to homework and play. The cookies go in my cart—as they do every time I shop.

Directly related to keeping a child alive, of course, is the question of what to feed him. The truest answer, "Whatever he will eat," sounds much too glib to be taken seriously nowadays. Everybody expects a response as complicated as the latest food pyramid.

And why not? In a world where you can't control the government or the rate at which cool purses become rapidly outdated, your child's diet is a handy place to roll up your sleeves and take charge. After all, the stomachs keep grumbling and the mealtimes keep coming. You are the food gatekeeper. You make the choices. And what a lot of choices there are.

Somewhere between anorexia and obesity, we're led to believe, lies a happy-medium diet for our children that's free from trans fats, sugar, refined grains, additives, pesticides, and artificial coloring, a diet that will stoke optimal growth and development, boost brainpower, fuel performance on the playing fields, reduce the likelihood of dread disease in their adulthood, and extend longevity— all without breaking the bank.

But will they eat it? That's what I care about, along with "How fast can I drop it down their gullets?" I zap (Tyson Southern Fried Chick'n Chunks chicken nuggets). I snip (watermelon-kiwi Go-GURT). I pop tops (Chef Boyardee Cheesy Burger Macaroni). I draw the line at Pringles in bed, but then I never said that being practical about feeding kids should involve slovenliness.

I am all for good nutrition. Yes, I am a pro-nutrition kind of mom. I absolutely believe we should nourish our children. No starvation. No stuffed pigs. Equal opportunity for all food groups at every meal.

But beyond that? There's more misguided attention given to feeding children than there are moms with guilty consciences.

That I am a cookie-dispensing mother—which just a few years ago, let's not forget, projected an image of nurturing rather than the rankest irresponsibility—is something for which my kids have their great-grandmother to thank. My Gram, who never met a trans fat or a net carb she thought to count, kept a round tin perpetually filled with Oreos for visiting grandchildren. (That is, when the tin wasn't filled with *chruschiki,* a Polish pastry whose ingredients include "a jigger of whiskey to make the dough soft.") "And what would you like to eat?" she would ask the minute we trooped in her door.

Having thrown away the banana in her Ellis Island boxed lunch when she was nine because she'd never seen one in Warsaw and nobody suggested she peel it first, Gram took a no-nonsense approach to food. All she wanted to know was how it tasted. "I knew you were coming so I baked a cake," she'd beam as she brandished her signature pound cake (one pound of flour, one pound of 10X sugar . . .) or a glazed Bundt whose humped mold produced slices alternating one inch or two inches thick.

"Balanced" diet to Gram meant the comforting rhythms of breakfast, snack, lunch, snack, dinner, snack. She fed us fresh-picked raspberries from the bushes in her backyard and made mushroom soup from scratch on Christmas Eve. But she certainly never analyzed the nutritional content of her *nalesniki,* pierogi, and home-cased kielbasa. She never wondered whether any of my Wonder-fed siblings or I were consuming the right proportions of protein or calcium, let alone selenium or boron, two nutrients I've recently seen highlighted in what-to-feed-your-kids articles. (Boron? Isn't that a square on the periodic table, or gas station circa 1962?)

Not that she wasn't open-minded. Gram loved culinary experiments. If only she'd emigrated to Peoria, Illinois, the test-market capital of the planet, instead of East Detroit, Michigan. "It was new, so I thought I'd try it," she'd say by way of explaining the blueberry Toast'ems and Screaming Yellow Zonkers in her cupboards.

Gram didn't dwell on the "whys" when it came to food. She was satisfied with the "why nots?" Why not eat boxed macaroni and cheese so bright and happy that Crayola named a crayon after it? Why not shake and bake? Fruit ironed to the texture and color of stained glass? A new flavor of Hawaiian Punch? Let's give it a try!

Seasoning the articles I write with references to cookies and Pop-Tarts, alas, has proven a sure way to make editors nervous. "If we say that you let your kids sample the chocolate-chip dough, we ought to mention that this is only okay if you use pasteurized eggs," one pointed out, ever mindful of keeping her readers safe. "And how about we make them peanut butter cookies instead? No, wait! That's an allergy problem. Oatmeal?" Mentioning that I feed my children bright orangey pasta and meatballs from a can is tantamount to confessing I let them ride motorcycles without helmets while carrying Confederate flags and wearing fur.

Once I wrote a line in an essay paraphrasing Margaret about how the best things in life, to a child, end in "o": Dorito, Frito, Cheeto, Tostito, Ho Ho, Cheerio, LEGO, Daddyo, and of course, Oreo. I had thought this was a brilliant bit of mental sorting for a three-year-old. "Too much junk," came the editor's reply along with her red pen. You could tell she lived in New York because she unhelpfully suggested "Bugaboo" in place of the snack foods.

Quantity never enters into the critics' conversation. Neither does balance. Or the notion that cheerfully chomping the occasional color, flavor, or texture not found in nature is one of the prerequisites of childhood. An after-school Oreo or a seven-year PBJ jag never killed anybody. The best advice I ever heard on handling my finicky son came not from a nutritionist or a pediatrician but a Harvard ob-gyn—who'd had just such a boy herself: Wait. By the time he's dating, it's not very likely he'd try to impress a babe on prom night by taking her to Chick-fil-A.

Unfortunately most magazines are looking to give their readers more immediate solutions. If you have a child who will eat only foods that are the color of an unadorned pasta noodle, the presumption is that you need to tempt him out of it. (Imagine if Picasso in his Blue Period were handled the way we do a toddler in his white

one.) The fact that pickiness is chiefly a problem in your own head goes unmentioned. Nobody ever starved or developed scurvy from garden-variety pickiness. Whether the topic is eating quirks or after-school snacks, anything you're bound to read on the topic presumes a dietary utopia where kids can't get enough pineapple-teriyaki baked tofu and parents actually care.

I don't. And that's probably why I've written fewer articles about feeding children than any other aspect of their care. There never seemed much worth exploring, aside from my strong feelings about breast-feeding (very few excuses not to start it but if you don't want to do it for a whole year, the new ballyhooed magic goal, who on earth could blame you?) and my anxiety about Henry's lifetime of chicken nuggets and Jif (as documented in chapter 4).

When I'm assigned feeding-your-child stories, it's like sending an Eskimo to describe the equator: I may know seventeen words for snow (snow cone, flurry, ice cream, soft serve, custard, frogurt, gelato, sorbet, sherbet, ice pop, Bomb pop, Popsicle, Dreamsicle, Creamsicle, Fudgsicle, Ben, Jerry) but they're useless to me in a land where nobody even believes in dessert.

Once the editor of a newsletter for kids asked me to write about stocking your family pantry. So I did, careful to include such wholesome items as beans, raisins, dates, canned vegetables, and instant brown rice.

EARNEST EDITOR: You left out the hoisin sauce.

APPARENTLY FOOD-ILLITERATE ME: Whose sauce?

EDITOR: Hoisin. We need to give a few more ideas here. Condiments to have on hand for variety.

ME: Oh. Okay. Sure.

EDITOR: Like how about chutney? Balsamic? Chinese chili paste?

ME: Ummm . . . [*not to be confused with "Mmmmm"*]

EDITOR: Olive paste? Clam juice? Coconut milk is always good to jazz stuff up.

ME: You did say this newsletter is for families, right?

EDITOR: Yup.

ME: As in, people who live with kids?

EDITOR: Huh?

ME: Just checking. So, um, what is hoisin anyway?

EDITOR: Sauce. I think it's made of soybeans, garlic, chilies, maybe a little flour. It's really good in stir-fry or as a glaze before you broil fish, or—

ME: Wait! Your kids eat stir-fry? They eat glazed fish?

At this point the editor confesses she has no children. "But the idea is to broaden kids' palates! Expose them to new tastes! Let them help with the mixing and the stirring so they will take ownership of the meal! They've got to eat more fish! More fruits and vegetables, you know."

"Then you've got to trust me. The only condiment we've left out that any parent is going to believe is ketchup."

"Oh no. It's half sugar!"

"That's why kids like it so much!" I say, though ever professional, I suppress an accompanying "Duh!" Instead I add, "Think of the lycopene! Hey, I have an idea—why don't I loan you my kids for a week to feed?"

Well no, I didn't say that last bit. I fulfilled my assignment, turning in a story that described Alice Waters's fantasy pantry, though not one found on any cul de sac I knew. Still, it got me thinking. Maybe I wasn't giving my kids' palates enough credit. So I served up a stir-fry the next night. Nothing too exotic—broccoli, diced carrots, snow peas, mushrooms, and chicken in soy sauce. We'll work our way up to hoisin, I figured.

> ELEANOR (*suspiciously*): What's this?
> ME: Stir-fry.
> MARGARET: Why is it brown?
> ME: That's soy sauce.
> ELEANOR: Ew-u-ww! Get it off my plate!
> EVERYONE ELSE IN EARSHOT (*ever louder*): EE-U-WW!

The stir-fry thusly scorned, I felt dashed—and a little vindicated. For the next six weeks, I quizzed everyone I knew about whether their kids ate stir-fry. The first mom said "Sure!" and I was pricked with guilt. But she was Korean, which I thought might skew my results, so I undemocratically omitted Asian parents from the rest of my sample. Two other moms said yes, their kids eat stir-fry, "except for the vegetables." Twenty said no way.

One said sometimes, if she put a little ketchup on it.

Do you want to feed your family or your guilt? Most of us who have made it to our childbearing years have a pretty good grasp of the basics of nutrition. There are not too many malnourished Americans. There are, I concede, too many fat ones, but this is more a mathematical problem of eating more calories than are expended, not a matter of nutritional illiteracy.

The basic problem with worrying what-to-feed-the-kids lies in the word *what*. Here's what I ask instead:

Key Feeding Question 1: *Is* There Food to Eat?

Generations of people—probably my Polish and Moravian peasant forefathers—couldn't take this basic fact for granted. We should spend more time counting our blessings that we were born in well-fed homes in the Western Hemisphere than counting our kids' calories. We might well have landed in Sudan or North Korea or, God knows, certain corners of my home state.

After giving thanks for it, I want mine to enjoy the food, and move on. Refuel. Do the next thing. If they're thinking about food too much, it's because they're worried over restrictions (and might end up fat). Or they've turned it into the currency of a power struggle (and might end up messed up). If I dwell on it, the odds seem likely that they will, too.

Key Feeding Question 2: Will They Eat It?

It's become trendy to blame our "toxic food environment" (in the words of one diet researcher) for our veggie-rejecting kids. As if there were a golden past when kids said, "Please, sir, may I have some more kale?"

To be sure, food marketing to kids is more manic and sophisticated than when I was urged to eat my Sugar Frosted Flakes because "they're GRRRReat!" Cross-promotions now spin an endless, seamless web of gotta-have-it, gotta-see-it, gotta-wear-it, gotta-eat-it kid culture, and it's a rare family where nobody gets ensnared. To paraphrase that well-packaged band 'N Sync, It ain't no lie, baby buy buy buy. Which is not the same as saying we all have to lie down, open our gullets, and pour it in. Along with teaching

our kids how to tie a shoelace and how to share, parents are forced to train kids on how to be discriminating consumers. ("Just because I wouldn't let you see the movie about a belching green monster who uses a book of fairy tales as toilet paper, Page, doesn't mean Shrek cereal is any better for you.")

"Just say no" can apply to more than drugs. Though I personally have nothing against cheese crackers shaped like SpongeBob SquarePants, for example, I tend to nix them from my grocery cart because they cost more than the faceless round kind. And no amount of whining will influence that decision. It's my call. If the Center for Science in the Public Interest doesn't like potato chips and soda, it doesn't have to order any.

But advertising can't get all the blame in explaining why kids favor politically incorrect foods. There's also another reason: They're programmed that way. Kids are born liking anything sweet, starting with that lactose-rich baby drink, breast milk (*lactose* being a word that means "milk sugar"). Babies root eagerly for a rag dipped in sugar water but screw up their faces if you try to offer a sour lemon. A pediatrician once pointed out to me that when he offers toddlers a choice between a red lollipop and a green one, they'll pick the red one almost every time. Red is sweet. Red is strawberries, watermelon, cherries. Red is red pop. Green is broccoli, spinach, endive, and (lemon–lime Gatorade notwithstanding) *yuck*.

Somewhere a parent is now saying, "But my little Juliet doesn't like sweet things," and this may be so. Her taste for spinach and tofu has less to do with vigilant nutritional brainwashing, however, than with the taste buds she was born with. Each of my kids has a different-sized sweet tooth. Henry's is as tall as Willie Wonka's fantastic factory, while Eleanor turns down chocolate so indifferently that I marvel how she can possibly be the flesh of my flesh.

But here's the incredible part about worrying over kids' food choices: There's no proof that it matters. How can a toddler live on air? How can a boy make it to age eighteen on jam sandwiches (or to age ten without a single veggie) and still be hale and hearty? The latest research is: No one knows. They just do.

I, for one, am willing to trust biology on this one.

Key Feeding Question 3: *Where* Do They Eat?

When studies began to pile up that kids who eat with their parents are better behaved, get better grades, enjoy better nutrition, and are less likely to smoke pot, I promptly pitched the story to a family magazine. Whose editor even more promptly passed. "Too many families are eating on the run and moms don't have time to cook," I was told. "We don't want to lay any more guilt trips on them."

I'm the last person to want to lay more guilt trips on mothers. But when did breaking bread with the ones you love—the ones you maybe haven't seen since breakfast (if you even ate your Toaster Swirlz together)—become just another chore on the to-do list? A *Wall Street Journal* article actually used the headline "Family Dinners . . . How Not to Dread Them." Among its helpful suggestions: Buy a $39.95 kit, which includes a "dineometer" to record the number of family meals. Serve meals in which all the foods share a particular color or begin with the same alphabet letter.

Guilt inducing? Hard work? Something to dread? Believe me, I hate to cook. I spend as little time in the kitchen as possible. Daddyo, on the other hand, has been known to mix batter from scratch at 10 p.m. so he can have waffles ready to pour for breakfast and thinks it's "fun" to de-ink a squid. (Guess who tends to whip up more meals in our house?) But even a cookbook illiterate like me can set roast chicken, brown rice, broccoli, salad, and cooked carrots on the table in ten minutes—fifteen if I take the time to heat the oven and crack open a tube of biscuit crescents. The chicken comes rotisseried at the supermarket, the salad comes premixed in a bag, the vegetables steam in minutes, and the rice microwaves in ninety seconds. (Rice in ninety seconds! Thus it earns a Paula's Perfectly Practical Product Award, alongside such classic momsavers as the disposable diaper and the one-hand-only collapsible playpen.)

You can even divide the meal in half and do it twice, if the kids are starved at 5 p.m. but all parents aren't home till 6:30. The point is that you're together.

Around the table is where you get to catch up, give thanks, hear complaints, discuss the weather and which teachers were "evil" today, reinforce manners, share sustenance, impart values, attempt to broaden palates, and learn from one another. It's a civil little oasis in a wacky world.

You don't have to make like the Kennedys and come to table prepared to debate the fine points of foreign policy, although that's one idea. We settle for domestic policy here. Only yesterday there was a lively exchange about which kind and shape of pickles taste best. Margaret defended pickled okra and Page proposed a new gherkin-only rule. At the same meal it was learned that boys do not wear hats to the table and girls do not wear pajamas, and Daddyo was prevailed upon to pronounce everyone's names backward, a particular talent of his. Sometimes it's a wacky world right at your table. But it's *your* wacky world, and that's what makes it great.

(Too busy with basketball practice, electric guitar lessons, SAT practice tests, and competitive folk-dancing rehearsals to gather together more than twice a semester? Advance to chapter 10. Do not pass GO. Do not order pizza to be delivered on the practice field.)

Key Feeding Question 4: *How* Do They Eat?

Just as there are red states and blue states in American politics, there are kid-food households and non-kid-food households when it comes to American cupboards. There are houses that aspire to wild salmon, flaxseed, Kashi Go Lean, and hoisin sauce for all, where dessert never passes a pediatric lip, at least until the child is old enough to bum Twinkies in the school cafeteria. And then there are those of us who would rather spend our limited mealtime energy on getting the kids to sit up straight and say "please."

The food rules I care about are these:

No eating while zombiefied in front of the TV.

No knives in mouths, no forks on sisters.

No using the verb *sucks* in connection with the meal (or anything else, for that matter).

No passing a roll as if it were a football.

No slumping, slouching, leaning, hat wearing, or singing at the table.

No toys, blankies, or elbows on top, either.

No putting food back in the serving dish after you have sampled one bite and decided you didn't like it.

No fingers in the pickle jar.

No licking the ice cream stuck to the container lid.

No snarfing all the raspberries in the carton before anybody else has a chance to know they're there.

No dogs near the table.
No putting milk jugs back in the refrigerator empty.
No arguing with your mouth full.
No dessert first.
No Oreos without milk for dunking.
No Pringles in bed.

Key Feeding Question 5: *Whose* Decision Is What My Kids Eat Anyway?

The craziest food phooey is that what your children eat is not a private matter anymore. The whole world is making mountains out of cupcakes.

Used to be, on your birthday your mom brought a snack for your whole class—brownies, Rice Krispies treats, or if you were lucky, the jackpot, cupcakes. My mom always baked M&M cookies, which featured candies in place of Toll House chocolate chips, a stroke of genius that had every classmate in Pennow Elementary School counting the days to March 12.

But no more. Sweets have become the hottest contraband substance in schools since butter knives and Tylenol were taken away. You can bring in a class-disrupting cell phone or a copy of *One Dad, Two Dads, Brown Dads, Blue Dads,* but please, keep those ruinous cupcakes away!

In my own school district, sugar anxiety is running so high that all classroom birthdays for the month must now be celebrated at a single event. ("This is the worst day ever!" Henry declared, on receiving the news.) And even at this unibirthday, cake and cupcakes are disinvited. Among the alternative suggestions: a "make-your-own-pizza party with chopped vegetables, fruits, and low-fat cheeses" or "donate a book to the school library or classroom in honor of a child's birthday." Yup, that's a real source of excitement to a third-grader.

As a result, bake sales have gone the way of cassette tapes. PTA funding took a nosedive when the annual candy sale was nixed. High-sugar cereals and cookies are now officially banned from many public-school-provided meals. (What they make of the revamped whole-grain, one-third-less-sugar formulations, I don't know. Sugar Frosted Flakes may be new and improved and, like the Sugar Pops and Sugar Smacks I grew up on, has dropped the offensive s-word word from its name, but it still goes by "Frosted," a defiant "Nyah! Nyah!" to those who would tamper any further with such a classic.) My friend Tara, whose kids attend a Montessori school, once lovingly placed a Hershey's kiss in her son's lunch box as a first-day-of-school treat, only to have it confiscated by a teacher on junk patrol.

"It would be twenty-three times during the year that other families would not be anticipating that their kids are going to be eating something sweet," said one Massachusetts principal by way of explanation of her birthday cupcake ban. Here's an easy way to get around that unpleasant surprise: Just count the number of kids in your child's class at the beginning of the year. Now you know how many days you can count on your child eating something sweet. (It averages out to less than once a week, when you figure all those summer birthdays in.) Anyway, anybody who's been to a birthday party knows that kids never eat the whole darn cupcake. They just lick the neon blue or yellow icing off the top. So they get a little sugar rush—sugar being a fancy name for glucose, the fuel the body uses to run and figure out arithmetic.

Some snack grinches aren't content to stop at traditional treats like cupcakes and potato chips. A columnist in my local paper recently excoriated the county's after-school program for daring to serve the innocent children *fruit-and-oatmeal bars* and *apple juice.* Oh the irresponsibility! The horror! "The last time I checked the ingredients on those bars, they contained partially hydrogenated oil," she groused. "Healthy they are not." The juice? "No fiber." The graham crackers and pretzel crackers served on alternate days? "Empty calories." And what should the hungry children be served instead? Fruit and water, she suggested. Mmm, that will tide them over until they ride the bus home and eat a family dinner at 7 p.m. when mom and dad are finally back from work.

It makes sense that schools shouldn't have soda-pop machines (but then, I don't think kids should be carrying cash to school either). And deep-fat-fried main dishes five days a week on the lunch menu is too much for any stomach. But regulating birthday treats and reaching into lunch boxes? If we're really serious about ridding the schools of junk, we might start with the same old time-sucking units on recycling and bullies that the kids endure every year.

My Oreo-friendly Gram, for the record, fared quite nicely on her daily doses of butter and sugar. She developed no chronic diseases, never needed a day-of-the-week pill box. Although she aged more like a saggy Jane Russell than a nip-'n'-tucked Jane Fonda, she didn't seem to notice. (Her grandchildren and great-grandchildren rather liked her ample lap.) Into her nineties, she tended her raspberries and roses and crocheted afghans in patterns so complex the end result looked like tweed. When she broke her hip at ninety-five, it was the first time in her life to be admitted to a hospital (not even to give birth; my mother was born at home). She died missing the century mark by a matter of months, basically of old age.

In one of her last years, I told her that a lawyer had tried to ban the sale of Oreos to minors in California, on account of the trans fats they contained. "Life's too short!" she chuckled. "Now, what would you like to eat?"

Momfidence...

. . . is packing Fritos and Little Debbie Snack Cakes in the ol' lunch box every once in a while . . . just because.

. . . is being a good role model and eating lots of fruits and vegetables and protein yourself without making a big deal about it—which would be the sure kiss of death that would make no child inclined to follow.

. . . is bringing the fake juice you bought on sale when it's your turn for snack day instead of the 100 percent juice suggested because you don't have time to make a special trip to the store so that twenty-two five-year-olds can sip six ounces of natural sugar water instead of six ounces of fake sugar water.

. . . is choosing to spend your mealtime energy on really important things, like noticing who's kicking whom under the table during the blessing.

Bless This Mess
On Upkeep

8

> If you waited until your children started school to take them to the dentist, you waited too long . . . Parents cannot afford to be cavalier about baby teeth . . . even a toothless baby should receive regular dental care.   —*Jane Brody,* "Dental Advice: Start Early. Very Early." *New York Times, 2004*

The editor-in-chief of a baby magazine once gave me a brilliant tip on bathing little ones. Not that I ever read it in her magazine.

"So last night I was so tired I just wiped the kids down with baby wipes instead of giving them a bath," I overheard her mention in a hallway as the conversation turned, as it always does when two or more moms gather, to how time flies when you're having kids. "Do you think that's really bad?"

Bad? At the time, I was horrified. But not because my friend's job as High Priestess of the How-to Headline evidently left her feeling as much self-doubt as the rest of us. (For that knowledge, I was relieved.) What unnerved me was that she so cavalierly dared to deviate from the basic standards of proper baby care. Didn't her magazine devote an article to the subject of bathing practically every other issue? Hadn't I received five baby bathtubs and untold hooded towels as shower presents to remind me of my duty to keep my infant smelling like Johnson & Johnson, not to mention ward away killer germs?

I was still a brainwashed newbie who couldn't appreciate a clever shortcut when I saw it.

Back then, I changed my three-month-old's clothes the minute they were soiled. No driblet of spit-up nor dot of strained peach was too insignificant to escape my critical eye. I'd remove not only the offending stained top but the T-shirt underneath it, the pants, and the socks, too. If I wasn't going to let my child be dirty, I certainly wasn't going to let him go around mismatched.

Nowadays I'm satisfied if everyone is simply wearing clothes. And occasionally I'm not too picky about that.

Quickly I discovered that babies do not get dirty enough for the ordeal of a daily bath. That older children are oblivious to that itchy feeling we grown-ups get without frequent shampoos. That using a shirt front as a napkin is an inborn reflex, not outgrown for many years, no matter how often you tuck the paper kind into their laps and collars. That running around the house naked never hurt anyone. That kids *like* to name the dust bunnies under their beds.

Now I think, *Wet wipes instead of a bath? How did my mother get along without them?*

There is no right or wrong way to do most of the business of parenting. There is, however, almost always a more expedient one.

Especially when it comes to the upkeep of small children, I've discovered what's really necessary and what I can pretty much let slide.

Bathing

....

Babies who can only bat their mobiles and have yet to taste a strained pea don't get very dirty. Even the more mobile ones only get the veggies in their hair every third day.

Older children do get a bit filthier, but here's the thing: They don't notice! A preschooler can go for twenty-three straight days without washing more than his fingertips. (I know. I counted.)

That's not to say bathtime should be dispensed with entirely. It can be a mom's most relaxing time of day. At least, it can during that span of time *after* you wrangle them into the bathroom, out of their clothes, onto the potty (important!), and into the nice, no, it's not too hot, it's just-right water—and *before* you must then coax or threaten them out again, towel them off while they howl, struggle to work close-fitting pajamas over resistant damp skin, assure them the wrinkles on their fingertips will come off soon, and dry their hair and all their Barbies and their plastic gorillas.

Those in-between moments are so worth it! Take your perch on your command post, the closed commode. Now you can peruse the mail and sip the hot or cold beverage of your choice while basking in the happy knowledge that everybody's momentarily contained. Siblings of either gender bathing together are a must because they amuse one another, thus extending the bath's usefulness, so long as the youngest can at least sit in a bath ring and the oldest hasn't discovered privacy.

What you *don't* do: Crouch down with a washcloth and scrub. The bubbles in the bath—really, they won't get urinary tract infections from a single capful—will do the cleaning. They'll splash enough water around to rinse.

"How long do I let them stay in there?" I remember asking my mother, early on. Although I had dutifully read up on safe water temperature, the importance of supervision, and appropriate bath-safe learning toys (including how to sterilize them between uses, not that I ever did this once in ten years), somehow this particular detail—recommended length of soak—had been left out!

"Until they get cold and complain," she shrugged.

My record is ninety minutes. (Bubbles are key.) I try to keep it in mind to tempt me onward those nights when I'm too pooped to even think about running the bathwater in the first place.

Oral Hygiene

Fair warning: All dentists and dental hygienists may now cover their eyes and skip ahead a few pages.

I have never used a specially designed fingertip toothbrush to wipe a baby's gums after a feeding.

I have never improvised by using a bit of sterile gauze or a clean, wet washcloth for this purpose, either.

I have never lovingly brushed each pearly baby tooth as it appeared.

I did not take my children to a pediatric dentist at age one. Or two. Maybe when they were three.

I don't stand over their shoulders every single night making sure they brush until the tooth timer dings.

I don't own a tooth timer, though once a dentist gave us a minute-long hourglass to time toothbrushing by. Nobody could outlast it because somebody always grabbed it or knocked it over halfway, but it was a very popular toy.

I do not floss their baby teeth.

No junior mouth rinses.

And so help me, Dr. Fain, I almost never remember to pack their toothbrushes on sleepovers and vacations. Although by the third night on the road, I do spring for new ones.

They are fine.

Even though I know they are fine, because they have one cavity among their four mouths, as revealed by twice-a-year checkups, admitting I am dentally lax is not easy. The PR campaign urging parents to seek dental care before there are dentals has been nearly as effective as the De Beers family's assertion that an engagement ring ought to be a diamond costing a month's salary. Unless your child is sucking a bottle past his first birthday 24/7, drinks no fluoridated water, never sees a sealant, and doesn't even own a toothbrush, his teeth aren't very likely to rot out because you were too sleep deprived to do the gum rubbing.

I'm not a total slackard. At least twice a week I remember to initiate a conversation like this:

ME (*yelling upstairs*): Did you brush your teeth?
HENRY: Yeah.
ELEANOR (*sidling in*): No he didn't! I didn't see him!
HENRY: Yes I did!
ELEANOR: Did not!
MOM (*coming nearer, catching whiff of Jif breath*): Henry, is that true? Are you sure you brushed?
HENRY: I did!
MOM (*entering bathroom*): I can tell you didn't. Don't lie to me.
HENRY (*under breath to sister*): Squealer! (*To me*): How can you tell?
MOM: Because your toothbrush is dry!

Here Henry smacks head with amazement at my detective work.

MOM: And Eleanor, where's your toothbrush?
ELEANOR: Uh, I left it at Auntie Patti's last week.

Vacuuming, Dusting, Mopping, Ad Nauseam

My mom wasn't what you'd call an obsessive housekeeper. When she pulled out the vacuum, we'd all ask, "Who's coming over?"

When I pull out the vacuum, Daddyo goes outside to see if there's a blue moon.

You might say I care more about neat than clean. You can't eat off my floors—though, Lord knows, many do—but I'm all for the calming influence of a tidy surface.

Here's how to "clean" a room in sixty seconds flat: Round up all loose papers into one pile on the counter. You can fish out the phone bill and today's homework later, as needed, and dump the rest on garbage day. Heap all stray toys and shoes in the nearest toy box and all small plastic unidentifiable objects in the trash. (Preinstall a toy box—a laundry basket works nicely—in every room a child may wander.) Plump throw pillows; stash stray socks behind them if visitors are already pulling into the drive and you don't expect them to stay long enough to sit. Pick the largest bits of lint and half-chewed crackers off the rug so the eye doesn't rest on any one object. Kick smaller mystery bits underneath the rug. Ignore dust; most people do. Now banish children from this room, or else in ten minutes you'll have to start all over again.

To be obsessive about cleanliness, on the other hand, is to spend a lot of time I don't have. Oh, I wipe down the table after we eat and I sweep the kitchen floor when I can't walk two paces without hearing the distinctive crunch of a Cheerio. When my children were at the stage of checking everything out with their mouths, I made sure there were no pennies or week-old dropped chicken nuggets lying about.

But there's a difference between so-clean-you-can-eat-off-the-floor and so-neat-that-nobody-will-trip-on-a-small-plastic-car-and-die. The latter is clearly more important.

Everybody has different standards, so I'm not saying you should follow mine. My dear husband, for example, grew up in a house that looked like a museum, with a mother who stands on desks to dust curtain rods—*for fun.* She packs her rubber gloves and bibbed apron when she comes to visit. Lucky me! If scrubbing my house makes her happy—and it does, for housecleaning is her hobby just as lying around reading Jane Austen is mine—then who am I to stand in the way of her pleasure? Her son, my husband, shares her ability to see disorder that's practically invisible to me. Margaret once turned heads at the local Toys "R" Us by squealing rapturously, "Look, look! A toy vacuum, *just like Daddy's!*"

Now—drumroll, please—it turns out that science is on the side of slackards like me. My dust-coated furniture and those sticky mystery spots on the floor might just be doing my children a favor: A growing body of research seems to show that ultraclean conditions are *bad* for kids.

Not so fast with that Lysol Brand Disinfectant Antibacterial Kitchen Cleaner! Dirt is good!

I'm so tired of warnings about rogue germs halfway around the world. And who hasn't heard by now not to put mayonnaise on a lunch box sandwich in June or drink unpasteurized apple juice? Here, at long last, is some good bacterial news and nobody's shouting it from the rooftops!

Children exposed to dirt are apparently less likely to develop asthma and allergies than those who grow up in ultraclean conditions. Some researchers even blame tidy households for sicknesses you'd never think had a link to filth, like multiple sclerosis, type 1 diabetes, and Crohn's disease. Something about ultracleanliness not priming a child's immune system properly, leaving him more vulnerable to pollen, dust, peanuts, and even his own body tissue.

You can bet upon learning this that I zipped off a happy column titled "And Now for Some Really Good News . . ." (Also discussed: new findings that motherhood seems to make women smarter, and video games boost kids' brainpower. Happy revelations indeed!)

Even animal hair is a health benefit to children, according to the hygiene hypothesis—a lucky break for Brownie. Lately Daddyo's been insisting he's a death trap because he's always underfoot, especially when one is cooking or cleaning. (It's almost impossible not to be underfoot when you are only ankle high, even to a child's ankle.) Although I haven't heard of anyone ever killed by tripping over a hovering miniature dachshund while manning a vacuum, it seems like another good reason to keep that kind of behavior to a minimum.

Bedroom Cleaning

There is neat, there is dirty, there is cluttered—and then there is the look of a room that appears to have been decorated by Christo and then trashed by a college fraternity partying with toys instead of beer. By which I refer to the native state of a child's bedroom, which warrants its own subcategory of cleanliness.

In third grade, my best friend Therese often could not play on Saturday mornings because she had to wash her bedroom walls. Not just clean her room. Wash her walls! My mother was impressed, though thankfully not enough to put the practice into action around our house. I just thought it was weird.

Kids don't care whether their walls are clean—or if their underwear is folded in the drawer or if their beds have hospital corners. Nor should mothers. We have enough on our hands making sure guests can make it from the front door to the living room sofa safely.

Every so often, though, guilt and disgust trump my ability to look the other way (or company's coming over) and I explode.

> ME: You need to clean up your room.
> BELOVED CHILD OBLIVIA: It is clean.
> ME (*staring incredulously at a minefield of headless dolls, mateless shoes, wadded clothes, wet bath towels, and balance-threatening UPOs—unidentifiable plastic objects*): You call this clean?
> CHILD: (*Shrug*)

A friend once tried to get a jump on the jumble by buying one of those toy organizers—two low shelves that each hold five clear plastic bins. The idea was that her boys would be able to easily see and select the toys they wanted. So she carefully sorted their trucks into one bin, LEGOs in another, balls in a third. Sounded like a smart idea to me. Then her husband noticed that it was taking her longer than ever to clean up at night. "They don't care which toys are in which bin," he pointed out. "They just like dumping."

Dump, pour, pile, dump. Stack, knock down, stack again. Sort, fling. It's what kids do. For Page, dropping toys down the far, unreachable corner behind her bed is a science experiment: Will a plastic Piglet fall as fast as a stuffed one? If Teddy Bear can be yanked back up again by his large furry brown arm, can a tiny Beanie bear?

What about a bear sticker? Once I heard her wail so inconsolably that I raced up the stairs two at a time, thinking that *she* had fallen out of bed. No, she had tried sending her beloved lovey Ratty down the black hole. By the time I fished him out he was almost unrecognizable—a sticky rubber goo rat tangling with grey dust bunnies is not a pretty sight. That's an experiment she never repeated.

It's not that I've learned to look the other way at messy rooms. I've learned to look at them *their* way.

In children's rooms you see the undisturbed evidence of their primitive, live-in-the-moment nature. A shirt is removed—and ignored until the next time it's needed, days or weeks away. ("Mom? Have you seen my soccer socks?") Board games are upended by the loser—and forgotten in the tantrum that follows. Snacks are scarfed—and their wrappers abandoned on the floor like squirrels' half-gnawed acorns. If my kids started regularly returning hangers to closets or game pieces to boxes, I'd take their temperatures. Or worry they'd been replaced by robots.

Once when Eleanor was two, I discovered every drawer in her room hanging open and empty, maybe thirty minutes after I'd straightened up in there. But before my steam could shape itself into words, she piped up, "Do you like my outfit? I got dressed all by self!" And so her self had, right down to her socks and her shoes. Which were buckled. This was no disrespectful disorder. It was the side effect of self-mastery in progress.

It was as if I'd been handed a toilet paper tube from one of their laundry basket ships. Only it wasn't cardboard at all; it was an enchanted spyglass through which I discovered nothing was exactly what it first seemed.

Those sheets flung carelessly over chairs? To them, it's a fabulous fort. The deflated balloon on the floor? Page's new pet, Balloony. Those lined-up baby dolls with green and purple faces? Cosmetology school. Those stinky socks? Nothing. (Stinky socks are invisible to a child. They can't even smell 'em.)

Where I once saw only a bed littered with little green army men, I now realize that Henry sees the Normandy landing, with himself as General Eisenhower. That array of blocks on the floor is a zoo Margaret is saving to show her daddy. And never mind the paisley swirls of Play-Doh pancaked on the floor. Now, like my children, I only see the art.

So what if they sleep in the eye of a hurricane? I've got a daughter who dresses herself, a boy who leads men into battle, and a baby who understands the principle of cause and effect. Not bad trade-offs, if you ask me.

Just so long as I can make it from the door to the bed without wrenching an ankle on a UPO.

Momfidence...

. . . is reading home-decorating magazines for the entertainment value, because you have no delusions about changing your style from "early lived in" any time soon—at least not before you can walk though a room without picking up five stray socks, a granola bar wrapper, six books, many shoes, an impressive toy assortment, all the throw pillows that used to be on the sofa, and a pair of Strawberry Shortcake underwear.

. . . is being open to improvement, however. I swear I'm going to crack down on Cheez Doodles in the den or redecorate the room to better coordinate with those orange-stained throw pillows.

. . . is directing the barber to give the boy a buzz even when the prevailing style is a mohawk or mullet or Woodstock redux because a buzz is low maintenance and you're the one who has to look at it.

. . . is moving promptly to wash off ballpoint-pen tattoos, chocolate pudding traces, and unidentifiable substances (gum? yogurt? Elmer's?) in the hair, at least before any birthday party, church service, or grandparent visit.

Silence Is Fool's Golden in a House with Kids

On Bedlam

Love & Logic parents look forward to their children's misbehavior. Why? The path to responsibility and wisdom is paved with mistakes.
—*Jim Fay and Charles Fay,*
Love and Logic Magic for Early Childhood

This parent looks forward to the end of the day. Why? No more misbehavior!
—*Paula Spencer, mom*

"You can tell kids live here," says Jed, the refrigerator repairman.

No kidding, I think as I pile chipped melamine plates and crazy straws into the dishwasher. Was his tip-off the fleet of plastic wagons, bikes, and scooters that he'd had to navigate in order to park? The sidewalk chalk that sent his feet skittering? The sticky brown mystery globs adorning the lower half of our Kenmore side-by-side?

Maybe he means the long piercing howl that just floated down from a distant corner of the house. It sounds like Brownie when Page accidentally steps on his tail during a rousing game of Let's Pretend We Are Puppy Brother and Sister. But today Brownie has been relocated outside, far away from Jed and his tool belt. What the dog lacks in size he makes up for in courage, defending our home against invading repairmen with the energy of a Doberman and an insistent bark that's the most annoying sound I've heard since colic. What the repairman hears is merely children at play.

"Oh!" Jed exclaims suddenly.

I look over. His voice doesn't have that "aha!" tone that indicates he has solved the mystery of why our Go-GURTS don't freeze solid anymore. This "oh!" is more like "eeewww." Except Jed is too burly and grease stained for his horror to come out sounding squeamish.

He's holding a large dead newt. Jumbo! A former pet and aquarium evacuee. Now Jumbo looks like a dehydrated ingredient bound for a fairy-tale witch's cauldron. You'd think we would have smelled him there under the refrigerator, since he's been missing for months. Apparently, however, old newts don't die a stinky death; they just shrivel away. Henry had looked all over the living room for the critter, never imagining he could have made it clear across the house to this deceptively cool spot under the fridge. Bits of telltale carpet fuzz still cling to the creature's desiccated skin.

I wrap the unfortunate amphibian in paper towels and start to tell Jed the story of Jumbo's escape (possibly a feeding hatch left open, possibly some small hands trying to pet him). Then I explain how we came to have newts for pets (I'm allergic to cats) and, just to make conversation, my theory about how newts and dachshunds look suspiciously alike.

Jed doesn't seem to be listening. His eyes drift skyward. "Um, do you need to get that?"

"Hmm?" Neither the phone nor the doorbell are ringing.

"That. I think somebody's calling you."

Another scream floats down from a far upper corner of the house. "Ahhhhheeeeeeeeee!"

I listen but do not act. It's too far off. Wait to see if it comes closer. Wait to determine if there is a corresponding shriek of pain. Wait for the sound of Eleanor's bedroom door slamming once, twice, then faster threefourfivesixseven times. Bambambambambambambam! Bam! Eight times. Wait for the sound of Henry's diabolical laughter. "Mu-ooo-ah-ha-ha!" Listen for signs of real trouble.

Sometimes I can make out words. Well, mainly one word, stretched out in endless variations as if a funhouse mirror were revving up for takeoff on the O'Hare tarmac. Yes, here it comes: "Maaaaaa! Maaaoooooom! MAAAOOOOOOAHHHHHHHMM-MMMM!"

Many a worried visitor has, like Jed, paused in midsentence, waiting for me or Daddyo to intervene.

"Oh, they're okay," I assure him. I'm trying to decide whether a dead newt is too big to flush down the toilet, like a goldfish. It seems disrespectful to just throw him in the trash—he was, after all, a pet—but if I toss him into the garden someone might find him and insist on an elaborate burial service.

Jed looks dubious. He busies himself with his tools.

I tune out most of the incessant squawking and squabbling that is the sound track of my everyday life. Even when it's my name being reflexively yowled, the matter rarely has anything to do with me. The rumpus thunders and passes like a summer storm, all on its own. It's called building social skills. With practice, and I've had plenty, you can pretty much tell when a wailing child is maimed or just mad. There's a telling desperation to the screams of the mutilated, as opposed to mere loud frustration.

The condition of truly hurt children tends to be announced by another child who appears like an emissary from an ancient battle-field, who has run a marathon's distance, bearing dispatches for the Empress Mom. This child usually appears breathless, pauses, stands at attention, and says something like, "Mom, sir! Page fell off of the wall, and her leg is on backward, sir!"

I will also jump in at the sound of breaking glass or the twenty-fifth consecutive door slam. To act too soon, though, would be jump-ing the gun. For most often, we merely have a girl crying wolf.

On cue, Eleanor appears, bloodless but shimmering with injured pride. Lights up, and action: "MOM! MOM! He *kicked* me! Make him stay out of my room!"

Jed looks up, coughs nervously. "Gotta go get something out of the truck," he mutters. Maybe he's thinking I'm a terrible mother to have ignored the distress flares. Maybe he thinks I'm a terrible mother for raising children who howl like moon bats in the first place. I choose to imagine he's just unnerved by the terrible quan-tity of our under-the-refrigerator crud. Actually I don't really care what he thinks, so long as he fixes my freezer so that my fish sticks will freeze and all will be right in our world again.

I chuck the newt, wash my hands, and assume the sheriff pose, hands on hips, hat high, trigger finger ready.

Henry is right behind Eleanor, so close, in fact, that he might as well be attached to her shoulder as though they were escapees from a freak show.

"She won't stop calling me Booger Boy!" he huffs.

"Booger Boy," she mutters, low. "Stay out of my room, Snot butt!"

He kicks her again. Hard on the calf. Right in front of me.

Secretly, the cavemom part of my brain is proud. *My children strong. Fight good. Defend self. Strong! Kill animals. Me teach good.* Sadly, however, my public reactions cannot be so primitive, for I am a well-brought-up, Montessori-tuition-paying, trick-or-treat-for-UNICEF kind of highly evolved mom. When the situation comes to blows, especially in plain view, I am obligated to lay down the law, for lo, I am the voice of reason, civilization in toto personified, the law giver and transmitter, keeper and protector of culture, morals, human decency, and the American way. At least in this house.

"You," I say, poking a finger at my son. "Do. Not. Kick. Under. Any. Circumstances. If you have a problem with her, you tell me." I remind myself I have been saying this to him since he was not yet two and I caught him applying a Little Tikes hammer to a helpless seven-day-old Eleanor's soft skull. For months, she never so much as squeaked unless she was hungry or being pinched, bopped, bitten, or otherwise "loved on" too hard.

"And you," I continue, turning to the wilier party. "Stop teasing him. Treat people the way you want to be treated. And stop slamming those doors before somebody gets hurt." Left unsaid is the rousing "or else": *Or else I will indenture you to Jed so you can make yourselves useful fixing leaky faucets and backed-up septic systems until you are eighteen and free!*

I take a breath before meting out the sentences. "Now: You each go to your own room, and find something quiet to do." I escort them upstairs. If I am deft with this homily, it's because I've delivered it several hundred times. It's like my stump speech on disciplinary policy.

On my way back down, I pass Margaret and Page in the bathroom. They are quiet as dust bunnies. Unlike spine-tingling pseudoscreams, *this* is cause for alarm.

As much as I crave calm and quiet, it's fool's gold. Sure, it's theoretically possible that they're voluntarily napping. But at the same time? As possible as it is for me to win the Publishers Clearinghouse Sweepstakes without even entering. Noise in any form—

the sound effects of tigers and explosives, the wheels of a doll car scratchily careening over polished floors, TV laugh tracks, computer mouse clicks, arguments, the ceiling shuddering overhead— says all's well.

Silence only means that somebody's up to no good.

Or two somebodies. When I double back, I notice a baby doll and a play high chair. In the bathroom. Oh and yes, here we have baby's bib, and baby's potty, and baby's bottle full of bright yellow liquid. In a nanosecond I take it all in, for this is the drink-and-wet baby doll that the girls love because of its "realistic" bodily functions. You don't want to know how the usually clear bottle came to look realistic, too. You just want to know that I moved quickly. Luckily the doll had not yet been fed. The yellow bottle was removed from the house and the girls were directed to the hand soap.

Five minutes later, while I'm Cloroxing the bathroom floor, I hear Henry's time-out door open. "Hey, Eleanor," he calls, "wanna go play with Brownie?"

"Sure!"

I smile. *Josh-ay loo-bay, josh-ay choo-bay.* That's what my Gram used to mutter in Polish (or what it sounded like to my ears) whenever my four siblings and I lit into one another. Like the ship she immigrated to the United States on in 1912, which had been hit by an iceberg just like the *Titanic* a few weeks before it, Gram tended to steam placidly onward. Whether we're talking suspect Oreos or sibling squabbles, this woman had perspective.

Loosely translated, her saying means "You always pick on the ones you love." Or, alternatively, "Can't live with you, can't live without you."

Meanwhile, downstairs, Jed has cleaned the condenser coils and thus saved the day. Now we can make another week's journey to Costco to fill the larder with frozen yogurt sticks and pizza rolls. As he hands me the bill, he mentions proudly that his own baby is just three months old. Ah. That explains his uneasiness over the screams. He doesn't know yet that hubbub is the natural by-product of having children. I consider assuring him that the cries of babyhood are just the warm-up exercises. But I don't want to scare him too much. When you're doing two loads of laundry a day and running the dishwasher after every meal, you depend on a guy like Jed. I hope I don't need him to come back. But if I do, I hope he will.

Momfidence...

. . . is being cavalier but not careless. The kids must be strapped and buckled into every car trip. We finish all the medicine in the bottle, I lock away poisons, and I keep pot handles turned in. No punching, biting, or use of "stoopid poo poo head" goes unaddressed.

. . . is inviting lots of kids to your crowded house to play because even though the noise level is higher, the overall vibe is actually calmer thanks to the novelty factor of a fresh face.

. . . is the eye of the hurricane.

Ready, Set, Stop the Mompetition!

On Enrichment

> Many of the women felt that what they were doing was ridiculous. But they—but we—couldn't stop. To stop—to let go—would have been to let things spin out of control even more than they already seemed to be.
>
> —*Judith Warner,* Perfect Madness

"**M**argaret wants to play with Sarabeth," I say to Sarabeth's mother. "Can she come over?"

My own mom used to turn me outside with instructions to come back in "when the streetlights come on." I'd cross the street and stand on my friend's stoop yelling, "Mare-EE-E! Mare-EE-E!" until Mary appeared. But now that children don't just hang out after school anymore—let alone cross streets willy-nilly until dark—my maternal intervention is sometimes begged for, to set a playdate in motion.

Annoying word, *playdate. Date* implies planning, structure, obligation, and spending two hours in front of a mirror agonizing over what to wear—concepts not normally paired with children's *play.*

Sometimes you luck into a mom on the other end of the line who says, "Sure, what time?" Mission accomplished.

More likely, she whips out a planner. "Well, let's see. Today? Oh, I'm sorry, Sarabeth's at gymnastics. Tomorrow she's got swim team and math tutoring, and Wednesdays we're back to gymnastics. Oops, and an organizational meeting for Children Promoting World Peace—she's representing America in Italy during spring break, did she tell you? We'll have to skip arts-and-crafts class for that (she does that one for fun). And she has to practice piano." She laughs. "What does your book look like?"

She is startled when I say that any afternoon will work fine. My "book" is so blank at the moment that I keep our schedule in my head. There's no T-ball. No Suzuki violin. No voice lessons. No synchronized swim. No world peace.

"Oh, how did you manage that?" she says lightly. At first I mistake her tone for envy. Then she adds, "I can't imagine Sarabeth not doing anything," as if reevaluating whether this news of my daughter's loafer lifestyle renders her suitable to run with her own well-groomed thoroughbred.

But Margaret is very funny, creative, and agreeable! I want to assure her. *She's good at math! She learned to read at four! She can think up more fun things to do with sticks than any child I know!*

"Well it's just one of those flukes," I limply offer instead.

"I'm sure that will change," Sarabeth's mother says briskly. "Doing nothing isn't very realistic for long these days, is it?"

"It's not?"

"Not when everybody else is doing things. It's keep up or be left behind, right?" As if realizing she's been a bit too candid, she hastily adds the standard rationales that parents believe only because we've heard them so much. "And of course I want Sarabeth to be Well Rounded and Take Advantage of Opportunities and Try New Things. Besides, She Loves It. It's Not Like I'm Forcing Her. She Wouldn't Have It Any Other Way. How about a playdate a week from next Sunday between three and four?"

Left Behind. It's not just a best-selling book series and a predicament of the faithless. It's the pitiful fate of kids whose moms are losing the Mompetition. That would be those of us not galloping fast enough toward the finish line with our well-rounded Renaissance kids on our already overburdened backs.

(Who? Me?)

We were off to the races—whether we knew it or not—from that first anxious glance at a developmental milestones chart. Sitting up at five months? Walking at ten months? Advance two laps. Did you buy only black and white nursery toys? Watch all three Classical Baby DVDs *and* follow the parent tutorial in the Baby Babble speech development video? Enroll in toddler yoga? Make your own organic blender baby food? You're in first place! Maintaining that lead will be tricky, though. Will you nudge toward rowing or lacrosse? Piccolo or clarinet? Pre-algebra? Pre-med? Pre-nervous breakdown? So many options! So little time!

Raising a kid isn't child's play, you know.

I guess I'd run faster toward the Winner's Circle if I "got" the prize. But I'm not even sure what it is. A fat Ivy League acceptance envelope (complete with $160,000 in instant debt)? The marriage of well-credentialed equals that makes the *New York Times* Weddings/Celebrations pages? The last professional jobs that haven't already been outsourced to India? The sheer pride and satisfaction of knowing I've got a thoroughbred in the home stable, too?

Or are we just running around like turkeys with our heads cut off because every child deserves to be Well Rounded and Have Opportunities and Try New Things? After all, They Love It!

We Wouldn't Have It Any Other Way!

Maybe I should get on the stick about enriching their minds and developing their talents, I muse after I hang up, idly at first, and then with growing unease as I realize that Sarabeth isn't an exception. Most of my kids' friends' schedules are jam packed, even in the dead of winter. *Shouldn't I be expanding their horizons? Discovering their great gifts? Getting them in on the ground level of something? And golly, what about Harvard?*

For a minute it seems irrelevant that I myself never went to a single organized activity outside of school. I took no lessons, except for a few weeks when my older sister ran a dancing school in our basement, until my younger sister and I were kicked out for acting like younger siblings. Never went to a day camp, or an overnight camp for that matter, unless you count the time the whole fifth grade went to Camp Tamarack together. In February. In snowy Michigan. (What was *that* all about?) All summer long I engaged in marathon Monopoly, rode my "horse" (a Schwinn bike named Apple), and visited grandmothers. I grew up thinking tutors and summer school were for the slow kids, not the college-bound ones.

That kind of laxness is so last century!

Aren't I a hip modern mom who wants her little gifts of nature to blossom into their best selves? Why should my cool, cute, amazing children be left behind?

A chamomile-scented smoke signal curls up from my mug: SOS! Stop obsessing, sap! I hear a lively game of Let's Chase Brownie in the next room and a basketball hitting the pavement in the drive. Somewhere the pages of a Harry Potter book are being turned. I sip.

Of course every child should have things to do and be exposed to new experiences. But does it always have to be something I pay for? Why aren't trips to the library or a detour to an old fort on summer vacation sufficient? It only seems to count as enrichment if somebody else is in charge. Ordinary parents and ordinary experiences don't cut it anymore. All across the land, toy boxes are bulging. Backyards bought with children in mind stand waiting. The safe cushioned playgrounds fancified with tax dollars are calling. There's plenty to do, if only the kids weren't all booked up.

I sip again.

There is nowhere else I need to be right now.

No hectoring anybody to find shoes let's go now we're late what do you mean you don't feel like going hurry up!

I am spared the drop-off, pick-up dance in which two thirty-minute lessons mysteriously consume two and a half hours.

I develop no bedsores from sitting in the driver's seat or a gym bleacher long hours on end.

I can actually do laundry. Both washing and drying in the same day.

I save considerable cash—all those tuition fees, clothes, and equipment add up, even before you buy gas for the minivan or spring for special foods-on-the-go designed to fit in the cup holders because nobody's around to eat at home.

I can excavate the backpacks while the kids are still awake instead of on my way to bed at midnight, which means I can ask Henry face to face why he still hasn't turned in this note to his teacher.

Oh, the benefits of a blank family planner for a mom (aka the one who signs the registration forms, acquires the paraphernalia, and does the carting around)!

And the idle kids? Poor dears don't seem to realize how I'm depriving them.

Before I fork over my dollars and my sense in order to make child improvements, I've learned to ask a few hard questions.

Why?
·········

(Why? Why? *Why?*)

It's not, let me hasten to say, like I never sign my children up for *anything*. It's that half the time I wind up wishing I hadn't. Through most of elementary school, anyway, they remember nothing and pick up relatively few actual skills.

Helpless Henry was fifteen months old when we enrolled him in his first extracurricular (or "extrafamiliar" as I now like to think of them, since they gobble up so much family time). It was infant swimming class. I don't know why—something about mommy-baby bonding and making him "water safe." Temporary insanity is more likely. For six weeks the little guy wailed through each 45-minute lesson. It never occurred to me that I might splash around with him in our bathtub or a backyard baby pool for just as much benefit (and a lot more pleasure) as he got out of being hauled to the local university and cajoled to "kick, kick, kick!" while he bawled and I stressed.

Parental anxiety is to the enrichment business like blood to a shark. They sniff it. They close in. They make a killing. Extracurricular activities aren't just a way to pass the time (although for many families that's another plus). They "cultivate self-esteem for a lifetime of successful achievement" (Yoga Kids). They "develop character" (Suzuki music). They "encourage your child to problem-solve, think creatively, gain self-esteem, and grow to be an independent learner" (Gymboree). Who can resist?

And since that anxiety starts in the womb, so do the countless ways you can improve upon your basic-issue child. A *Music for My Baby in Utero* CD, anyone? But let's just start with the postutero child. Baby swim? Ballet at three? Ice skating for preschoolers? Daddyo and I have been there. And all I have to say is, *What were we thinking?*

A combination of restraint and coincidence has left my family calendar blank across four children for now. Henry—ex–Cub Scouts, ex–karate, ex–ice skating, ex–piano, ex–swimming, ex–golf, off-and-on soccer—seems perfectly content spending his after-school hours in the dull splendor of bike riding, ball kicking, checkers, and computer games. (And yes, TV watching. Advance in horror directly to chapter 13.) Eleanor—ex–ballet, ex–tap, ex–ice skating, ex–swimming, ex–Brownies—does the same. She also paints rocks, stages plays, invents secret codes, runs an ant farm—and goodness knows what else, since I don't have to sit there watching her do it.

Not coincidentally, my younger two kids have yet to be enrolled in much of anything other than swim lessons for safety reasons (and not a minute before age three). When they're old enough to develop a bona fide interest, we'll talk. But I'm not springing any bright ideas of my own on them any more.

We're talking kids who haven't reached their double-digit birthdays yet.

It's not that this stuff isn't fun, which it can be. Or incredibly cute, which it is, especially in the youngest age brackets. You aren't human if you don't smile at the sight of a pinked-out preschool ballerina doing "creative movement" (i.e., running around just like she does at home, only with her arms held aloft and a dozen other cotton-candy girls alongside her, while a tall woman with perfect posture exhorts the girls to quit trying to go en pointe like every picture of a ballerina they've ever seen). That is, it's cute until the third lesson when she throws a tantrum because she'd rather stay home and play with her stuffed Angelina Ballerina toy set instead of putting on her leotard and hopping into the car.

If you want to fork over money better parked directly into a college fund on leather slippers that will be outgrown every six months, and spend your free time ferrying around a tot who'd be just as stimulated hanging out in her room, more power to you.

I did.

But like I said, I just wish I hadn't.

Do They Want to Be There? Do I?

"Oh, but they like it," parents quickly insist when I look agog at the twenty-five hours a week they put into Little League or competitive cheerleading.

But if I ask "How do *you* like it?" I usually get a blank shrug. Something as tangential as a parent's life is not supposed to get in the way of children's happiness and achievement. (I concede that spending all my free time sitting on dusty bleachers and washing smelly uniforms *might* be a blast, if only I'd give it a chance.)

If you both like it, really really Sally Field like it, have fun! But if you're issuing threats and bribes to get your child to a crosstown practice or you're muttering obscenities behind the wheel of the minivan while your head pounds, your stomach growls, and your pager beeps, then may I suggest turning on a sprinkler in the backyard and pouring yourself a cool tall one? Middle school—with its abundance of supervised clubs and after-school options—will be here soon enough.

What Does It Cost—in Dollars and in Sense?

Call me selfish, but I'd rather blow $100 at a Talbots sale than on acting lessons for a kindergartner. (Mom can't go naked, but Hollywood can wait.) I almost signed Eleanor up for a local jump-rope squad, until I read that upcoming team activities for members, ages six and up, included not only thrice-a-week practices but also demonstration clinics in Peru and competitions at Disney World and maybe, with luck, the world championships in Australia. It's not enough to become a proficient double Dutcher, you have to prove it in New South Wales? (And guess who pays? Times two, of course, since I can't imagine any parent in her right mind letting an eight-year-old skip overseas supervised by strangers. "Sorry gang, Mommy and Eleanor just have to run Down Under this weekend—but you've got your own tournaments in Paris, Tokyo, and Vegas to look forward to!")

I'm sure it's a swell program. But I don't know that kids in elementary school need to give that much commitment to a teddy bear, let alone an after-school hobby.

Then there are the basic logistics to consider. If my four kids were each in two or three activities meeting two or three times a week, I'd need to hire a freelance air traffic controller to make it through each afternoon.

Are They Really, Truly, Uniquely, Amazingly Talented?

This is the one that deludes—I mean, tugs the heartstrings of—us all: the natural talent rationale. If your preschooler shows a knack for drawing, providing her paper and pencils isn't enough. She needs art lessons. If she likes to dance, you can't just buy her a tutu and watch her twirl around the den; she must have studio time. Kids with ages in the single digits compete for spots on traveling teams— as in, traveling around the state, the nation, and the globe. And not just in sports. In science. In baton twirling. In Irish dancing. In spelling.

They can't *all* be national champions.

I know, I know. Tiger Woods practiced putting from his crib. Mozart was turned on to piano by his court musician dad. Brooke Shields was brought to casting calls for Ivory Snow before she was one. Who wants to be the parent who nips all that raw potential in the bud?

Who wants to settle for a happy, well adjusted, and merely talented child when, with just a little sacrifice and scheming on your part, you can trade up to a driven superstar? Fame! Glory! Scholarships! Recording contracts! Modeling careers! Burnout! Injuries! Peaking early! Lost childhood! Blown fortunes! Dysfunctional family dynamics!

How many wrecked family meals, weekends, and vacations is success worth? How much money? How many disgruntled tagalong siblings?

I'm all for prodigies. But I always thought they were the exception rather than the rule. Of course, that was before my kids started school in a district where fully 30 percent of the students qualify as "gifted." Clearly we're enjoying a talent explosion, a genius epidemic. What else could explain the huge range of activities available to even the most geographically obscure families? Or the dramatic increase in space allotted to the recapping of children's activities in the average Christmas-letter novella? Or the run on bumper stickers that read "Proud Parent of a Baby Who Can Sign 200 Words"?

Certainly it couldn't be mundane old oneupmomship.

Sarabeth's mom calls back. She forgot to ask me what I plan to have the children "do" on their playdate.

Is this a trick question?

"Well," she explains, "Sarabeth doesn't like to play with dolls or play house. And she does a lot of artsy projects at the arts-and-crafts center downtown, so maybe something active would be a good idea. If they swim, I could bring a suit. If they're bike riding, I can bring her helmet. But wait, maybe that's not so good because her violin recital is the next day and if she broke an arm that would be a disaster. How about a movie? What do you think?"

What I think is that we're talking about an afternoon a week away. I don't know what two five-year-olds will find to amuse themselves and I don't care, as long as it does not involve anything antisocial, illegal, or against house rules and does not require my carting them anywhere. I'm sure the multitalented Sarabeth can come up with something.

I can always tell when a child guest hasn't been left to her own devices very much. She spends half the visit seeking me out to complain or to tattle or sometimes just to make conversation because she's more comfortable around grown-ups than the other kids whizzing past her in my halls. She expects to be *entertained* as if she were the minister dropping by for tea instead of, um, a little kid.

I decide against telling Sarabeth's mom about my daughters' favorite new activity, messing around in the mud pit in the backyard. Whether they like it so much because they come out looking like three-foot Hershey's Kisses or because no grown-ups will go near it, I can't say.

Thanks to runaway Mompetition, parents feel way more responsible for their children's amusement and enrichment than my mom ever could have imagined when she'd hold the door open and shoo us out (though she couched it as "go get some fresh air"). In fact, Mompetition is so entrenched that it's almost hard to see. Some kids don't even know what they're missing.

Or do they? Assuring Sarabeth's mom that the girls will be fine winging it, I'm reminded of the summer we enrolled Henry and Eleanor in a program all our friends were raving about. From 9 a.m. to 3 p.m., peppy teen counselors hustled them from tennis to swimming to arts and crafts. All the things I'd heard they should be "exposed" to, in one handy, well-organized package. Sounded like fun to me.

"Please don't make us go back there," they begged the following year.

"But didn't you like tennis and swimming and sculpture?"

"It was okay," allowed Eleanor, who was six. "But there was no time to play."

Momfidence…

… is seeing your child as a short human, not a long project. There's no formula for success, no year-end bonus if you exceed anyone's expectations.

. . . is realizing that there aren't too many adults running around in tutus or karate-chopping boards in two.

. . . is proudly watching your kids put on a play in the basement . . . mess around with Play-Doh . . . catch crawdads in the creek . . . play four-square . . . cut out paper snowflakes . . . run a lemonade stand . . . transform a cardboard box into a remarkable likeness of a movie theater, complete with plush felt seats . . . or have a blast doing some other hopelessly old fashioned thing that will count for diddly on a college application form ten years hence.

. . . is sleeping in on Saturday mornings.

Happiness Is a Gun and a Naked Bimbo
On Toys

> Equipping children with realistic-looking guns, swords, shields, and other tools of warfare is tantamount to setting up a training ground in aggression. — *Laura E. Berk,* Awakening Children's Minds

"**S**o what do you want for Christmas?" Grandmom asks Eleanor and Henry. They are two and four, mere consumption novices. Henry's been crafting a mile-long wish list from the snowdrifts of holiday catalogs that have fallen upon our house, but Eleanor has no memory of last Christmas and little idea about what's ahead. So I'm surprised when she chirps an answer first.

"Ba-ee! I want Ba-ee!"

"A baby doll? How nice," Grandmom nods. "Would you like a little stroller, too?"

Eleanor shakes her head. "Ba-ee!"

"She's saying Barney, Mom," I translate. "That big purple dinosaur on TV."

"No! Ba-ee! BA-EE!" Eleanor insists, louder. My mom and I exchange blank looks.

Finally Henry pipes up. "She wants a *Barbie,* Mom."

Duh!

I never expected my daughter to clamor for a fashion doll while still in diapers herself. Not that I was displeased. Barbie had easily been my own favorite childhood toy. My sister Patti and I gave ours new names (April and June), husbands (my tall plush Snoopy and her teddy bear named Ta Ta), and jobs (stable owner/detective/ dress-shop proprietress for June; mother of the fifty-four shorter dolls for April). In our hyperactive imaginations, their sporty cars resembled Nancy Drew's glamorous roadster, not lowly shoe boxes, so long as you ignored the NASCAR effect of the "Payless Shoe Source" advertisement along the sides. Our dolls and their shaggy menfolk lived in Tinytown, a corner of our basement with its own phone directory and newspaper.

Though I gave away my Breyer horses and Mystery Date board game as I grew up, I saved my vintage Barbie carrying case stuffed with tiny cocktail dresses and bridal gowns. For my daughters. For someday.

For *now?*

Full of fond memories and holiday cheer, I plunge into the Pepto pink zone at my neighborhood Target. I stumble out an hour later. To think that my Barbies had sat on wooden spool chairs and lived in cardboard boxes—albeit nicely decorated ones, with walls papered in harvest-gold Con-Tact shelf liner and a groovy rabbit-skin rug. Today's fashion doll has it all, fashion being the least of it. I marvel with leftover third-grader envy at the long aisle of careers and beaux available to her, not to mention the mansions, trains, planes, and convertibles. So complete and realistic is the world the modern Barbie inhabits, I half expect to see tiny plastic charge cards and diaphragms along with her cutlery, food, and consumer electronics.

For Eleanor, though, I leave with a simple starter Barbie, in a tutu.

As I'd imagined, she loves it. She carries the doll everywhere, along with her blankie. What I don't foresee are everybody else's reactions.

First, Babs is frowned on at PC school. I mean *pre*school, the Montessori where toys are made of wood and nobody wears anything clingy, spangled, or synthetic.

"We'd rather she left the doll at home," I'm told by Eleanor's teacher, Earthina. (Names have been changed to protect the innocent—me.)

"But I thought it was okay for them to bring toys from home if they just brought them out at naptime."

"That's true. But most kids bring blankets or stuffed animals. Not—" her lips twist as if the very word tastes bad—"*Barbie.*"

"Actually Eleanor calls her Polly Bannerina."

"Yes, Mrs. Spencer, but—"

"Because it's a ballerina. Get it? Polly Ballerina?"

"Yes. But you must agree that a Barbie's different."

"How?" I ask. (I do realize she's not exactly plush.)

"All the other girls want to see it and play with it."

"Does Eleanor let them?"

"Well, no, she just goes to sleep, but—"

"Well, can't the other girls bring in their own Barbies if they want?" One little boy, I know for a fact, stashes a rubber-banded pack of Pokémon cards in his naptime blankie.

"Actually the problem is, well, Mrs. Spencer, I'm not sure your daughter is identifying with Barbie in a healthy way."

"Oh!" This is the first encounter I've ever had with a teacher describing my child as subperfect. (Remember they're only two and four here; there would be other encounters.) Identify? I consider. Both daughter and doll have blond hair. And Eleanor does come to class in a tutu sometimes. "What do you mean?"

"She says she wants to be Barbie when she grows up."

"Who wouldn't?" I quip—too quickly—thinking of the mansion, the wardrobe, the one-inch waist.

Earthina is not amused. I decide this is not the time to point out that Henry wants to be a rifle-totin', b'ar-rasslin' Davy Crockett when he grows up (though I am sorely tempted). Instead I assure her that I am not too worried about Eleanor's future. And I promise to remind her to keep the doll to herself at naptime. After all, I tell her, it's so wonderful that the school allows children to bring comfort objects from home at naptime to strengthen their sense of security and help them make developmentally appropriate transitions, blah blah blah—*whether they attach to a fair-trade handmade Peruvian baby doll or a naked plastic fashion babe!*

I don't actually say that last part to the teacher. I do slip it in when I run into the usual knot of other mommies in the lobby and sigh about the exchange. Bad move.

"Toddlerhood *is* early for Barbie," opines a mother whose own two-year-old still sucks a bottle and a pacifier.

"I worry about body image," concurs another.

"And all those sexy clothes," chimes in a mom in a baggy T-shirt.

"Doesn't it bother you that she sets such a blond and narrow standard of beauty?" asks a fourth (this one blond, wasp-waisted, in a form-fitting tee).

Gee, I just thought the doll was fun to play with.

Remember play? That's what kids used to do before they got enriched. They still like it, when they get the chance. Unfortunately parents spend too much time obsessing about what the kids are playing with and too little time just letting them be. I never realized how many sleepless nights the local Toys "R" Us inspired until I began doing interviews for a toy story. Startled by the snarky reactions to Eleanor's Barbie, I pitched an article on the topic. Something like "How to Pick a Doll Your Daughter Will Love."

"There's something there. We can always use toy articles for the holiday issue," coos my editor. "But this is a much bigger story than Barbie, you know."

"It is?"

"Oh yes! Gender stereotypes! Violence! Crass commercialism! Aesthetics!"

"Wait—are we still talking about preschoolers here?"

Indeed we were. I was still new to the world of child's play back then. But this editor knew where her readers' hot buttons were.

Who knew, as my research soon revealed, that Winnie the Pooh is, to some people, too *ugly* and "historically incorrect" to pass muster in a nursery? ("The old-fashioned Pooh is okay, it's just the Disney-ized version I take away from her," this anti-all-things-Mickey mom was careful to distinguish.) Who knew it's a short sashay from dress-up clothes to murder, as another mom darkly reminded me of little Jon Benet Ramsey, the six-year-old beauty queen whose life was tragically and mysteriously cut short, though not, as I recall, while she was decked out in a rhinestone tiara and a shiny net play-princess dress. Even a toy based on cheery Dora, the bilingual explorer, is suspect, earnest moms told me, because "it's just an ad for TV watching."

At first I feared these were just the extreme overthinkers. And then I realized everybody's overthinking. After a particularly scorching diatribe by a Marin County mom on the lack of nutritional role modeling wrought by the Easy Bake oven, I got another earful from the other end of the psychographic spectrum in the Bible Belt. Who knew that Power Rangers are inappropriate, because they get their power from the earth, in direct conflict to what is taught at Sunday school?

So much for the toy aisles being like a walk in a candy store. There are land mines out there, I tell you!

These are the seven things I worry about in a toy:

1. Is it going to kill or maim anybody?

Safety first and all that. No babies loose around the LEGOs bits. No toddlers attempting cinnamon buns in the Easy-Bake Oven. All big kids using jackknives do so under adult supervision.

2. Is it age appropriate, more or less?

The recommended ages on the packaging usually have safety, not common sense, in mind. So you have to take a closer look. A high-fashion doll is fine for a toddler when she spends her time twirling it around (like her sock monkey, like herself) to the Waltz of the Flowers. A baby doll, on the other hand, can be a big "no way." Consider the Bratz Babyz, the baby dolls that wear a thong instead of a diaper because they "already know how to flaunt it." These dolls' ad copy also enthuses that they're "keepin' it real in the crib." Somehow I doubt this refers to colic or diaper blowouts (though the latter is easy to imagine in a baby wearing a thong). Some toys aren't appropriate at any age.

3. Does it have a sound-off switch?

I have nothing against noise. I'm the mother of four. Noise is the very sound of happy children at play, and not hearing it can only mean two things: naptime or trouble.

But since kids are perfectly capable of raising the roof with their own vocal cords, why add unnecessary decibels?

No to drum sets, cymbals, or maracas. (They will make the

latter out of beans at some point in school anyway, in case you're worried about their being deprived exposure to rhythm instruments.) No talking books. No play cell phones. No karaoke. And, please, no singing stuffed animals. The talking Teletubbies were bad enough. But if I hear "Let's Get Physical" from Workout Care Bear one more time today, he'll be sweating it out on a shelf at Goodwill tomorrow.

4. Does it have some imagination left inside?

Every girl knows that Skipper and Kelly are Barbie's little sisters and Midge is her perma-freckled best friend. And Ken— well, Ken is just the boy doll, the standby groom for when Barbie wears her wedding gown, the guy you prop next to her when you put her in one of her five thousand sparkly dresses, assuming you are fortunate enough to own a Ken and don't have to use your teddy bear for this purpose. Beyond that, her life is what you make it. You get to make up where they're going in those Corvettes and cruise ships. You supply the conversation. You invent the adventures. Even if you have Doctor Barbie, NBA Barbie, or Barbie as Batgirl with Motorcycle, those prefabbed careers tend to be short-lived. Eventually the clothes come off and she looks like all the rest of your Barbies, the stars of your own personal Tinytown.

Which is why Mattel broke my heart when it announced a couple of years ago (just before Valentine's Day, no less!) that Barbie had "dumped Ken" for an Australian surfer named Blaine. Actually at first I was more puzzled than outraged. *Barbie has a story line?* "Like other celebrity couples, their Hollywood romance has come to an end," said a company VP of marketing. She added that the pair "feel it's time to spend some quality time—apart." Icky enough is the inappropriateness of introducing breakups and the ways of the celeb culture to eight-year-olds, much less preschoolers, the main Barbie consumers. But why does a toy manufacturer feel the need to do all the thinking for girls in the first place?

So much for the old idea that "play is the child's work." There's nothing left to work out when all your toys come pre-plotted.

5. Do we not already have five or ten or fifty of the same thing lying around this house?

Sometimes I'm not too stringent about this one. There must be dozens of two-inch-tall, flocked Calico Critters lying around my house, for example. I don't know how they all got there. But it's true a large proportion of them are rabbits. And none of them are ever wearing the tiny clothes they came in.

One way to avoid the multiplication thing is to avoid any toy that describes itself as a set. *Set* means there will be a zillion tiny plastic parts that will be oohed over once and then lost forever to your dog and your vacuum. Ever see a Playmobil cannonball? The typical newborn's fingernail is bigger.

Also beware the fateful exhortation "collect 'em all" (or the Pokémonic variation, "Gotta catch 'em all"). This means that the perfectly fine toy in your child's sticky little hands is insufficient, unusable, and worthless in its isolation. A single Bionicle trading card is like a Lay's potato chip—you can't have just one. And how much fun could Thomas the Tank Engine have circling the tracks by his lonesome? The child must have more, more, *more!*

Not that I've held the line with any impressive success. My Little Pony should be renamed My Endless Stable. No sooner do Beanie Babies and Battle Bots streak across the sky and fade than they are replaced by some new alliterative addiction. And you can only hope your child passes out of the targeted age group for the fad du jour before catching on.

Good luck.

6. Do I secretly covet it?

I tell myself that the reason my house contains enough baby dolls to populate an orphanage is that I have three girls. Except that would only explain three of the dolls. As for the rest, the truth is that I am the one with the weakness for baby dolls, from the vanilla-scented Corolles of all sizes to the best-dressed Madame Alexanders to the exceedingly accessorized Bitty Baby, whose abundant catalogs arrive in our mailbox even more often than bills. I love the glee on a girl's face when she opens the box and meets her baby for the first time. I love how iconic the limp dolls in their velvety rompers look tossed atop a bed or toy chest. I love their cradles and bonnets and high chairs and . . .

Ahem!

If Moms and Daddyos are going to shell out all that money on toys for every birthday and Christmas, we might as well pick out some stuff we like. This is not just a mom thing, or my house wouldn't also contain more Star Wars spacecraft and Godzilla-type monsters than seen in any movie. Whether the kids like it, too, is immaterial; when they're small, they'll play with anything. It's one of the silver linings of parenthood, now that you're in charge of the budget, to stock up on the childhood treasures you were once denied. Clever marketers know this, of course, which is why they brought back Holly Hobbie, Strawberry Shortcake, Transformers, Dream Pets, Pound Puppies, and every other relic down from the attic toy boxes of Generations X, Y, and baby boomer. So take advantage!

7. Are parents necessary?

Finally, if you're expected to sit down there with your child and play with the toy yourself, it can't be such a great toy. Parental co-playing must be optional. The whole point of a toy is to keep a child out of your hair.

Oh, I'm resigned to spending long minutes wresting the toy from its abundant packaging and many twisted wires while my child pants with rabid anticipation—if she hasn't already broken it while trying to wrest it free herself. I'm even prepared to spend some time constructing it (having learned this lesson my first parental Christmas, when we blithely ignored those three little words—"some assembly necessary"—at our own sleepless peril). But post-infancy, once the thing is up and out and running, you should be able to step away. Needless to say, siblings are one of the best toys around. No booking playdates two weeks in advance. No enduring Candyland!

The article I wound up writing was a balanced and understanding look at the quandaries parents face about the toys that make them cringe. I did try to give extra weight to the guy I thought made the most sense, the toy historian at Penn State who begged parents for "a degree of toleration and good humor about toys." This being a balanced piece of journalism, however—and because I had twelve hundred words to fill—merely saying "Let 'em play, for goodness sake" wasn't sufficient. So I also tracked down other perspectives. One was a women's studies coordinator who declared she was "not out to ban Barbie but to encourage healthful and realistic play with her." I did not tell her, in the interview, that there is nothing realistic about pretending your doll is married to an orange Snoopy and drives a sporty shoe box. Play is not supposed to be "realistic." And I believe it is almost always intrinsically "healthful."

Let 'em play, for goodness sake!

Which brings me to one last kind of toy worth singling out, if only to show that parental meddling in play infects both genders. I'm talking weaponry.

No, I don't especially like guns. I don't own a gun. I've never fired a gun. They scare me. Nevertheless, we keep an arsenal in my house. Over the years we've had six-shooters, cap pistols, squirt guns, Super Soakers, silvery space blasters, the aforementioned reproduction of Davy Crockett's "Old Betsy," and countless action-figure-sized revolvers and rifles. Battalions of well-armed little green army men have been known to occupy the dollhouse.

Boys are drawn to gunplay like rats to the Pied Piper's tune. Give one of my daughters a stick, and she'll rock it to sleep or wave it like a magic wand; give the same stick to Henry and "pow!" Without a toy gun handy, he'll fashion a remarkable substitute out of Duplo blocks or his sister's splay-legged Barbie doll. Which pieces go missing first out of a map of America puzzle in a preschool class? The gun-shaped Florida and Oklahoma, of course, according to the gentlest preschool director I know. One mom—a preacher's wife—reports her son can gnaw an accurate blunderbuss out of his cheese sandwich in ten bites.

Yet admitting I'm okay with toy weaponry can be like saying I'm pro–al Qaeda. "It encourages violence," goes the usual argument. Or "It desensitizes them to violence." As if boys aren't naturally rowdy. It's not like the moms are out there teaching them how to play Capture the Fort. The famously pacifist Dr. Spock advised parents to nix toy guns by telling the child, "There is too much meanness and killing in the world" and "We all must learn how to get along in a friendly way together." What's next? "Don't hurt the nice wormies when you dig them up to go fishing"? "Let's shake hands with the terrorists and promise not to be mean anymore"? Nice in theory, anyway.

It's always awkward when a pacifist comes over to play. A play-mate with pacifist parents, that is. I've never met a boy who turned down a chance to make war or hunt Indians in our backyard. A first I wondered what the mommy protocol was. Do I hide all the wooden swords and vinyl holsters in advance? Hospitality is all about mak-ing the guest feel comfortable after all—though the guest's PC mother, I finally decided, is another story. If I had to hide every pi-rate machete, pistol, and Three Stooges DVD (more violence), not to mention all the sugary snacks, buxom dolls, "sexist" toy vacuum cleaners, and other potentially objectionable pleasures in my house, I could skip spring cleaning for the next year.

"But what about the murder rate? What about death in Iraq?" a mom once cornered me. To which I counter: What about the Civil War? What about cowboys? What about our soldiers in this war on terror? It seems contradictory (not to mention a little controlling) to teach kids about headlines and history but forbid such themes in their play. Play is how kids work things out. Was it only a genera-tion ago that a parent in some parts of the country routinely sent Junior out to hunt a rabbit for supper?

I do insist on a few rules:

> No pointing a weapon at anybody not in the game.
> No hurting anyone.
> And no squirt guns in the house!

But ban toy weapons altogether? That doesn't promote peace—it merely deprives kids of a creative, energetic outlet and gives guns the allure of the forbidden. Soon enough, boys will find other ways—heavy metal music, athletics, cars, girls—to vent their testosterone. Meanwhile, G.I. Joe and Davy Crockett sound like pretty good role models to me.

And in a pinch Joe makes a decent Barbie husband, too.

Momfidence...

... is seeing the bright side of the ugly reality that kids just like garish plastic versions of toys better than the attractive wooden ones: plastic costs less and you feel less guilty tossing it when they're through.

... is walking softly and carrying a big trash bag. Periodic sweeps of the toy box are essential to make room for the next six months' worth of birthday presents, Happy Meal junk, and other toys that infiltrate the house like grains of sand in a Saharan home. ("What purple teddy bear with the ear that the dog chewed? What little plastic thingamabob? Gee, it must be around here someplace, honey.")

Do Be a Spoilsport
On Kids' Sports

Trenton's father, Craig Irwin, works five jobs to be able to finance and participate in his son's football training schedule. Mom Sharon Toups invests around $15,000 annually toward daughter Sarah's goal of becoming a National Champion Cheerleader . . . TJ Knox plays the role of both mom and coach for her daughter Lindsay's promising basketball career.

—*premiere episode summary of the reality TV show*
Sports Kids Moms and Dads

It's a glorious spring weekend. Warm sun, cloudless sky, a day made for watching your muscular husband man the Weedwacker while you lounge on the back patio reading the Sunday papers with a Diet Cherry Vanilla Dr Pepper on ice. A day for the kids to cavort on the play structure and draw with pastel sidewalk chalk until they grow tired of making self-portraits and devolve into writing semirude things about one another and you must make them apologize and hose everything away. It's a picnicking kind of day. A hiking day. A day to do the week's laundry and pack tomorrow's lunch boxes. A day in which any number of potential plans have been torpedoed because we are at . . . the tournament.

146

"I'm boooored!"

Page wiggles onto my lap, upsetting the bag of Skittles I'd set there to cork earlier whines. Then she wriggles off again so she can pick the jewel-colored bits off the ground. Why is everything more appealing to a small child when it's on the ground? If only I had thought years ago to serve finicky Henry meat and potatoes from the floor instead of a table. "Hey, Pagey, don't eat the ones with dir—"

"When are we leaving?" Eleanor demands. As she has demanded every ten minutes since we got here to the Green Acres and Acres and Acres Soccer Complex three hours ago.

"It's almost over," I say.

"But if they win, don't they go on to the finals?" points out Margaret, quite accurately.

"Well, yes. But it's a tie game and it's almost over," I try to explain. "The other team scored more in other games, so if we tie, they'll get to go to the finals and Henry's team comes in second. And then we'll all go home."

Home! *Please please please let us go home,* I silently pray. *A tie is just dandy. A loss—oh well. I'm sick of soccer. It's been lost weekend after lost weekend all spring, as it was all fall before that. If we get knocked out now, I can still say to Henry in a supportive, congratulatory tone, "Second place in the whole tournament. How about that!" And then we can leave!*

One eye on the field and the other on Page crouched over the candies in the mud, I try to do some subtle pelvic tilts to loosen my gnarled back. It's not that I don't want my pride-and-joy boy to know the thrill of victory. I just want to salvage my weekend.

When is the referee is going to signal that this eternal game is over? If we get out right away, maybe we can make it home without having to empty our wallets at the Winston-Salem Sonic Burger. Maybe the Skittles will tide them over so they're not staaarving. I wonder which Page has ingested more of by now—sugar or fertilizer?

It's not like I'm an unsupportive mother. Why, I was here at these very fields only yesterday, 126.8 miles from home, watching the preliminary rounds. Daddyo and I take turns going to Henry's games so the girls—who thus far have shown little interest in organized sports and have not been coaxed by us in that direction—don't have to get dragged along every time. Maybe once a season, like today, we decide to drag them anyway in the name of a family outing.

Which they just love.

Because we won Saturday's two games, our "reward" was driving all the way back home and then back here again today—to the Church of Our Lady of Soccer Moms. You'd think, since I live in the God-fearing South, that there might be resistance to Sunday morning soccer games, but none of the teams appears to be shorthanded. The coach advised us months ago to book one of the rooms blocked by a considerate team parent for our group at the Econo Lodge down the highway in just this fortuitous event. But the only thing less appealing to me than spending two glorious weekend days watching a bunch of ten-year-olds kick a ball around a field two hours from home is to spend the night in between sleeping in an Econo Lodge. So we made the two round trips, muttering the whole way.

Did I mention that this is not a "travel" squad? It's just the ordinary city league. If we were a higher-level club we'd have the privilege of crossing state lines every weekend instead of just county ones. Nor has this been the first tournament of the year. By fourth grade my son has accumulated more trophies than his grandpa collected in fifty years of playing in both the General Motors *and* Knights of Columbus bowling leagues. Win or lose, kids get trophies just for showing up.

Now, of course, with one minute left in the game, our mighty Kamikaze Arsenal score the tiebreaking goal. *Of course.*

(*Correction for the record:* Kamikaze Arsenal is what the boys wanted to name the team when the coach was soliciting suggestions. But what do kids know? After several parents objected to the name's "militaristic overtones," a call went out for alternatives. Soon my e-mail box was flooded with more conflict-free possibilities—all from parents. And I'm sure you'll be relieved to know that the team now more peaceably, although somewhat less intimidatingly, goes by the name of a large furry mammal.)

In fact it is Henry who kicks in the winning point. It is cool— way cool—to watch the fruit of your loins become the hero of the hour. I clap. I beam. On the outside, I look like a walking cliché, fanatic mom in ball cap and shades, rising from her collapsible chair to stand and cheer. On the inside, I am bummed. *Another* game! And this final match won't even start for another hour. We won't get home for four hours—just in time for the evening dance of bath– pj's–snack–toothbrushing–stories–back rubs–kisses–lights out–one more kiss–okaybacktobedthistimeIreallymeanit!

All around us now, whooping parents are getting up to run to midfield and form a tunnel with their arms for the victors to run through. Having already done this three times this weekend, it's starting to look a little corny. I busy myself with my folding chair in order to avoid catching the eye of anybody who might urge me to join in, as if placing my maternal loyalty on the line should I dare to refuse.

And then, deliverance! Sibling revelry requires my diplomacy.

"Mom! Page ate a bug!"

"Did not!"

"Did so! I sall it!"

"Unh uh!"

"Bug eater!"

"Unh uh!"

"ARE WE GOING HOME NOW?" Eleanor began gathering the girls' crayons, coloring books, dolls, Fruit Gushers wrappers, and Uno cards the minute it was obvious the game had ended. She'll make a better organized mother than me someday.

"No, guys. Guess what? Did you see? They won. Henry scored the winning point! And, uh, they get to play one more game!" I muster a peppy soccer Mom smile.

Soccer sisters—who haven't watched a minute of the tournament—are not amused.

Finally Soccer Dad folds up his crossword puzzle. "We should have brought two cars."

Okay, yes, Daddyo works crossword puzzles during soccer games. I like to read books myself, when I'm not keeping the girls out of mud banks or parking lots. We do look up at the field pretty often. We gaze proudly at our beloved son and murmur the occasional "Nice shot" or "Good job." As if he could hear us. As if any of the boys running around out there on the enormous adult-sized field can hear the helpful cacophony rising from the sidelines.

"Good job! Nice kick! Way to go!"

"Scott! Tie your shoe!"

"Atticus! Drink lots of water!"

"They're open on the right!"

"Two minutes left, Roscoe!"

"Head up! Watch that forward! Excellent!"

"Way to go on that shoe-tying, Scottie!"

Cautionary tales of dads who kill one another at hockey practice or go to jail for attacking the Little League coach may win the gruesome headlines and make people ask, "What are we coming to?" But scenes just a notch less grisly can be found at any local park where youth sports are played. Don't watch the kids. Keep your eye on the parents.

Every soccer team fields the same members. Here's Camera Dad, who has never seen a minute of game play with his naked eye. He's too busy recording it for posterity—and the team parties where the tapes will be replayed so the adults can analyze and point out everything the kids did wrong. All in the name of "skill development." (Game-tape-viewing time presumably does not count toward the two-hour-a-day TV maximum recommended for the lads.)

There's Broadcast Mom and Dad, who give a running commentary of the action: "Oh! Josh was right there, and then that kid with the ponytail came out of nowhere! Get it! Get it! Oh, would you look at that defense. Now that's the way to work together. Sam's running, he's kicking, he's passing . . . Beautiful pass! Oh! Oh! It's over Finn's head! Get it! It's out!" This is a handy parent to have within earshot if you've brought a particularly good book to the match, so you can look up when you hear your child's name.

Can't forget Head Cheerleader Mom. Not that she'd let you. She roots for everybody's kids as loudly as her own: "Go Jon-a-thaaaaann! Go Loo-cas! Go, go, GO! All right Hen-reeee!" I try to park my folding chair far away from her, unless I've brought my migraine-formula Motrin along.

Groomer Mom and Dad have their eyes on the big picture. He silently takes in the proceedings with a set jaw while she rags on the coaches, the calls, the other parents who were late to the game or dared to skip this tournament altogether because their grandma was having heart surgery or some other lame excuse. Later you hear their son also plays in two other leagues, including one above his age level, and has a private goalie coach (former Olympian now teaching high school three towns over). He's spending his summer at soccer camp. All summer.

There's also, regrettably, a knot of Confused Ones, who rail as if they were watching the Manchester United with several pints in them. "Holding! *Holding!* PENALTY KICK! Are you blind? Call him! Call him, you nearsighted candy striper!" These parents—they come in both male and female forms—are curiously oblivious to the fact that the referees are often high-schoolers a handful of years older than the players, teens who love the game and are just trying to earn some extra cash for iPod downloads. The spectacle of fat forty-something fathers verbally sparring with earnest seventeen-year-olds is somehow not the sort of "healthy competition" I had in mind when I signed up my son to play. I just wanted him away from his sisters and burning off his prodigious energy for a few hours a week.

At the start of each season I ferret out my fellow Traitor Moms. We burst with pride watching our amazing kids on the field, but don't believe we will inflict any harm by looking away half the time. We furtively ask one another the score because we're never exactly sure. We're too busy talking sales and weekend plans and complaining about the absurd state of kids' sports.

We complain, we gripe, but here we are. Giving up our weekends and a small fortune in order to watch our kids play. During one memorable regional tournament hours from home, our opponents for an 8 a.m. kickoff turned out to be another team from our town. From our very school system, in fact, the same kids we'd been playing during the regular season. "Luck of the draw," shrugged the coach. "We'll have a good sense of their strengths and weaknesses!" So there we all were, dozens of families who'd driven hundreds of miles at the crack of dawn in order to watch our neighbors' boys run around with our own.

And why do we do this?

For a College Athletic Scholarship!

Only the most candid parents admit this, but everybody seems to be thinking it. The payoff is the brass ring that coaxes hockey parents out of bed at 4 a.m. and sends millions of others to log endless hours at pools, gyms, and fields while complaining they have no time to exercise themselves. College ain't cheap after all. And Mikey does seem to have the knack . . .

My own brother, in fact, won a full-ride athletic scholarship to a Big Ten university. But not in basketball, the sport in which he made the All State team. And not in track, where he set school and district records. John was signed to five free years of first-rate college to play football, the third sport he played back in the golden-oldie days (barely a generation ago) of three-letter athletes. (That's when one season completely ended before a new sport began, so a kid didn't have to choose between football and basketball, much less try to play both at the same time, or pick "his" sport at the ripe old age of ten in order to perfect his skill at it in around-the-calendar play.) John accomplished his scholarship feat despite playing football only four months a year, from August to November, and without any private coaching or skill-burnishing specialty camps. My parents didn't attend every practice or write letters to scouts. They never pulled him off a team because the level of play wasn't challenging enough for him. They certainly didn't start him on weight training or steroids to beef him up. (If anything, as I recall, my mom used to wish he'd *stop* growing so she didn't have to buy him new shoes every six weeks.)

Most incredibly of all, John never played any team sport until he was in sixth grade! Unless you count the pickup stickball and curb ball in the middle of our street, games that were remarkably organized considering they didn't involve a single adult. In fact, divvying up into "sides" and arguing endlessly over who was "out" or "safe" probably developed more useful life skills than any youth coach's efforts could. Organized teams for elementary schoolers simply didn't exist in our all-American suburb, except for maybe Little League or the occasional Knights of Columbus youth basketball game. And nobody noticed!

No specialization? No conditioning? No skill development? No performance-enhancing caffeinated sports drinks? No year-round play? No scholarship today!

If my son is a natural athlete, which he is, and he never goes pro, which he probably won't because his parents are such spoilsports, I guess it's all our fault. But that's guilt I can live with.

Fast fact 1: Forty-one million kids play sports; fewer than 126,000 receive athletic scholarships—of any amount.

Kids' odds of college scholarships would be better if they spent the amount of time now devoted to hitting balls to hitting the books and cramming for the SAT instead. Oh wait, they're already staying up till midnight doing that, too.

To Snare a Spot on the Varsity Team!

Pity the naive parent (me) who thought "tryouts" meant your kid is supposed to show up for the sport, try it out, and see if he likes it.

My rude awakening to the wild world of sports came early. I

was reaching for a canapé at a cocktail party when I was cornered by a huge man shoveling corn chips in his face.

"Henry's getting big! So what does he play?"

"Oh, you know, he likes chasing lions and Indians and stuff. He likes Davy Crockett—"

"I mean sports."

"Oh! He's ball crazy! Loves anything with a ball. He just got one of those T-ball stands for his birthday—"

"Ah! Baseball!" my companion pounced. "That's what I meant. What level?"

"Um, pretty low still," I say, trying to picture the ball stand in our driveway. "About this high." I hold my hand down around my knees.

"No, no—what level of play? Machine pitch? Coach pitch?"

I have no idea what he's talking about.

"You mean he's not in Little League? He looks old enough. You don't want him falling behind in his skills."

"His skills?"

"To keep up with the other kids! They'll all get better! Don't worry, he can catch up if he works at it!" He offers me the number of the local league office. And the name of his eight-year-old's private pitching coach.

Henry was five.

Addendum to chapter 10: Mompetition is not limited to moms. While my poor kids spent their early years chasing tigers and careening down our driveway in plastic wagons, some of their peers had been hauled around the state competing in one adult-hogged sport or another for years. In my town nobody blinks when elementary-age kids enter swim meets across the country or hop a 767 to Israel for competitive *jump-roping*. These kids are good. They should be: They spend more time at their chosen sport than the average 1945 pro athlete did. We'd been counting the years until Henry is old enough to play on his middle school team—no more of these expensive club squads—when a neighbor burst our bubble by telling us that most kids in our district played both school *and* club leagues simultaneously. To stay competitive.

Twelve-year-olds!

Fast fact 2: Some observers predict high school teams won't even exist in the not-so-distant future. With all the best kids fielding "elite" club teams that their parents pay for, it's thought that nobody will be left to fill the school squads. Yup, I'd much rather have my children exposed to a "better level of play" and wear fancy uniforms that I pay for than have them be able to hang around after school to practice with classmates. I'd much rather haul them all over creation myself in air-conditioned comfort than have them get to games on their own in a smelly old team school bus. I mean, what kind of mother am I?

For Their Health!

Children today can't walk to school—no sidewalks. They can't ride their bikes—too many crazy drivers on the road with dashboard TVs. Nor do they run around outside—aside from the babynappers, the lure of playing in the NBA right on your Nintendo system is too strong. And now that schools are dropping PE and recess in order to cram for tests, signing up for a well-run sports program is the least a conscientious parent can do in the great fight against obesity.

So why wait till they're ten if you can find a team for five-year-olds? Or threes? Why play your child against her age-mates when kids slightly older will give her even more of a challenge? Why join a weekend rec league when they could get in twice-a-week practices at the next level of play? Why settle for a few months of play when you can maintain skill level by playing year round?

After all, being active is good for them, so extreme activity must be even better!

Fast fact 3: Overuse injuries, once seen only in pros, are now the cause of half of all sports injuries in middle- and high-schoolers. Each year more than 3.5 million kids under age fourteen suffer a sports injury needing medical attention.

To Keep 'em Out of Trouble!

Fast fact 4: Seventy percent of kids quit organized sports by age thirteen because they're no longer having fun, according to *Sports Illustrated for Kids,* which ought to know.

That's exactly the age at which I *want* my kids to start sweating with a group of peers while doing something organized and exhausting under the watchful eye of an adult with a whistle. Puberty should be the starting place for trying out different sports and maybe finding one you love—not the quitting point. But if you've been wearing cool uniforms for a decade and you're burned out on practices and torpedoed weekends, what's the possible draw to a school league?

Not even halfway to their growth spurts, I see kids already sorting themselves into who's "good" at sports and who's not. Who can say which hockey superstar at eight will still be fast on his skates at eighteen? What if the six-year-old gymnastics prodigy blossoms beyond perfect balance in puberty but would swim a powerful butterfly? You can't know if you don't even think you can try.

To Have Fun!

. . . .

This is what the coaches say, right? "We're all here to have fun!" "Fun is the only thing that matters!" And then they give their young athletes lists of rules, strategies, game plans, practice schedules. I've known coaches who recommended certain sports drinks to provide a competitive edge at tournaments (*Shhh, don't tell the competing team from town that we're sipping something new!*) and coaches who scout the upcoming opposition and issue reports to the team. (*Watch out for the center in braces and pigtails; she's a killer! And don't forget to have fun out there!*)

Meanwhile these same boys and girls—I'm still talking about the ten-and-under crowd here; don't get me started on the bigger ones—have no idea how to organize themselves into a sandlot game. Nobody knows how to play kickball, much less Kick the Can, which somebody's mother would probably object to anyway because the can is a hard object that might fly up and hurt somebody, seeing as protective gear, elaborate rules, skill-balanced teams, esteem-enhancing uniforms, and adult coaching don't yet exist for local Kick the Can players. Besides, it's a game best played in the middle of the street, where nobody is allowed to go. And there's no chance of the game achieving Olympic, college, or ESPN status.

So why bother?

Momfidence...

. . . is waiting to sign up for the team at least until your child brings it up first. You may be able to spare yourself a year or two of practice hauling this way.

. . . is realizing that the average kid gets more exercise bicycling to school, digging up fossils, or messing around at the local pool than playing centerfield.

. . . is letting your family plans dictate how many practices and games your child makes it to, not the other way around. A family is a team, too.

Turn On, Tune In, Take 30

On TV

> Excessive TV-watching cuts into family time, harms our kids' ability to read and perform well in school, encourages violence, and promotes sedentary lifestyles and obesity.
>
> — *TV-Turnoff Network*

I willingly give my kids large doses of a drug.

I am knowingly rotting their brains.

I am risking lives of obesity, aggression, stunted imaginations, and lousy social skills.

Or so I hear.

My household is a user. We *like* that "plug-in drug," the television. "Scooby Dooby" was among Page's first words. There's no stringent two-hours-a-day maximum around here. We don't comb through the *TV Guide* together on Saturdays to plot the upcoming week's ration. We don't sit and watch together so that at the first Power Rangers karate kick I can say, as one brochure on responsible family TV viewing suggests, "I wonder if there is another way to solve that instead of fighting."

If you're watching Power Rangers, the fighting is the whole point!

Yet on the day that Henry and Eleanor bring home from school permission slips to participate in TV-Turnoff Week, I start to fill them out on autopilot. An endless parade of paperwork rides home every day in their backpacks. And since these forms don't require me to go out this evening to buy twenty-five paper plates or four white-cotton T-shirts, much less drop everything in the middle of an upcoming workday to watch a puppet show or chaperone a field trip, I'm only too happy to oblige.

"Here you go. It says you're supposed to sign right below me and give it back to your teacher."

"What for?" Henry asks.

"To show you agree to go without TV for a week."

"What's the point?" echoes Eleanor.

"Well, because your whole school is doing TV Turnoff Week."

In unison they crumble the papers. "That's so lame!"

"Wait! Don't tear those," I say, still in dutiful mom mode. "Don't you want to help your classes reach their goals?"

"Like that's going to prove anything!" they snort.

Gradually it dawns on me that they might be ahead of me on this one.

Anyone in the parenting game long enough to have formulated a love-or-hate opinion on Barney has heard all the damning statistics about how many hours it takes to bake a couch potato. I don't want even a couch Tater Tot. On the other hand, my tube-fed tribe seem pretty healthy and normal. Would a week without make a difference?

I send my defiant third- and fourth-graders out to watch *Toonami* while I do a little research. Ironically, their very school is singled out for its impressive participation rate on the Web site of TV-Turnoff Network, the nonprofit group that concocted this event in 1994 to save America from the evils of the tube. More than 7.63 million people "took the plunge," the site notes, as if clicking off the remote were the equivalent of quitting smoking or swimming the English Channel.

It's more like, 7.63 million people (mostly coerced kids) abstained for a week from a benign activity—and tuned right back in for the next fifty-one weeks.

What *is* the point?

Maybe I'm biased about TV because I grew up high on it. Back in those Neanderthal days of three channels and no DVD players ("No, kids, not even VCRs!"), my tender years' viewing ranged from old Bette Davis movies to *The Match Game, Petticoat Junction,* and far too many *Flintstones* reruns—nothing nearly so lofty as *Blue's Clues.* I can hardly remember seeing a blank screen on the big Magnavox cabinet in our living room. We even watched during meals. Yet despite the depravity, I managed to develop an addiction to Nancy Drew and the Scholastic Book Club. I went on to graduate from both high school and college, and made Phi Beta Kappa to boot. What's more, I managed all this without degenerating into an obese, violent, or (I hope) unimaginative and antisocial cretin.

Though it could have been dumb luck.

Telling kids to go cold telly for a week implies that the medium is so toxic it must be shunned completely, its good with its garbage. I freely admit there's lots of the latter. But PBS or Animal Planet the entertainment equivalent of cigarettes? ESPN or Turner Classic Movies on par with drugs? Not even Homer Simpson is that degenerate.

I know families who successfully ration TV time like candy bars, one program a day. Unfortunately I have neither the temperament nor the energy for micromanagement. I know others who boast of having no set at all. But I can't say that their children seem any more charming, intelligent, creative, or well adjusted than mine. I admire the parents for enforcing rules that they believe in (even as I secretly wonder how they manage). I also feel a little sorry for the children who lack cultural references to *Caillou, American Idol, Rubbadubbers,* and Bill Nye the Science Guy.

Fact is TV deserves some rarely received credit. The label "electronic babysitter" is always tossed out so derisively. But I think it's a pretty swell bargain to buy thirty or sixty uninterrupted minutes at a stretch without having to check references or fork over $10 an hour. Nor do I have to worry about this sitter calling her boyfriend all night or not being able to speak English.

Television is underpraised as a relaxant, too. When the racket is rising on a rainy day and there are too many hours left before bedtime, I can't think of a quicker way to engineer a group wind-down. And when a kid comes home from a hard day of singing songs at Circle Time, making paper collages, and serving as line leader or fish feeder, why not veg out with *The Backyardigans* for an hour before hitting her own backyard?

The Teletubbies had Page counting to four well before she was two. Mister Rogers showed her how to drum a pot and use the lids for cymbals. Barney taught all four to sing (a fact that pains them now, but gosh, I loved that "Clean Up" song). "Cumulonimbus clouds—looks like rain," observed Margaret, the Weather Channel addict, as we headed into the grocery store one sunny afternoon. Sure enough, we came out twenty minutes later to get soaked. A new skill or bit of knowledge isn't automatically better if gleaned from a live human. Heck, I wish there were shows that gave instruction on shoelace-tying and bed-making.

And how can they say TV ruins a child's attention span when

there mine sit, as focused as scientists, well into their third straight hour of Cartoon Network?

TV is a fact of modern life. Ironically, though, it's way less central to childhood than when I was growing up without other time-sucking diversions like computers, video games, and so many organized activities.

Ultimately, it's not the machine itself that's the devil. It's how it's used. So why not a campaign for *responsible* TV viewing? It would be unhealthy if a child did nothing but read 24/7 or play soccer to the exclusion of everything else. But nobody's pushing Close Your Book Week or Shed the Shin Guards Week.

The rules around here:

1. No TV in the morning before school

It takes all the concentration my kids have to get dressed and find shoes.

2. No TV when friends are over

The point of inviting a friend over is so that you're not so bored you turn on the TV.

3. No TVs in the bedrooms

Incredibly, more than two thirds of kids over age eight have a set within a remote click of their pillow. So do more than one third of kids six and under. But I prefer to retain the right to send them to their rooms when they misbehave, and it hardly seems like punishment if they get to hang with the Disney Channel. (That's part of the reason there are no computers in there either, though that's another story.) Besides, I can't see what they're watching behind a closed door. (See next item.)

And no, I'm not just saying this because I have four kids

and don't want to shell out for four TVs. In fact, when we moved to a new house we consolidated down to a single cable outlet. Side benefit: There is only one juice-stained, pitted-out sofa in the house with sticky wrappers concealed deep under the cushions.

4. No free run of the remote

A few short years after a baby discovers cause and effect by pressing a button on the DVD player and watching the disc drawer eject—over and over and over—comes a greater TV discovery: that there are more channels on the set than PBS and Nickelodeon. That's when we started to block the more problematic ones. Even then, you have to poke your head in every once in awhile to make sure they haven't stumbled on anything too objectionable, like promos for prime-time network shows that are racier than old R-rated movies. No *South Park*. No MTV. No *Sex in the City* reruns. No poker championships. No sitcoms portraying parents as doofuses. Which pretty much limits them to the likes of PBS and Nickelodeon, come to think of it.

And of course parental preferences always trump kids', especially when there's an approaching hurricane, a national crisis, a spaceship launch, or a tasty old *Bonanza* episode featuring my first crush, discovered while watching reruns when I was thirteen, Pernell Roberts as Adam Cartwright. (Swoon!)

5. No arguments

Remote-controlling is Darwinian. The biggest, strongest person in the room tends to dominate it, whether you're a couple alone in the room or a pack of small children. Henry would lead his sisters into a steady diet of G4, the all-video-game TV channel, if I ignored their rightful protests. And so when the squabbling gets high, he knows to switch over to a benign cartoon lest I swoop in and turn it off entirely.

I like to think that in this way television fosters cooperation and sharpens their negotiation skills.

6. No TV in the car

If I wanted little ones who were plugged in 24/7, I'd have skipped labor and bought an aquarium. And though being buckled up qualifies as "downtime," I can think of cheaper, more productive ways to spend car trips. Like drawing, reading, napping, or staring out the window.

And let's not underestimate human interactions. Wacky as it sounds, I'd rather hear kids screeching "Mom! He's looking at me!" than see their glazed eyes and frozen slumps for hours on end as the miles roll by. At least I know they're alive.

Inevitably "There's nothing to do!" shrills up from the backseat like steam escaping from a pipe. So I say what my mom always told me: "Look at all the beautiful scenery!"

And the kids echo my old line: "What scenery? All we see is trees!"

And I say, "Yeah, but aren't they pretty?"

Then they disagree. But now we've got a conversation. And that's one of my favorite ways of all to pass the time on the road.

I especially resent the TV Chicken Littles' suggestion that TV "undermines family life." Because Daddyo and I love to lure everybody with popcorn into Movie Night with us. Our picks. Group view. So far, dorky old musicals starring Shirley Temple, Doris Day, or Fred Astaire have been surprisingly popular, although Henry leans to vintage Godzilla. They loved a long streak of animated flicks by Hayao Miyazaki, the Walt Disney of Japan. *Heidi* and *The Miracle Worker* left big impressions, too, once they got over the distressing surreality of a world in black and white. (Henry and Eleanor had many probing questions about the blind and deaf, while Page and Margaret seemed to relate to the scenes of the feral Helen Keller.) And we've all found that those reissue sets of old TV classics beat anything on prime time today. (Unlikely hits: *Lassie, The Outer Limits,* and *Lost in Space,* though watching an entire year's episodes of the latter in two evenings is not quite as thrilling as having to endure a week-long wait after each episode-ending cliffhanger.)

"The three most funniest things ever created are Bill Cosby, the Three Stooges, and the Little Rascals," Henry, then seven, declared after a satisfying evening of tubing with us.

Turn off opportunities for cultural references like those?

That's why, in the end, I never forced the kids to turn in their TV-Turnoff Week pledge forms. Instead, I spent the week with SpongeBob, Larry, Moe, and Curly—and a couple of kids smart enough not to follow the herd into a box-free canyon.

Momfidence...

. . . is finding MTV, CNN, soaps, and unlimited Internet access scarier viewing for kids than unlimited Wile E. Coyote and the villains of Kim Possible.

. . . is buying the occasional Care Bear underwear, the Teletubbies bath towel, the Nicktoons computer game, the Yu-Gi-Oh! cards, or stuffed Powerpuff Girls because even though you're hip to the tiresome cross-promotions of the marketing game, your kids just think the stuff is cool.

. . . is punching the "off" button and banishing everyone outside when *you* feel like it—even if it's the middle of a program.

"Please Don't Jump on the Dead Whale!"

On Discipline

I will not treat a child in a way I myself would not want to be treated.
— *Barbara Coloroso,* Kids Are Worth It!

Unless nobody is listening.
— *Me*

Some moms are good at scrapbooking. I keep lists of sayings. This includes the occasional unbelievably funny line that springs from my kids' lips, as well as the just plain unbelievable ones that, more often, come out of mine.

Previous entries to the annals of Things I Can't Believe I Just Said:

> Don't run with a pickle in your mouth.
> Stop licking your sister.
> Dogs don't like their ears tied in a knot!
> We drink milk; we don't gargle with it.
> We drink milk; we don't lap it with our tongue.
> We drink milk; we don't hide peas in it.
> Keep your ear wax to yourself.

We don't hit babies on the head with a hammer. (For the record, it was plastic.)

I don't remember my mother ever saying things like "No running with a fork in your pants." Then again, I don't remember my mother repeating herself twenty times per minute per child either.

I must not have been listening.

Which brings me to the subject of discipline. Nowhere in the parenting canon are there more prescriptions for how to handle your children, except maybe when it comes to getting them to sleep. But sleep is mostly an issue of infancy, whereas discipline just goes on and on and on.

It's one thing to read, in the calm rationality of the printed page, about star charts and a 10-point Behavioral Makeover Pledge and Plan. It's another thing altogether to try to find the suggested script on page 147 for dealing with an erupting Mount Toddlersuvius when the hot lava is exploding right in front of you. What these helpful guides fail to mention is that in the heat of the moment, if you can remain more or less humane, winging it is usually sufficient.

It's vacation time, and my kids are doing what kids do at the beach. They're running half a mile ahead of me hunting for buried treasure.

They find it, all right. Pirate booty? No. A starfish? No. An abandoned bucket and a shovel, maybe, or the dying embers of one of last night's campfires? I should be so lucky. Because my children are trouble-seeking missiles who home in on every possible danger and source of disgust, they find a dead whale.

Yes, a dead whale.

"Aiiiiiiiiiii!" shouts Henry, charging up the fleshy mound as if it were Bunker Hill.

Eleanor follows him. She always does, even when it's not in her best interest, which is most of the time. It's not her fault that her big brother is as forceful and obstreperous as she is gentle and accommodating.

"Watch me!" shouts Margaret, not about to be left out. She prefers to invent her own game, which seems to involve long-jumping over the flank. Her kindergartner's legs, however, are not quite as long as her imagination. Still, what Margaret lacks in inches she makes up for in persistence. She tries the jump, over and over.

The whale is barely recognizable in its decayed state, having washed ashore weeks earlier. It's buried in the sand except for an exposed rise of flank the color and texture of well-chewed bubble gum. I only know it's a whale because I overheard local fishermen talking about it in the tackle shop—never dreaming it would make the perfect trampoline for my children.

Page and I are still a few yards back. She keeps stopping to pick up every bit of clamshell she sees—there are many bits, this being a beach—and hands each one to me. I'm supposed to add them to the bulging pocket now scraping against my thigh. Every few feet I take one out and nonchalantly toss it behind us when she isn't looking. But somehow she keeps finding them faster than I can unload them.

I squint at her leaping, whooping siblings. They are beautiful as they run, straight limbed, hair flying, totally unselfconscious. So what's with the anxiety climbing from my gut to my throat? I should be satisfied that they've finally outgrown trying to eat the sand. Nobody has dared to dive straight into the surf oblivious to waves taller than me. Yet. Nobody has taken off her bathing suit because "it got wet."

They're having a blast. On the other hand, I'm the responsible adult here. (*Wasn't Daddyo walking with us just a few minutes ago?*

Where is he—and what would he say? What am I going to say?) Their behavior hardly seems eco-respectful. Granted, it's not as bad as the time they wagered Milk Duds over the fate of a fire-bellied newt caught in our creek which they pitted against our four pet hermit crabs. Still, carcass jumping doesn't seem very nature-friendly.

Mainly, though, I'm terrified that the kids will bounce too hard, break through Moby's skin, and sink slowly into a pit of decomposing guts and blubber.

"Hey, don't do that!" I say as soon as I am near enough to be heard over the surf.

No response.

The wind is sandblasting years off my wrinkles as it whips down the island. So maybe it's hard to hear.

"Guys! Stop!"

Nothing changes.

"Mom! Mom! Mom!" *Boing. Boing.* "Look what we found, Mom!"

"I see. That's enough. Stop."

Boing. "Stop what?"

"Playing on the whale!"

"This is a whale?" Variations of "Cool!" and "Gross!" and "How can you tell?" ensue—but nobody gets off.

"Yes. It's a whale that washed ashore and got covered by the sand. Let's leave it alone and keep walking."

"Why?"

"Because it's a whale. Get down."

"Why?"

Time for the big guns: "Because I said so."

Boing.

"NOW!"

"But it's fuuuuuuuuuuuuun!"

"That's enough. Get dow—Page! Get back here!"

Page has let go of my hand to beeline toward the others. Having learned how to whoop and jump at the hands of masters, she's not about to miss this opportunity. Running start. Bounce. Run down the other side. Bark, bark. Scream.

Funny, all of the other kids on the beach this day seem content to hold hands with their mommies.

Funny, none of the other mommies can be heard saying, "*Please don't jump on the dead whale!*" (while her children shout, "Dogpile!").

These are the same children whom teachers praise: "A joy to teach." "The light of the classroom." "So sweet." (These are all direct quotes. I'm so startled each time I hear one, I jot it right down in their baby books.)

These are the same children who reportedly use fine table manners and help clean up the playroom before they leave their friends' homes.

These are the same children who hang their heads shyly when introduced to strangers, who fall mute at grown-up parties.

It's only with their hapless parents that they completely fall apart.

Among family is where the name-calling begins, where karate chops commence, and where nobody walks around a piece of furniture if he or she can skywalk over the top. If one child practices climbing the outer edge of the stairs or bailing bath water onto the floor, you can bet he or she will find company. They tear through rooms like twisters, scattering crayons, game pieces, sofa cushions, and Fla-Vor-Ice wrappers in their wake. Maybe it's because there are four of them that the chaos feeds on itself like a California brushfire. Although I swear it was just as loud when there was only one.

If only we'd walked in the other direction, I would have avoided this whole annoying scene. I'd be sitting by the surf right now watching them play, mellowing out with my Jane Austen cracked open . . .

Or so I fantasize. Forget that be-here-now mindful parenting. If I didn't have a rich fantasy life of regular mental escapes, I'd be locked up by now. The reality, though, would unfold something like what happened during yesterday's beach outing:

It is a truth universally acknowledged that a . . . Mom? Mmm. MOM! What? Who's the Person of the Day? There is no Person of the Day today, Page. Mom? What? Look at that bird! Mmm. Mom? Mmm? Where's your father? Can I have some water? Here. . . . *a single man in possession of a good fortune must be in want of a . . .* OW! Mom! He spilled it on me! She grabbed it, and it spilled. Mom! Make him stop! Mom? Who's the Person of the Day? There is no Person of the Day yet, Page. . . . *wife. However little known the . . .* Is Henry the Person of the Day? No. Put the top back on the water. Mom? Have you seen my Hello Kitty towel? . . . *universally acknowledged . . .* Mmm? I need my towel! Did you bring it? Mom! You're sitting on it! Oh. Can't you use that one? It has Teletubbies on it! No, that's Page's! Where is your father? Mom, you're sitting on it! . . . *feelings or views of such a man may be on his first entering a . . .* On what? My Hello Kitty towel! . . . *It is a truth . . .* Mom? Is Eleanor the Person of the Day? We haven't picked one today, Page. Eleanor! Keep that shovel in the sand! But there used to be a Person of the Day . . . *neighbourhood, this truth is so well fixed . . .* yes, yesterday Henry was the Per—Mom! She hit me with her shovel! It was an accident! Did you hit her? No! Yes! Liar! Am not! Baby! . . . *in the minds of the surrounding families, that he is . . .* No hitting. Why don't you work on this side, and Margaret can work on that side? (Makes sense to me.) . . . *It is a truth universally acknowledged that a man . . .* where's Henry? Go find Dad! Where's Henry? I don't know. I don't know.

Out there on his boogie board in the surf. Thank you, Page. Can I be Person of the Day? Mom? Mom! . . . *is considered as the rightful property* . . . Mom! Did you see that? Did you see me wipe out? Man, I need a new board. Watch this! Are you watching? . . . *of some one or other of their daughters* . . . Of course, I'm watching. Go get Dad. I'm cold! Mo—o—o—m! Make Eleanor stop! Mom? Is Eleanor the Person of the Day? No, Page. Eleanor is definitely not the Person of the Day. There is no Person of the Day. . . . *My dear Mr. Truth universally first entering a neighbourhood possession fortune want a rightful property* . . . Mom, why is Page crying?

One time while they lay flat on the sand making sand angels with their arms and legs, I made it through five whole pages without looking up. When I finished, Page was standing in front of me naked. She'd lost her favorite Teletubbies bathing suit. "The water took it," she shrugged. It never did wash back ashore.

Daddyo says their friskiness means they are happy, that their inner ids and outer egos are blended as seamlessly as batter on chicken nuggets, with misbehavior being the necessary natural greasy by-product. He's always spouting wise rationalizations like that. Easy for him; he has the longer fuse.

I glance around the beach. I half-expect him to sidle up and remind me that unless I'd rather raise a robot or a show dog, I have to do a certain amount of just letting them be. Provided that no one gets hurt, of course. And that's the rub of this blubber dilemma. That's why my mama radar is going *Whoop! Whoop! Whoop!* The odds of impending disaster seem closer by the leap.

Sometimes even we benevolent mothers have to harpoon the fun.

I start with the path of least resistance, selective ignoring. As in "Ignore the bad behavior, reward the good." So I walk ahead without them. And it works about as well as it does when I try to leave a tantrumming child who doesn't want to go home from a store. That is, they are unmoved (physically or emotionally) while my anxiety increases (because now I can't see them).

A few steps more and I hear Margaret crying. I freeze. *She's fallen into the blubber! Oh good God. Will Henry dive in after her? Will I lose them both, like the fallen skater and noble rescuer who both wind up lost in an icy pond? How will I clean them off? What if the entrails are poisonous? And how would I know?* I turn and run back.

She's been bloodied all right. But only by her big sister scratching as she pushed her away from becoming Queen of the Carcass. I mean Hill.

Somehow I thought "selective ignoring" was supposed to be about me ignoring them, not them ignoring me.

Clearly a more active intervention is called for. Next I try distraction. I target the head of the operation. "Henry! Come on now, let's go. How about trying for Person of the Day two days in a row?" I use my most cajoling mummy voice. It's not exactly bribery. I call it appealing to his interests. The Person of the Day is one of our fine Spencer family traditions. We have many such inventions, like Group Hugs (like a mini–mosh pit without the jumping) and Family Folding Night (sock and laundry sorting while broadening their horizons with never-seen-before DVDs, like classic episodes of *Green Acres*). The Person of the Day is an honor given to a family member who has made a remarkable achievement, say, voluntarily scrubbing all four toilets in the house without being asked. As you might imagine, it doesn't happen very often. As a result, the Person of the Day is announced—kazoos, please—with great fanfare at dinner. The reward: a hearty handclasp. That's it. No prize. No special treat. Just a little positive reinforcement. It's not quite as desirable as Children's Choice dessert night (to each his own fave), but strangely they clamor for the honor just the same.

"C'mon, Henry. Lead your sisters off the whale. Let's go make a castle. And you'll definitely be Person of the Day!"

"Who cares?"

O-kay. Here's where I'm supposed to "play back" his feelings. I'm supposed to acknowledge that I understand him, make him feel respected, so that he will be in a receptive frame of mind to absorb my message. I'm supposed to say, with a sweetly empathetic tone and a straight face, "You are angry because you don't want to stop. I know it is so much fun!" And then he is supposed to say "Sure thing, Mom! Thanks for understanding!" This may be very effective in child development labs or on other planets. But I am on the beach. With a dead whale. As the wind blows sand in my eyes. The pocket full of Page's shells is bloodying my thigh. My husband is AWOL. And no one is listening. No one is paying any attention to me at all. I'm in no mood to humor anybody's frame of mind. I just want them off the damn whale. Now.

"Guys!" I bark.

I wait a minute. "Hey!" This time, I stamp my foot on the sand. It feels good. Then I draw my proverbial line in it. "If you don't get off the whale there will be *no* TV. No cartoons.

"Dead whale or SpongeBob—you choose."

A cartoon sea creature is obviously no match for the real deal. They're still cavorting as if I weren't there.

Finally, I scream, "STOP JUMPING ON THE DEAD WHALE *RIGHT THIS MINUTE!*"

For the first time in this whole salty drama, all four children look up. Page starts to cry. "You don't have to shout! Why can't you use nice words?"

Why indeed? Maybe because sound waves don't always penetrate my children's ears at lower decibels. (Their hearing has been checked and all is fully functional, though as my pediatrician points out, hearing and listening are not the same thing.) Interestingly, some words come through louder and clearer than others. Words like *dessert* and *toy,* for example, trigger full and instantaneous attention. It's the requests and commands that I may as well be mouthing in mime. Maybe if I had tried "Please stop jumping on the—*ice cream*— whale," this would have been over a long time ago.

Yelling is the dirty little secret of parenting. Everybody does it, at least sometimes, but it rarely happens publicly. Certainly not while we're on model-mom behavior at school or day care. Definitely not within earshot of Grandma or the babysitter. Not (so help us God) in the hushed aisles of the grocery store. Never on initial playdates. On the beach? Yeah, sure, go for it.

The tide is coming in. In a rare show of teamwork, the kids have been building a castle. Its moat fills with water again and again, smashing the fortress's walls. The tide meets its match in Henry, Eleanor, Margaret, and Page. They furiously rebuild the foundation with the blind optimism that only children have. The tide will win, of course, just the same way I will win—eventually—in civilizing these wild rascals. But they won't grow up—or give in to the tide—without a good long struggle.

"How was the beach?" Daddyo asks, swallowing the last of his beer as we all troop back to the house, where he'd apparently slipped off to ages ago. He swears he told me, though I never heard. Must've been that wind.

"Awesome!" says Page, displaying her shells. "And I didn't lose my bathing suit."

"We built a castle," shouts Margaret.

"We found a dead whale!" yells Henry, louder.

"Margaret is a big baby," Eleanor sneers.

And tossing Daddyo a wet sneaker, I say, "And Mom is the Person of the Day."

Momfidence...

. . . is knowing which child responds to a calm reprimand, which won't pay you one whit of attention unless your neighbors can also hear you yell, and which will burst into wide-eyed tears if you so much as glare at her—and disciplining accordingly.

. . . is being completely amnesiac about the day's exasperating transgressions when you peek in your children's bedrooms at night and watch them sleep.

. . . is remembering that kids who are disciplined feel safe and loved—a maxim so true I cannot crack a joke about it.

From the Mouths of Babes...Lies!

On Kidspeak

> To focus on children's needs, and to work with them to make sure
> their needs are met, constitutes a commitment to *taking children
> seriously*.   —*Alfie Kohn,* Unconditional Parenting

A preschooler tells me I am a "meanus weenus what eats flies
and boogers."

A first-grader cuts right to the chase—and closer to the heart:
"I hate you!"

An older child rolls his eyes and says for the twentieth time of
the day, "Times have changed, Mom!"

To think there was a time when I couldn't wait to hear each of
my babies' magical first words.

Children, we are told time and again, speak the truth. They
must be listened to. "Out of the mouths of babes" and all that.
Most of the time they deserve our swift responsiveness, of course.
Trouble is, what they're saying isn't always exactly what they mean.

Take them literally at your own risk.

Since no one hands each new mother a secret decoder ring

along with her newborn's hospital discharge papers, we're left to figure out the true meaning behind our children's words (and epithets) on our own.

Luckily, I've had plenty of practice. Now that all four of mine are speaking in full sentences, I have plenty of time to listen, because I can barely get a word in edgewise.

"I hate you."

....

Translation: I love you.

No, really! I love you so much I feel free to tell you how mad, disappointed, overtired, distracted, envious, or whatever the h-*word means to me to vent my state of mind on you right now.*

Congratulations! Your child feels secure enough to rip your heart to shreds! Not that knowing that this naked emotion is a sign of healthy development provides any consolation the first time you hear it. My mother, who's so cavalierly fuzzy about most details of rearing her five kids, recalls with perfect clarity and a pained expression the moment my older sister broke her in with those three little words—and that was a half-century ago. The wound is obviously still tender.

There was a time when had I overheard a child say "I hate you!" to his parents, I would have assumed that Ma and Pa were skunks, the child a handful, and juvenile detention or military school were clearly in this family's future.

That was before my own learned how to talk, of course.

ME: Let's get dressed. Here are your underwear.
PAGE: I don't want Care Bears underwear.

ME: Well your Hello Kitty panties are in the wash.
PAGE: I don't like Care Bears underwear. I hate you, Mom!

A few minutes later, we've advanced to socks.

ME: Can you find your socks?
PAGE: I don't want to wear socks. I hate you, Mom!

Well good morning to you, too.

The younger the speaker, the more the indictment stings. At 7:15 a.m. you're kissed and proclaimed "my very best special mama." By 7:35, you're mud. And what was your horrible transgression? You insisted on shoes.

In winter!

Meanie!

It's not so much the words that smart; it's the contempt. The vitriol. The turncoat nature of the business.

You can see, though, how it happens. Toddlerhood brings the full flowering of unbridled affection—puckered lips, python embraces, body-slamming hugs. Which is precisely the problem. Everything about two-, three-, and four-year-olds is larger than life. They're big-time happy, big-time sad. They can also be big-time cranky and big-time mad. At the same time they're learning that words have power. Words get things done. ("More juice!") Words make your point. ("No!") Words can hurt. ("I hate you, Mom!")

Guess who's the most convenient target?

Usually I chirp something like "Well, I *love* you, no matter what. You're just mad because you can't find the socks, aren't you?"

I've heard I should explain how *hate* is a hurtful word and must never be used, but that only seems to fuel its potency. So I tend to name the feelings and move on. *Don't take it personally.* Don't assume a deeper unhappiness that must be psychoanalyzed.

"I hate you!" can also spring from the lips of a bigger kid, who should know better. When coming from an adversary in diapers, you can find some consolation in how comically incongruous they sound. When an older child says them, they can sound all too painfully believable.

That's because in the instant they're uttered, they probably are true. Not that the average ranting child is using *hate* in the evil-drenched sense of hate crimes and hate mail. (First clue: Ten minutes later they're asking for help with math homework and then a ride to Olivia's house.) They're describing their heat lightning feelings toward us the way we hate boring PTA meetings or hate it when the trash bag breaks on the way to the bin. The emotion is a flash across the sky that's illuminating without actually being dangerous.

Every mom, after all, finds there are also certain aspects of her children and their care about which she's less than fond. (Bed-wetting? Attending birthday parties at Chuck E. Cheese? A brown crayon in someone's pocket ruining an entire load of white sheets in the dryer? Who doesn't hate it when these things happen?) We just have more self-control so we don't say it out loud, is all.

To those who purse their lips at the very idea of using the word *hate* in close proximity to parenting, let me state plainly for the record that *I adore my children more than life itself!*

But I can still hate laundry.

Love and hate are two sides of the same coin. If a parent can feel both emotions at the same time, why can't a child? Calling your mom a "meanus weenus" is, in its own way, a baby step toward maturity (even if it does mean that we still need to work on the finer points of what constitutes socially acceptable speech).

So I no longer take refuge in the bathroom to cry over it. Hearing "I hate you" proves that my relationship with my child is, well, just as complex as my relationships with everybody else I know.

"I want that!"
. . . .
Translation: "I am a budding consumer at work."

It's a festive sound, an eager rat-a-tat, like popcorn popping. It emanates from the family room, and it signals that Christmas is coming. Though unlike the buttery aroma of popcorn, this sound stinks.

"I want that!"

"I want that!"

"Oh, I want that!!"

The season's new toy commercials are here. Nobody automatically switches channels during the program breaks anymore; this latest crop of toys is more fascinating than the 'toons, which have been seen a dozen times already anyway.

Time to haul out the DVDs for a few weeks.

If only "I want that!" were a problem limited to December, or only to TV. We live in a wide world of stuff, much of it marketed to kids practically intravenously. Overnight the latest movie character is on their cereal boxes and in their Happy Meals. It magically infiltrates every possible aspect of their daily life, assuming the form of toys, T-shirts, backpacks, video games, coloring books, snack foods, billboards, bed sheets, paperbacks, key chains, pajamas, even school lessons, until Character Du Jour is recognizable to even the youngest tot. More recognizable than Santa himself.

My kids have never known a day when you didn't pick your sneakers or your underwear based on which cartoon character they featured. They can't imagine that I once snarfed Nancy Drew mysteries without ever thinking to look for the girl sleuth as a doll or a junior fashion line.

The licensed kid stuff is overwhelming enough. Now the wider world of grown-up stuff, from SUVs to cell phones to iPods, has also been shrunken to child size and coated in candy pink and silvery boy blue. Who can resist?

Not my kids.

Which means it's up to me.

To misinterpret "I want that" as actually meaning "I want that" is the quick road to an overflowing toy box and an empty wallet. Not to mention an even more blithe appreciation for the value of stuff than is already inherent in twenty-first-century childhood (skateboards left in the driveway behind the car, dress-up gowns worn in the mud . . .).

There are really only five responses to "I want that."

1. "Umm hmmm."
   (Tone: distracted, benign)

2. "Really."
   (No question mark at the end, interested, noncommittal)

3. "We'll see."
   (To be used judiciously; mine are on to it already. "That means no!" Margaret shrieked the other day, and I half-expected her to show me the statistical tally sheet that proved it.)

4. "Not right now."
   (Lets hope flicker while nipping any rising whine)

5. "Dream on."

"I'm bored."

....

Translation: "I'm bored."

A complaint is to a child what a command is to a mom—a few syllables that leap practically reflexively from the lips. Kids complain about the indignity of having to go to school every single morning five days a week and set the table for supper to boot. About not having a home theater with widescreen console and a popcorn machine. About the flavor of juice box that I happened to buy last week.

Mostly I shrug and offer looks that attempt to covey a mix of empathy and "Tough luck, buddy."

One complaint, though, gets my goat: a claim of being bored. It reveals a certain lack of imagination that tries my patience like none other.

Some say that kids have no right to complain in the first place about anything; they should be grateful for what they have and the mere fact that they feel otherwise is evidence of their moral depravity, which is obviously my fault.

I disagree. I think kids complain because they feel powerless. It's an automatic response, like whining. They can't go out and buy a TV the size of a Ping-Pong table. They can't control whether or not they enroll in second grade. So they gripe. We grown-ups do the same thing, though unlike kids most of us have learned that nobody's going to do a darn thing unless we're moaning about a bona fide emergency or, miracle of miracles, have managed to get through to the right department.

But complaining about boredom is different. That's one they can fix themselves.

Certainly it falls under the job of "mother" to do a certain amount of Coming to the Rescue. I bandage skinned knees promptly (and often), for example. I console bad dreams no matter the hour. I can cut the scratchy tags out of a shirt or fashion a Greek warrior costume out of an old tablecloth and rope in the nick of time for a social studies project, even if the thing was requested by the teacher three weeks ago but only mentioned to me last night. When it comes to meeting needs of hunger, thirst, cold, heat, sickness, or siblings in altercations that have come to blows, I'm there.

I do not, however, do boredom rescues.

Call me callous, but I find it hard to look around a playroom stocked like a toy store and work up any pity. If I wanted to program every hour with exciting things to do, I'd have been a cruise director or a camp counselor. As a mom, my entertainment responsibilities are limited to providing the time, space, and raw materials for fun, along with the occasional vacation, weekend outing, or surprise after-school ice-cream cone. I like to think that in giving my children siblings—aka built-in buddies—I have already gone above and beyond the call of duty.

When I hear "I'm bored!" I'm apt to parrot the suggestions once made to me in my ponytail days:

> Go twiddle your thumbs.
> Go try to kiss your nose.
> Go try to bite your elbow.
> Go play Spit and Catch.

(That last one sounds disgusting, I know, but every one of my many pleasant Polish great-aunties used to make this same suggestion, each with the same benign smile on her face.)

In other words, you're complaining to the wrong person. If you're bored, go find something to do. If you can't, I'll be glad to come up with something for you—but you're probably not gonna like it.

You'd be surprised how many amazing drawings get made, how many games are invented, and how fast a child makes up with her best friend or sister when the only other alternative, the one coming from Mom, involves cleaning supplies. Or spit.

"Knock knock."

Translation: "I am about to drive you mad."

> "Knock knock."
> "Who's there?"
> "Me."
> "Me who?"
> "Page!" *(Many giggles)*

> "Knock knock."
> "Who's there?"
> "Gorilla."
> "Gorilla who?"
> "Gorilla crossed the road!" *(More giggles)*

> "Knock knock."
> "Who's there?"

You get the idea.

There's no such thing as a solitary knock-knock joke. Even when there's only one child in the room. If siblings or friends are present, the "knock knocks" start flying off the walls like a flock of mynah birds in the Catskills, each trying to upstage the other with more, louder, dumber, cruder caws. I can't decide which are more crazy-making:

the young-child jokes that make no sense or the big-kid versions. The latter, it's true, at least have punch lines (sometimes funny ones). But big kids' longer memories means they have more jokes to tell. A sweet-faced child can hold an unsuspecting mommy hostage with three straight hours of stand-up, no sweat, if she's not careful.

The child development rap on jokes is that they're evidence of a budding sense of humor, improving language, and advanced logic. The joke on child development raps is that nobody cares about those things when trapped in a minivan with an inexhaustible little Jerry Seinfeld.

I usually let them knock around until the dull thud in my temples makes itself known. Then I fling myself dramatically on the sofa and plead for a pillow and a few minutes' silence. I get both. The silence lasts twenty-nine seconds. But by then the merry jokesters have been distracted. If a wayward "Knock kn—" slips out, I moan loudly.

I'm still working on an escape plan that works while driving, though.

"Wasn't me."

....

Translation: Guilty as charged. Not that I'll ever in a billion years admit it.

Who stashed a half-eaten cherry Popsicle, since melted, in the dollhouse?

Who made off with my pen caps and my tape?

Who carefully cut a fresh-baked brownie from the pan, smack dab in the soft gooey middle?

Or scattered opened Band-Aid papers all around the bathroom floor?

No one around here is 'fessing up.

Which means Hans must be at it again. Who's Hans? No, not the fifth child whom I've waited until the middle of this book to spring on you (not to mention on poor Daddyo). Hans is the other being all parents bring home from the hospital along with their new baby.

Little Hans—as in, *little hands* that touch what they shouldn't, move what they oughtn't, and meddle where they aren't supposed to—is his own life force. He's a disruption of the very atoms that once lay still and changeless in a house before children.

An unseen superpower of mystery, exasperation, and comic genius, Hans bides his time while you get the hang of sleeplessness and diapers. Then you begin to find rattles in your shoes and the TV remote in the trash. Crayon hieroglyphics appear knee high along the walls. Before long your missing mouse pad turns up as a dollhouse carpet and your box of sanitary pads lies ransacked on the bathroom floor, every one unwrapped from its pink cover as if someone had been practicing for a birthday.

Hans loves toilet paper, saltshakers, CD cases, pads of Post-it notes, and the strings that tie the seat cushions onto the kitchen chairs. If it can be untied, unraveled, upended, scattered, emptied, or otherwise undone, he's there.

His most distinctive feature is invisibility. Oh, you know he's been around—the evidence is all around you—but you somehow never catch him in the act. Hans doesn't go for "Look Ma!" activities. (He leaves those to your children.) With Hans, things just . . . happen. You're left wondering how a box of wooden blocks, many residents of Noah's ark, several used Popsicle sticks, and the entire fifty U.S. states puzzle came to be scattered across the universe of your den when you weren't looking. (Oklahoma blew all the way to the kitchen sink, and California will mysteriously reappear three weeks later in the driveway.)

Hans is fast. Once I stayed up past midnight organizing my bookshelves—fiction in one place, biography in another, and so on. By breakfast they were piled onto the floor like so many Devils Towers.

Hans is not neat. His specialty is clothes flinging. I wouldn't mind the scattered socks so much if only they landed in matched pairs. And yet he's drawn to the accoutrements of neatness. He once pumped out the entire contents of the liquid hand soap onto my bathroom counter. He's especially fond of hairbrushes, headbands, and barrettes—I find them everywhere. He uses toothpaste like tile grout.

Yes, Hans is an inventive fellow. For several weeks I lived in a depressed panic because a small sapphire pendant Daddyo had given me years earlier was missing. I tried to think when I had last worn it and clearly remembered placing it in its tiny box afterward. On hands and knees, I scanned the floor. I mourned alone, avoiding confessing I'd lost the gem. Imagine my surprise to finally see it—of all places—hanging from a doll's neck in Eleanor's room.

"How did this get here?" I asked.

"I have no idea," she replied, her face blank.

Hans!

Mystery is his forte. I've never figured out how or why my pillow, of all places, was damp one evening. All possible suspects were sound asleep, so after sniffing to rule out wee-wee (which would have narrowed the suspect list), I could only shake my head. Same thing the night I found the cereal boxes from the pantry arranged in an artistic semicircle down in the basement like a museum-ready installation: Snap, Crackle, and Pop at Stonehenge.

Sometimes Hans is downright endearing. Yesterday as I went

out to the street to get the morning paper, I happened to look back at the house. Sometime in the last twenty-four hours, the iron grill-work posts on the front porch had been quietly festooned with rhododendron blossoms. The festive sight made up for the beheading of every crocus a few weeks earlier.

On my weariest days, I flirt with a certain fantasy. (No, Colin Firth is not involved; this is the reverie of a tornado survivor.) I step inside a photo from one of those home magazines—you know, the kind where everything has been upholstered in white and the carpet looks more like an expansive, sun-bleached dune than a dirty, end-of-summer sandbox. The pears in the lovely bowl on the table have not been furtively nibbled and cunningly replaced so that all the bite marks are hidden. I'm wearing a white dry-clean-only outfit and sneakers that still look brand new—not a single smiley face drawn on either one. My pens, all capped, are in exactly the same place where I left them three days ago. Then I notice something's missing.

No Little Hans.

Suddenly I shudder. If Little Hans is not around, it can only mean one thing. I am old. He wouldn't vanish until the kids have grown and moved on, returning the atoms in the house to their static, undisturbed state.

Hmmm. On second thought, maybe I can wait a little longer after all for spotless organization and dry pillows. Suddenly those goals seem a pale compensation for the cheerful chaos and got-to-see-it-to-believe-it antics of life with Hans.

He's not really so annoying, once you get used to him.

Momfidence…

. . . is listening to everything your child says, except when (1) more than one child is talking at once; (2) the talking is being done in shriek, whine, shout, or mumble; or (3) you have a headache (often because of 1 and 2).

. . . is keeping a straight face even when they crack you up because they're saying something hysterical with a straight face. And it's laughing when they are intentionally trying to crack you up.

. . . is the search for a finished sentence. During the first nine years of childhood you don't have time to get all the words out before you're interrupted, and during the last nine years, even if you do, no one seems to hear them.

Beware of Trick Questions

16

On Having All the Answers

Far more effective than passive listening (silence), Active Listening is a remarkable way to involve the "sender" with the "receiver." The receiver is active in the process as well as the sender. But to learn how to listen actively, parents usually need to understand more about the communication process between two persons. A few diagrams will help.
— *Thomas Gordon,* Parent Effectiveness Training

Motherhood makes you the go-to girl for answers. Not that I usually have them. But they keep coming anyway, so the least I can do is take them like a woman and suppress the urge to say, "Go ask your dad."

Sometimes it's not the kids' questions that catch me off guard; it's their timing. "Why is that lady so fat?" I'm asked within Lady Colossus's earshot in the grocery. Sometimes it's the setting that unnerves, as when somebody wants to know "What's a period?" as we're walking into church. And sometimes I'm caught off guard by the sheer thoughtfulness of the query. "Is a computer a living being?" Margaret wondered last year, possibly because I spend so much face time with mine.

Yes, you have to keep on your toes. ("Mom, when I grow up can I be a mom and grow hair on my toes?")

You have to realize that no part of life will go unscrutinized. ("Mom, do people close their eyes when they kiss because it's so gross?")

And you can't take anything personally. ("Mom, how many more days until you're an old woman?")

(The answers to those last three: yes, no, and more than you think but fewer than I do).

Sometimes a Mommy-on-the-spot can stall with a contemplative "Well . . ." or "Hmmm." Draw it out long enough and their attention might be diverted before they remembered they asked anything. Or if you say, "Why that's a good question!" in just the right praise-filled tone, a child in a hurry might be satisfied with that and run off before you need to supply an actual answer.

A firm "no" is another handy reply and works in more circumstances than you might think, provided you can steel yourself against the raging tantrum it often incites. The catch with a "no" is that there's no going back. Wishy-wash on a "no" and all future nos lose their power.

Many questions, alas, are more nuanced. They defy easy answers (or, if answered too easily, may be regretted forever).

Consider the following three cautionary examples.

Trick Question 1: "What Are We Having?"

At some point in the postschool, presupper swirl of soccer practice, homework, playing, errands, and creeping crankiness, a child will bring the merry madness to a halt with four little words: "What are we having?"

As in, What's for dinner?

As if I have the slightest idea.

I know. I am the mother. It's my duty to dispense the necessary worms into my baby birds' wide-open-and-waiting beaks. Trouble is, I'm kitchen challenged. (I hate to cook.) And I'm time challenged. (Who isn't?) The combination dooms me.

Breakfast is easy. I set out the bowls and the giant Costco cartons of Cocoa Puffs and Lucky Charms. Lunch is even easier. They buy it at school. But dinner?

It's not just me. In kitchens and cars across America, mother birds face down the Four O'clock Question with furrowed brows and feathers drooping. Doesn't matter if we've spent the day at home or at work. We're all doomed, and with good reason.

It's a trick question.

First, the dinner dilemma puts your domestic aptitude to the test. My friend Julia—as in Child, it figures—once astonished me by confiding that she begins thinking about dinner while sipping her morning OJ. I can't even think ten minutes ahead, let alone ten hours. Especially not when I'm busy pouring magically delicious toasted oats and marshmallow bits while simultaneously dressing, patrolling for missing sneakers, and fishing around in grody backpacks for field trip permission slips I was supposed to have signed last week. Besides, how can I know what I will be in the *mood* to cook, let alone eat, hours from now?

My inability to plan ahead means, of course, that the evening's meat remains frozen at 5 p.m. Nor are the ingredients for a given recipe acquired, so I wind up discovering at step 4 that I'm out of the necessary sour cream or condensed mushroom soup. So I skip it, which leads to everyone taking one look at the finished product and muttering "I'm not that hungry."

Your math skills are sorely tested, too, by the dinner inquest. Quick glance at the clock. Quick pantry inventory. What collection of foods in my understocked cupboards can I mix and match to impersonate a well-balanced meal? What will be the maximum number of mouths in the house who are likely to actually eat it? Maybe I could handle this brainteaser better if it didn't come around *every single day* like clockwork!

Should you succeed at advance planning and pantry roulette, you still face the Ee-u-ww Factor.

CHILD: What are we having?
ME: Lasagne (or "meat loaf" or "trout" or "chicken")
CHILD: Ee-u-ww!
EVERY OTHER CHILD IN EARSHOT *(ever louder)*: "EEW-UU-WWW!"

Their taste buds travel in packs. The day's dish could have been the child's favorite only last week, but a single "ee-u-ww," as infectious as Ebola, will ruin everything. Page adored "pink fish" (aka salmon)—until she heard her older sisters howl. There's also a little-known law of nature that says every family meal must have one dissenter. Tough luck for a child whose siblings all beat you to cheers for your favorite cheeseburgers; you must maintain family disequilibrium by declaring them "ee-u-ww," at least today.

Five o'clock. Dinner begins, ee-u-wws and all. Five ten, everyone's finished. And the meal angst is over for another day. Then:

"What's for dessert?"

Trick Question 2: "Can We Get a Dog?"

I should have held the line at hermit crabs. That's what I'm thinking as I shiver in the crisp 4 a.m. air and look up at the stars I haven't seen since the last time a baby was in the house, when Page was born.

I am waiting for Brownie to pee. Nobody forewarned me that new puppies don't have enough bladder control to "hold it" all night after being tucked into their crates. So my husband and I must take turns making midnight potty runs with a small shivering wiener dog.

At least our four human babies wore diapers.

The proper answer to the inevitable "Can we get a dog?" question is "no." End of discussion. That is, unless you are ready for another baby, and this time one who will never learn to speak, open the door, or clean up after himself (which is why I'm inclined to recommend the actual baby, who also has the potential to look after you in old age). The exception is if you are a Dog Person. Dog People seem unfazed by hairy sofas and kennel bills; when they say "honey" did this or that, you can never be sure if they mean their partner or their Pekinese. Then again, Dog People usually have dogs before they have children and thus avoid the "Can we have a dog?" wheedling altogether.

When a child begs for a dog, he's really saying, "Dogs are cute. Can I pet one?" Go visit a pet shop, which makes a fine (and free) petting zoo. Do not mistake it for a place to actually buy an animal.

So how did I—who never owned a pet in her life except amphibians, who is allergic to every hairy-bodied creature except Daddyo, whose mom took away his kitten after one day because animals are filthy beasts—wind up in one of the thirty-eight million dog-owning households in America?

We were worn down. Outnumbered. We even fell for those famous last words, "We'll feed it! We promise!"

My children have learned a lot from having a pet—as have I. Just not the lessons I expected.

Forget responsibility, for one. Kids and pets may go together like peanut butter and jelly. But it's the parents who wind up making the sandwiches, cleaning up the crumbs, wiping off the knife, and keeping track of when the jars are running low. Not to mention listening to the sandwich whine pitifully when the children go off to school and he faces a dull day of trying to get Mom to play Fetch the Filthy Monkey with a Tennis Ball Head while she's trying to work.

Kids go to school; pups still need to be taken out.

Kids forget; pups still get hungry.

Kids will do the work when nagged, but guess who's nagging in the first place?

In fact, between waiting for Brownie to do his business outside and cleaning up his accidents inside, he's more time-consuming than a baby, especially considering he neither gurgles nor coos as a reward for all the effort. He seems to cost as much as a baby, too, between vet bills, food, crate, leash, chew toys, replacement door screens, and tuition for puppy school (from which there was no refund when he flunked Leash Walking and Basic Commands). Many a night I am torn between wanting to get rid of the darned dachshund and feeling I already had too much invested in him to give him up.

The kids are the ones really invested—but not financially. Henry—too old for teddy bears, too cool to give hugs—curls up with Brownie and a book in bed for hours. Who'd have thought saying "It's time to clean his ears" would be the magic words to break a computer game trance? Eleanor, once too afraid of dogs to trick-or-treat at Halloween lest she ring the doorbell of a house with a poodle, now coddles the Brownster like a baby doll (and dresses him up like one, too).

They all get firsthand lessons in a small creature's fragility and neediness. They've learned to pet and play gently, more or less. Margaret unfailingly refills his water bowl. Page has learned that puppies cannot eat animal crackers. Or go down slides.

Page also—grudgingly—learned a lesson each of her siblings did earlier, that families can always accommodate one more. We're working through the rivalry issues slowly but surely. She hasn't shed her clothes and howled for attention for ten days straight.

This morning when Henry came downstairs, Brownie's tail began wagging like a metronome on fast forward. Henry never used to come down so promptly, or in such good spirits. "Hey Brownie! How's my buddy? You're my buddy!" he sang, nuzzling the pup's sleek otterlike fur. Brownie returned the affection with eager, wet kisses. Right on the mouth.

The hermit crabs didn't do that.

Trick Question 3: "But Why?"

Why "why" is the favorite question of all childhood is beyond me. Its brevity? The uptick at the end that employs the same grating tone as a whine? Because it drives the hearer berserk and they know it? Why? Why?

Why me, Lord?

Hearing "why?" for the billionth time doesn't make it any easier to answer than the first 999,999,999 times. I have, however, developed four reliable responses that tend to nip the madness in the bud:

"What do you think?"

Used when you have all the time and patience in the world and wish to prompt Socratic dialogues and insightful probes into the workings of your child's brain and challenge him to contemplate the world around him in order to stimulate those brain synapses and make him feel respected and loved. Also buys time while thinking of another answer.

"No one knows."

Used in a thoughtful declarative tone as if referring to the eternal mysteries of life (even if the question merely concerned the color of the sky), to nip further "but why?"s in the bud or when in no mood for Socratic dialogue. Most satisfying to those under age six who have not discovered Wikipedia.

"Because I said so."

Used when feeling time-crunched, put upon, and in no mood to argue; also to signal the mommy interrogation has come to an end.

"Go ask your father."

Used when having a marital tiff and therefore inclined to put *him* on the spot for a change. Or used when copping out. Also works beautifully for any of the other questions in this chapter.

Momfidence...

. . . is always being glad they asked.

Moms Need Time-outs
More Than Kids Do
On Escaping

> With the right planning, resources, and work ethic, you can, too, be
> a perfect and fulfilled woman, raising a perfect and happy child.
>   "I'm an alpha mom, yes," says Isabel.
>
> — New York *magazine profile of*
> *Alpha Mom TV founder Isabel Kallman*

I should be missing them. Pining! I should be petting their sweet,
tangled hair right here beside me instead of feeling like a mama
bear finally let out of her zoo cage. They are my babies! What will
they do without me? How will they manage? How can they stand
it with their mommy so far away?

How can I stand it?

In fact, I couldn't wait to get away—bad enough. Now here I am,
glad to be away. What kind of mother am I?

The damned if you do, damned if you don't kind, clearly.

I am sitting on the top deck of our beach house, gazing at the
blue Atlantic. After a few summers of renting—some places too big,
some too small, many too far from the water—we found our dream
shack four hours from home on North Carolina's coast. "Beach house"

is what the realtor called it, but shack is more accurate, cobbled together thirty-five years ago from a dozen different kinds of wood, all painted white in an optimistic optical illusion of expansiveness. On the other hand, the shack fronts fifty miles of sand (national seashore, not ours), which is all that matters when you have four kids and a dog who likes to dig up crabs.

The other beauty of having a vacation place to call your own is that the parents have someplace to go when they run away from home.

One small downside is that the bank still owns most of the house, so we have to rent it out to strangers for much of the year. Except for February. That's when we get to use our beach house. So here I am. Working, really, not vacationing. But I'm alone and that's the main thing.

That's the unbelievable thing.

It doesn't get much better than this. Most notably, it's quiet. Not only can I hear myself think, I can hear myself think in complete sentences. In whole paragraphs! I can carry on a whole conversation uninterrupted. Or I could, if I had someone to talk to besides Brownie. I talk to him anyway, although I try to refrain from nagging him to wipe the sand off his feet. I have downed an entire Diet Coke without anybody asking to share it. The sunset clouds are pink and orange, a fact I can delight in without anybody saying, "So?" or "Hey Mom, did you know the bathroom floor is flooded and it wasn't me?"

Hmmm. Sunset means bedtime is approaching. Night is when children are most vulnerable. Night is when their mother should be near. Did they have their "bed-night" snack (as it's known around our house)? Or brush their teeth? Will Page's story time pick up where we left off last night, on chapter 3, "In Which a Search Is Organized and Piglet Nearly Meets a Heffalump Again?"

(If I ask Daddyo he'll say, "I don't know," "I don't know," and "Don't worry, they just put themselves to bed.")

Oh, how could I be gone for four whole nights in a row?

Pricked with guilt—and unable to leave well enough alone—I call home. "Hi! How's it going?"

"Fine. Everyone's fine. Everything's under control," the daddy-in-charge says calmly. "Hold on." There is a faint shriek in the distance. Now a closer one. Muffled reprimands and marching orders. All throughout, I hear the repeated blasts of explosives, which I hope are the computerized kind. On the other hand, it being bedtime, they shouldn't be.

"I'm back."

"What's going on?"

"Nothing."

"Oh. It sounded like something."

"No, everything's fine," I am assured over the sounds of either a tantrum or a hatchet murderer loose in the playroom.

"So what's everybody doing?"

He shouts to the room. "It's Mom! Anybody want to talk to Mom?"

Nobody does. Henry is battling the forces of evil onscreen. Eleanor is at a friend's house. (*This late?*) Margaret is unaccounted for. Page is mad about something and refuses to speak. "But" [consolingly] "Page made you a very nice drawing of the two of you. Hey! Page! Don't tear that up! I thought you were saving it for Mommy."

"I hate Mommy!"

O-kay.

"Maybe we'll call back later," he says. Click.

I wait an hour. Nobody calls.

At eight o'clock, bedtime, I figure I will phone in to say good night. Daddyo seldom talks to every child every night when he's on the road and nobody seems to notice. They just accept that he is gone and will return some days hence bearing big hugs and Skittles. But I can't bear it. No matter how long I fantasized about escape, once I'm free they're still yoked to my conscience like phantom limbs. Or phantom octopus tentacles.

"Hi Mom," Eleanor answers.

"Hey sweetie! What are you doing? What's going on? I miss you guys so much!"

"Well, let's see. Daddy is putting Margaret to bed. She got mad because she wanted to finish her book and he said okay but then she didn't hear him say okay so she got mad and threw the book and it hit his head and he got mad and sent her to bed and she got madder and that's what she's doing.

"Page had a fit and went to sleep a long time ago but I don't know what she was mad about but I think she misses you and she didn't want Dad to read her Pooh book but maybe she was mad at Margaret because she hid her blankie in the dress-up clothes box and wouldn't tell her where it was and I wasn't here so I didn't know about it but I know that's where she hid it because that's where she hides everything.

"Henry is playing Xbox. He's so annoying. When I came home he hit me in the head with a dart and then he said it was an accident. But it wasn't an accident because he was aiming right at my head and he didn't say sorry so that's how I know it wasn't an accident. Anyway, well, let's see, I went to Leah's house and then we went swimming. It was cold at first but then it gets warmer if you get used to it. I think I left my bathing suit there. They are being foster parents for some kittens and they are so cuuuuuute! I wish you weren't allergic. They have really short fur and get this, they're free! Can we take one?"

I leap at the chance to get a word in. "No. No cats. Shouldn't you be in be—"

"Well anyway, there was this turtle in the lake . . ."

Ah, home. It's all coming back to me now. I toss in a few "Mmm, hmmms" and pour myself another Diet Coke.

It is one of the stranger paradoxes of my life that I love my kids, who require such constant tending, as much as I love to be alone.

Since I became a mother, delicious afternoons curled up with Jane Austen are mostly memories. Ditto weekends antiquing or leisurely soaks in the tub. For years, I considered it a minor victory if I managed to shut the bathroom door and pee all by myself without anyone toddling in or applauding "You did it, Mama! I'm so proud of you!"

Rare occasions when naps and multiple playdates coincide, or when Daddyo's running errands with all tykes in tow, represent nothing short of a minivacation. Never mind that I usually squander those precious minutes emptying the dishwasher or scraping Play-Doh off the floor.

It's the greatest push–pull of a mom's life: To give her kids all the attention and juice cups they need while carving out minutes for herself. Everybody heartily recommends it. But no matter how many ways I do the math, there's simply not enough time in a typical day to give 100 percent to them, him, work, my brain, my body, the house, the laundry . . .

If only they kept napping right straight till puberty, I might have a chance.

One of the first times I sent Henry to his room for some vile transgression of the family code, I felt an odd twinge. It wasn't guilt. Discipline is the one aspect of parenting I rarely feel guilty about, because they inevitably deserve it. No, sending a child to time-out made me . . . envious!

Imagine. Sent to the solitude of your own room, with strict instructions not to bother anybody else for five whole minutes. And as a consequence of momentarily taking leave of your senses. What a concept!

My senses leave me all the time. (That's how I got pregnant four times in seven years.) Where are the manuals and how-to articles extolling the Mommy Time-Out? There's a workshop I'd finally sign up for.

Over the years, I've tried carving out personal time. I've variously joined a morning step-aerobics class, a lunchtime professional support group, a moms' book club, evening yoga.

They were all great! Trouble is, I've never been able to sustain such wonderful liberations very long. Inevitably, I grow overloaded at work and feel guilty diverting even forty-five minutes to an hour toward exercise. Lunch gets preempted by grocery shopping, dry cleaning pickups, or pediatrician visits. Even the hour-long walk I manage regularly or a rare mall spree makes me feel negligent unless my kids are all asleep or playing so intently they don't notice I'm away.

Often, it's not that I want to be away from them so much as that I wish, desperately, to be in two different places at the same time. If modern medicine can achieve the miracle of pain-free labor, why not cloning upon delivery? One Paula could do the laundry and listen to knock-knock jokes while the other Paula continues reading nineteenth-century novels on the chaise lounge to her heart's content.

Maybe that's the trouble! Maybe I need a chaise lounge!

The reality is that, in a day crammed with priorities, it takes a smart mom with her head on straight to sashay herself to the top of the list on a regular basis.

Nope, not me.

I try to keep reminding myself: Workouts and haircuts are not frivolous if they make me feel great. Lunches with friends at grown-up places that don't serve chicken nuggets nourish the soul, and that's glorious, too. So why can't I follow through consistently?

Because giving birth is like gaining an indelible shadow, knit fast to your feet like Peter Pan's (or to your breast, your hip, your shin, or any other appendage it can find). Young children are so demanding and needy—and yes, so fun and delicious—that separations are laced with ambivalence, even when you crave them. The struggle to find the right balance of selflessness and self usually boils down to this: How little time to ourselves can we scrape by on?

We compromise: *If I can just get a long hot shower in the morning, I'll be okay!*

We rationalize: *An hour in the nursery while I'm at the gym three times a week won't hurt her.*

We justify: *My book club is just one night a week.*

We dream and scheme: *We'll do Paris, alone, for our twentieth anniversary. It's only eleven years away!*

Or we simmer and pout: *I've got to do something!*

Which is how I hit on the idea of running away from home every so often. The extended Mommy Time-Out. I'll spare you the usual treacle about refilling our gas tanks because mothers can't run on empty. I can't even think on empty. As much as I hate to be apart from my babies, I hate to be apart from myself for too long even more.

Obviously it's not very practical for most moms to up and vanish with any frequency. Although when you put your mind to it, you'd be surprised what kind of patchwork of coverage you can finagle in order to temporarily replace yourself. It doesn't even have to require packing a suitcase. One mom I know goes Wal-Marting at 8 p.m. to restore her mental order—hey, it's something. If my sister-in-law, a devoted mother of six who blithely travels around town driving an airport-limo-sized van with a Porta Potti stashed in the hatch, can figure out how to escape solo with girlfriends or church ladies every so often, that's inspiration enough for anybody.

I try not to abuse the extended Mommy Time-Out. I save it for really urgent circumstances. Such as:

• When I have repetitive stress syndrome
That's the nervous tic you get from moving through breakfast-snack-lunch-snack-dinner-snack day after day, punctuated by cleanup and restockings. And that's just the feeding loop. Overlay that with the bedtime loop, the laundry loop, the diaper loop, and before you know it, you're feeling loop-de-loop. The repetitions are part and parcel of motherhood, just like reading *Goodnight Moon* for the umpteenth time or biting your tongue once again from saying, "I told you so." Unfortunately, these are not the sort of planned redundancies that anybody's going to get fired over; your job as mom has a lifetime-guaranteed contract, with an eighteen-year learning curve. Which is why it's up to you to relieve yourself of the responsibilities—at least temporarily.

• When my sisters or friends need a time-out, too
Escapees love company and a good excuse. ("But Paula invited me!" counts as a swell excuse.)

• When I have a really big deadline
As much as I treasure my work-from-home setup, I envy corporate moms their airplane downtime on business trips (and their grown-up wardrobes, too). When productivity or deadlines beckon, sometimes I send myself on one, too, exiling myself to the beach to write. I know what you're thinking. Mom

drives four hours from home so she can write about being a mom? But I once read that Ernest Hemingway felt he wrote best and most truly about the place where he wasn't. So he wrote about Michigan's Big Two-Hearted River from Paris, about Italy while in Key West, about Spain from Idaho. Not that I'm comparing toilet-training journalism to war or bull-fighting.

And it's only three hours and forty-five minutes to the beach shack if I don't have any children in the car (no bathroom breaks).

My love 'em–leave 'em dilemma has given me new insight into my own mom. Despite raising five children, she never seemed to be without needle and thread. She's a virtuoso with cloth, yarn, and embroidery floss. She never had an office, but always a sewing room. I used to think that she worked so hard—making our clothes (even winter coats and blue jeans!), recovering sofas, designing needlepoint tapestries, knitting gorgeous sweaters—because we couldn't afford to buy these things. No doubt thrift was partly her motivation. But now I see that her handiwork was much more than that. It was her mental oasis, her way of being alone in a crowded house.

Not that I ever took up sewing or knitting or any of my mother's handicrafts. But I see that I did absorb a different legacy from her: the understanding that everyone deserves a little space all their own.

My own haven, when I can't get physically away, is reading. I used to flip through catalogs while breast-feeding or sitting on the picnic table supervising the sandbox. Now I keep one eye on a magazine as I color with Page or run Henry through his spelling words. I scan the newspaper while I cook. I catch up on magazines at soccer practices or on the playground. I stash a book in each bathroom—nonfiction, since there's no plot to forget; I manage only a few pages a day, at best.

Surprisingly, I never feel guilty over this particular bit of self-ishness. I figure that although I might be mentally absent (but only for a paragraph or two at a time), at least I'm physically present. Much of the time, that's what kids need more.

I also like to think my habit has the added benefit of good role-modeling. Maybe my children will grow up to consider reading as natural and essential as breathing. Why just the other day I was studying the morning's headlines over breakfast while Henry read Sports, Eleanor read the local Style section, Margaret took the weather map, and Page stared intently at a Froot Loops box.

If only I could figure out how to get the more necessary bits of my life done at the same time. Maybe if I jotted down notes while on a treadmill while simultaneously helping with homework and playing rock-paper-scissors?

Oh wait, that's what I'm doing right now.

Momfidence...

. . . is spending your big time away from home perusing the kids' section of every gift shop because even though you know your return should be their gift, you always carry your sweet baboos in your heart. (And it's delightful to browse free from worry about accidental breakage.)

. . . is not being too deflated when the sweet baboos clamor, "Did you bring me anything?" five seconds after their welcome home hugs.

You Can't Judge a Mom by Her Midriff

On the Jiggly Bits

Motherhood. It's hot!

— *ad slogan, Motherhood Maternity clothing store*

Greta buys her ticket first. We're at the movies, one without a G in its rating or a Burger King tie-in. Greta has no children (which is how she knew which film to see) and mine are home with Daddyo.

It's obviously been too long since my last Mom's Night Out. I'm giddy and we haven't even had a drink. It's that lightness that comes from turning off the part of my brain ordinarily programmed, like a beacon in a guard tower, to make periodic sweeps of the landscape to see if anyone is darting into the parking lot or punching their sister.

My purse is light, too, having been emptied of all wet wipes, crayons, year-old biter biscuits, Goldfish crumbs, rattles, and confiscated little green army men (recently used to attack unsuspecting sisters at church). I've traded up my all-purpose black stretch pants and denim shirt for a bright sweater set and clean capris. In a further attempt to leave mommying behind for a few hours, I've even added a necklace. I'd stopped wearing them years ago when the chains grew encrusted by sticky baby gums, and only recently rediscovered the pleasures of jewelry not made from macaroni or twisted pipe cleaners.

Greta is most impressed, however, by my shoes: "Leather soles!" (She's only ever seen me in Keds.)

Standing behind her at the ticket window, I'm having a happy déjà vu. I'm at another box office in another life, when I'd actually seen every Best Picture nominee by Oscar night. When I'd analyzed them afterward in long rambly dark-bar conversations. When I actually noticed cute guys working behind the ticket window.

My turn. "One for the same movie, please."

"Sure." The ticket clerk smiles with dimples even deeper than his chin cleft. I feel the unfamiliar flush of rusty flirtation receptors. As I fumble for my money, I idly calculate our age difference. That's when I discover a use for Botox not pictured in any cheesy ad: It would make impossible the frown that flits across my brow as I realize this boy is probably closer to Henry's age than to my own. *When did that happen?*

Never mind—back to enjoying the moment. He smiled! I smiled! I'm not wearing Keds!

"Mom's night out, huh?"

Pffffft! My hip-chick reverie evaporates. I suck in my stomach. "Why didn't you ask her that?" I try to joke, with a thumb toward Greta. Then I lean closer. "So what was the giveaway? The ten-year-old purse? The circles under my eyes? This?" I point to my stomach.

Greta tugs my arm. I don't usually grill strangers—let alone draw any attention to my archnemesis, my jelly belly—but I can't help myself. Anyway, there's no one behind us in line.

I have to know. Is my maternal state so obvious? Have I changed so much?

The clerk cocks his head with an expression of bemused disbelief like he might give, well, his own mother. I can see him tuning out her harangue about picking up the clothes off his floor or not putting the empty carton of milk back in the refrigerator. Finally he says, "Uh, your Band-Aid."

Left pinky. Piglet. And Pooh. Paper cut while removing spelling worksheets from backpacks.

On top of everything else a mom is responsible for, she must take pains not to look like one. Why this would be so awful I'm not sure. My own mom did her procreating during the youth culture of the 1960s and 1970s, and nobody asked her to waltz around in hot pants or Qiana maternity blouses.

But lately we're expected to look as scarecrowy and hyperstyled as Desperate Housewives. Unless we're pregnant, that is. Then the accepted model is a hyperstyled scarecrow revealing a "bump." That's the body part that used to be known as "great with child." It's a hard enough look to pull off for those who wear their last trimesters like "pumpkins," as one pregnancy guide charmingly puts it; for the rest of us "refrigerators," it's hopeless. Ever try to locate a bump on a refrigerator?

Maybe I wouldn't mind this new vision of foxy motherhood so much if I had come out the post-postpartum end of my four gestations looking different. Like, say, one of those buff celebramoms hoisting a cashmere-clad mini-me on a nonexistent hip. (How do those kids hang on?) Maybe I'd be less cranky if I, too, had a trainer, stylist, Botox-and-detox crew, Zen yoshi master, and personal baby wrangler all tucked behind the scenes. When asked how I manage to maintain my fabulously microscopic shape, I, too, could shrug and say, "Oh, just running around after my kids," as if that really did burn off 120,000 calories a day.

Believe me, if running around after kids were all it took, I'd have written the Chase After Your Kids Diet years ago.

But no. I came out of childbearing looking like most women. Unfortunately in the popular media, this means invisible. Aside from walking stick, the other acceptable version of Mother, Hollywood-style is the cube-shaped and/or goofy extreme. Think the doughy Raymond/Seinfeld/Roseanne sitcom moms. Think Marge Simpson's tower of blue hair or Didi Pickles's orange wings on *Rugrats.* Think of the hapless creatures turned in by their daughters on *What Not to Wear.*

I have to flip a lot of channels before I see somebody on TV who resembles anything close to the reflection in my mirror.

Side note of hope: Thank goodness for the occasional Jane Kaczmarek, the normal-looking *Malcolm in the Middle* mom who really is a mom. And I'm not saying this because she, too, is a brunette, forty-something Pole from the Upper Midwest who has a handsome husband with a receding hairline and lots of kids with ordinary English names and, according to an interview I once read, *my exact height and weight* (five foot seven and 145 pounds, which was probably an exaggeration of a bad day for her but a very good day for me). No, what impresses—astounds!—me is that she actually confessed these figures to a magazine. And the existence of her varicose veins, too!

Even if such an admission were all a clever publicist's plant designed to win her the undying admiration of real Clairoled-brunette Slavic moms in America's heartland, I don't care. She looks plausible. She looks like she might indeed spend her weekends busting up arguments over who gets the yellow cup. She looks like she might even—if I may be so presumptuous—wear the occasional pair of mom jeans, even out in LA.

And what would be so wrong with that?

I mean really. Who wants to see their mother's low rise, anyway?

If it sleeps like a mom and hollers like a mom and cleans up puke like a mom (not to mention goes by the name MOOOOOOM!), it must be so. Disguise if it you like. Inject your skin with botulism. Click around on kitten heels. Spend your precious sleep time doing the downward facing dog with your personal trainer. Squander your bunco money and risk your life by having a little nip and tuck. You go, girl—you may be able to sustain the vixen illusion for a few glam starter years.

Eventually, though the ultimate physical realities of motherhood will be revealed.

There are too many possible giveaways:

1. The jiggly bits (you know where they are)
2. The random food bits adorning hair, clothing, and any visible flesh
3. The muscular arm—just one, on either side, depending on whether you're a lefty or a righty, superstrong from lugging child, baby seat, and diaper bag and/or a handbag containing enough supplies for a family of six to make a Sahara crossing or go out to a movie
4. The touchy back (see above)
5. The tired eyes (which may be remedied with modern dermatologic medicine or a trip to the local Clinique counter, if you are willing to forgo college savings accounts)
6. The fuzzy eyebrows (because your tweezers haven't been seen since tick season last summer)
7. The fireworks spreading across your skin (no, nothing post-coital, I'm referring to big blue veins and spidery silver ones)
8. Did I mention the downward-facing breasts, the belly, the thighs, the J. Lo-wer butt, the lower upper arms (even, alas

on that one muscular side), the where-did-that-come-from
wattle . . .

Oh, sorry! That describes *my* body.

If you look like Teri Hatcher without going hungry or broke,
and your husband and child prefer sharp angles to breasts and laps,
more power to you.

If, however, you look more like the "Before" picture in a magazine makeover (and you'd like the kids to get to college someday),
why that's a fine vision of motherhood, too. Truth as beauty—
there's a novel concept. If we moms aren't authoritative representa-
tives of what moms ought to look like, then who is? Some gay
stylist in LA?

Let him (or her) experience breasts masquerading as hyperfilled
water balloons and hormonal shifts that permanently alter the very
width of your feet and then tell us whether clingy tops and super-
pointy shoes are really such a great idea.

Such are my defensive thoughts anyway, on the day after seeing the
movie with Greta. I'm home standing in front of a mirror as naked
as the day I entered motherhood, with a skimpy old towel standing
in for the skimpy hospital gown that loosely covered me that day.

I've seen better bodies. And I've seen plenty worse. Both in this
very mirror, attached to my own neck, as a matter of fact.

I hate my body. I hate that it doesn't even come close to the
prevailing blonde-cleavaged-abs-alicious standard of sexiness. And
no, I am not saying that because I played with Barbies as a girl. I am
saying that because I'm a magazine snarfer, an ad consumer, a sometime TV-and-movie watcher, a seeing person in this visual world.

I hate the inconsistent scale. I hate it when my pants are tight
and I have to wear extra Lycra to remind myself to go easy on the

100 percent whole-wheat reduced-fat Wheat Thins today. I hate that my hips are still wide now that my last tot is too big to prop there as camouflage. I hate the jiggly bits.

I also hate that I can't set out rat poison to eliminate these inane thoughts from my circuitry.

Because I love my body! My body has been very good to me! It snagged me my husband (who loves me for my mind but admits the first thing he noticed about me were my lips). This body has built four fully functional, marvels-of-engineering babies out of four invisible starter cells. It did things I never dreamed I had in me in labor—leaving me amazed that such a nonjock could ace such a grueling marathon and dizzy with pride that a weenie like me had done it without a drop of drugs to mute my exhilaration. Those droopy blobs on my chest may interfere with the clean lines of certain fashions, but my babies saw them as life-giving milk jugs. The pillowy thighs are, to them, an excellent lap. My body also still gives my husband pleasure, no small thing and, whoopee for me, receives it very nicely, too.

I love my body for getting me where I need to go despite its being well used. I love that though it attracts few wolf whistles, it doesn't draw snickers, either. It holds up respectably at high school reunions. It bears with me patiently when I haul it through spinning, yoga, mountain hikes, or whatever other crazy notions possess me now and again. It even runs on too little sleep and too much chocolate.

Yes, it's been a fantastic body so far, one for which I am eternally grateful, and one I hope to wear it proudly for as long as I am able, thankyouverymuch.

And so there, Teri Hatcher!

Suddenly I am aware I'm being watched.

"Whatcha looking at?" Margaret asks.

"Oh! Nothing."

"Whoa! You grew some big muscles up there," she remarks, impressed. I fix the towel where it briefly fell from my breasts.

"Are those your nibbles?" Page, who's right behind her (and even more naked than I am), wants to know.

"Yes. Nipples," I say, slipping into a bathrobe. I try to use the right anatomical names—to instill a healthy body image and all that. Only no matter how precise I am, the words always come out their mouths mangled. Probably just as well. That way, when *uneris* (uterus), *wova* (vulva), and *spinky* (penis) come up in their conversations with teachers or Grandmas, no one has any idea what the heck they're talking about.

"Hi ladies. What's going on?" says Eleanor, the mini-Gwyneth. "Are we taking a bubble bath in your tub? Can we paint nails? Can you braid my hair?" I don't know where she gets these ideas. I haven't taken a bubble bath since I was pregnant with Henry. I never polish my nails or "fancify" my hair. I am lucky to shave both legs on the same day. And this is why: *I am never alone in my own bathroom!*

"We're talking about Mom's big muscles," says Margaret, edging over to make room for her sister. "Were those your triceratops?"

"Triceps?" I echo. "Well, no. They're—"

Eleanor snorts. "For your information, the biggest muscle is called gloomiest maximumest." She shoots me a look of pride. "I learned that in gym class."

I reflexively pat my backside and hold back my smile. "It's *gluteus maximus*," I gently correct, though Eleanor's pronunciation sounds a lot more accurate in my particular case. "Your bottom. And your triceps are up . . . oh, never mind."

So long as my daughters' own glutes are young and cheery, I think they've had enough body talk for one day. I want them to like the skin they're in. "You know what? You can all take a big bath in the whirlpool tub. With bubbles *and* the colored squirty foam."

Times three: "Woo-hoo!"

It's not like how you look has any correlation to how fit or fabulous a mom you are.

Nor does how hip or perfect you appear correlate to how happily married you are. (And if you think it does, the answer may be less happily than you think.) Fit and fabulous are good things for a wife to be. Hip and perfect, on the other hand, are extraneous. Lip implants? Midday cleavage? Please!

I'm not advocating we all schlump around in shapeless housedresses and snap rollers in our hair. But I'd like to think there is a happy middle ground that doesn't make me feel like a 1953 leftover *or* weird out my kids. I'm all for looking your best, so long as "your best" doesn't mean *the* Best in the Greater Metropolitan Area as Defined by *Allure* magazine.

Anybody who's had a baby deserves to "live life large," as a friend of mine once described it, for a reasonable number of months, so long as, gradually, she snaps out of it. (Wasn't it Walt Whitman's mother who said, "I am large. I contain multitudes"?) I may have gained fifty pounds with each pregnancy—four times, which yes, adds up to one-tenth of a ton, as Daddyo once sweetly calculated for me—but afterward I did the usual sorts of things to eventually drop them again. I wanted to be able to chase the rascals and ride bikes and see them graduate from college. I wanted to breathe better. And I didn't want to wear saggy maternity clothes forever, no matter how "hot" they are.

Not least, I didn't want Daddyo to call me "Mommy" along with everybody else.

Admittedly I'm still working on the last ten post-Page pounds. But lately I'm thinking I've been too hard on myself even there. After all no one around here seems to notice them but me.

And if the slight extra padding is good for my mental health, there are also the physical benefits to consider. All this time I've considered myself a bit overweight, and now comes the latest glorious news from science that "overweight" is really "optimal" because a little padding protects us from breaking our bones as old ladies. Normal-sized women live longer than thin ones or fat ones, it turns out.

(The studies didn't comment on the ramifications of wearing four-inch stilettoes around the house, though if you ask me, heels and stray LEGOs are a dangerous combination that must subtract years from the average female lifespan.)

Maybe nature *intended* us to keep those last persistent jiggly bits after childbirth, as a kind of thank-you gift for the good work in perpetuating the species.

Or that's one chipper way to look at it anyway.

Momfidence...

. . . is knowing that if you're breast-feeding, you're already a "yummy mummy"; you don't need kitten heels and a miniskirt to prove the point.

. . . is covering your wobbly midriff with a supersoft cashmere sweater instead of beating yourself up about it not being belly-baring perfect.

. . . is giving your body a little credit for doing a really cool thing back there in the delivery room and in the suckling months afterward, contributions much more useful to the human race than fitting back into your favorite honeymoon bikini.

. . . is what's hot.

Every Marriage Has Its Love Toy Phase

On Romance

> Imagine waking up in the morning and gazing into each other's eyes, just you, your partner, and your baby, or just watching them sleep next to you, wrapped in their scent . . .
>
> — *Gurmukh,* Bountiful, Beautiful, Blissful: Experience the Natural Power of Pregnancy and Birth with Kundalini Yoga and Meditation

It's early morning. *Saturday* morning. Which means sleeping in. And it's been a great night's sleep, in fact. Eight thick, uninterrupted hours in which nobody fell out of bed, wet their sheets, or woke up screaming because "a bathtub sucked me down" or "a giant vacuum chased me."

I am vaguely aware of the sky brightening on the other side of the blinds, of distant birds chirping. I grow increasingly aware—yessss, definitely aware—of Daddyo's foot touching mine . . . now his hand reaching over . . . *mmmm, nice* . . .

"I want brefkist!"

It's not a come-on line. The words are accompanied by a maracas-like rattle coming from inside the head of Margaret's rag doll, Love

Toy. Standing at my side of the bed—always my side, even when this involves a longer trip from the door—Margaret herself arrives every morning with all the punctuality of a rooster, if roosters sucked their thumbs while clutching flannel rag dolls in their talons. Roosters don't know their Saturdays from their Mondays. They just know when it's time to crow for their chicken feed.

"Oh! Hi sweetie. Uh, up already?" I try to be nonchalant, not too breathless or audibly disappointed.

But Daddyo's ardor cools more slowly. "We're still sleeping. Go watch TV." Sometimes this buys the necessary few minutes. I snap my eyes closed again as if very drowsy and hold my breath.

"I'm hungry."

Keep 'em closed, you can do it, closed, closed, swallow that guilt over faking out your child . . .

"I want brefkist."

So matter-of-fact. So expectant. Both my mind and, alas, my body now shift from would-be sex goddess to their default mode, Nurturess.

"Yip! Yip! Yip!" Page—I mean Teeny, the Zero-Years-Old Puppy, arrives close on Margaret's heels. It's all over now. Teeny never waits expectantly at the side of the bed. Teeny jumps right up and begins to burrow under the covers. "Pant, pant!" (Teeny, not Daddy). "Pretend I am just being born and you say, 'Oh look, a zero-years-old puppy!'"

"Oh look, a zero-years-old puppy!" I echo on cue. "Hello Puppy!"

Daddyo sighs and rolls over.

"No! No! My name is not Puppy. Pretend my name is Teeny. And you are the Mommy dog and Dad, you are the Daddy dog, and you say—"

Margaret: "I want brefkist!"

The *Fairly OddParents* theme song suddenly blares from the

playroom TV. My first impulse is to holler for Henry or Eleanor to turn it down because people are still sleeping here; my second is to cajole Margaret and Page into joining them.

"Yip! Grrrr!"

Rattle, rattle, rattle. "Page! Get your teeth off Love Toy! Mom! Make her stop! Mom! Mom!"

"I'm not Page. I'm Teeny. And I am zero years old and it is my chew toy!"

Whop!

Wail!

I peck the man of my dreams on the cheek and get up.

No discussion of parenting would be complete without an examination of the process that made it all possible and which, defying all practicality and aesthetic logic (see previous chapter), seems destined to continue even after the procreation has been accomplished. By which I mean sex. For hand in hand with the new pressure that a mom should waltz around Sam's Club and soccer practice *looking* sexy is the old assumption that she is also actively *being* sexy (on the home front, that is, not at the grocery store).

There's no pretending, however, that things steam right along as they did before. And there are plenty of good reasons for this. Let's consider them.

In brief:

1. Pregnancy
2. Childbirth
3. Recovery from childbirth
4. Newborn
5. Baby

    6. Toddler
    7. Preschooler
    8. Child
    9. Child
  10. Child
  11. Child

Well, there's my list anyway. No matter what size the family, the general drift of this continuum is the same: There is a span of time in every marriage with children that I refer to as the Love Toy phase.

This name does not refer to the sorts of helpful romantic appliances now sold in ribald home parties the way our own mothers once acquired Tupperware. Nor does it imply you need such devices. Love Toy is Margaret's rag doll. "Doll" being a generous description—Love Toy consists of a kerchiefed head with a rattle inside atop two long strips of flannel. My daughter has not been seen without it since she developed a firm grasp at six or seven months old. Well, except for those three days when it stayed at a campground a little longer than the rest of us and had to be FedExed back home. (Whew!) Observing their baby sister's devotion to this first toy, her older siblings named it "Margaret's Love Toy." As in, "Look, Mom. She's loving on that toy." And "Margaret's crying! Where's her love toy?" Luffie—the doll is now familiar enough to us all to go by a pet name—has been to preschool, kindergarten, haircuts, doctor appointments, playgrounds, national parks, photographer's studios—pretty much anywhere Margaret has gone. Like TV's Lassie, there have in fact been seven Luffies so far, all subtle variations on the original; Margaret fingers their soft flannel so intently that she literally loves them to bits.

There's nothing like getting amorous and rolling over onto a

Love Toy (or a stuffed Piglet or hard plastic Transformer, or the toy's owner herself). This is to be expected for a few years in early parenthood. So you have to accept it and work around it.

Which is why "family bed" parenting has always sounded a bit too familiar to me. That's the group-sleep concept where you adore your children so much you can't bear to be parted from them day or night lest you damage their sense of security and faith in mankind. (One guide recommends skipping the crib and buying a larger bed for the whole gang.) I never could understand the attraction of hearing your baby snuffle in between you and your mate all night long or of having a bigger child toss and turn and kick you in the shins. We upgraded to a king-sized bed so we wouldn't kick *one another's* shins, not to make room for the more bodies. I see enough of my babies during the daylight hours, thankyouverymuch.

Come to think of it, I see them plenty enough afterward despite my best efforts to avoid them. During thunderstorms or when visions of "buffalo cars" chase them in their dreams, it's a family bed all right, at least until I muster the energy to get up and haul the interloper (sweetly, lovingly) back where she belongs.

"Why do you get to sleep with Daddy but I have to sleep alone?" a night visitor once complained.

Because I'm the Mommy, that's why. It's one of the perks of the job.

Besides expecting that there will be constant disruptions, one cannot overlook such marital aids as door locks and the midafternoon rendezvous. The latter works best on Saturdays, timed soon after popping in a fascinating new DVD that appeals to all ages while also laying in a stash of snacks in such plentitude they are sure not to be bickered over. Then you work fast.

Sexiness for a mom can't be only in the eye of the beholder. It must be what she herself sees in her reflection in the mirror, too—

or at least feels inside her soul. That lesson is what I got for my birthday one year:

I had eyed the enormous, fancily beribboned box all during supper: A new winter coat? A quilt? Something we needed for the house, like the year Daddyo had wrapped up a few planks, which he later made into a desk?

After a round of "Happy Birthday to You," all three big kids helped me blow out the candles on my cake and Page, who was only one at the time, applauded. At last I was handed the package—too featherlight to be wood, not bulky enough for a coat. From clouds of snowy tissue I pulled out a long, black silk nightgown and matching robe.

Oh.

It seemed more like the sort of thing he might have given me when we were newlyweds. What kind of present was a black silk nightgown and robe for a mother of four smallish children who lived in black Lycra stretch pants?

I imagined spit-up quickly ruining the liquidy folds. I saw sticky fingers reaching for a lustrous sleeve, spilled milk sopping the hem. Bath bubbles would stain it, toy cars would snag it, baby nail clippers might do unspeakable damage. It wasn't the sort of robe you wore to fetch the morning paper or pulled on to go comfort a sick child in the middle of the night. I struggled to mask my disappointment at such useless extravagance.

I really needed that new winter coat.

I left the tags on, intending to return it after tactfully telling my dear husband that, while I truly appreciated the gesture, didn't he agree that it was pretty impractical? Except I never got around to that conversation. I couldn't muster enough indifference to give up the silky set.

For one thing, it was gorgeous—not Frederick's of Hollywood

sleazy, but movie star elegant. The gown's bias cut made it float. The carefully engineered robe had an inner tie around its slightly gathered waist and a generous outer sash to finish into a big jaunty bow. The coyest bit of black lace edged up each sleeve. I liked just knowing I owned such a thing, the way some people revel in the possession of a Waterford vase or an antique chair or a first edition of their favorite book.

And it felt great. After everyone was in bed that night, I slipped the lingerie on, half-hoping it would look better on the hanger than on me so that I'd have a good excuse to give it all back. But no. Cut long and loose, of fabric more gossamer than a newborn's hairdo, the nightgown and robe were unlike anything that ever brushed against my skin before. It was like wearing a caress, to borrow a line from romance novels (since that's what I felt like I'd stepped into). Forget cleavage, garters, and four-inch mules. I've never felt so *comfortably* sexy in my life.

Probably because I felt so good, I looked good, too. Or at least that's what Daddyo thought. "Why don't you dress like this more often?" he joked.

Okay, half-joked.

I kept the nightgown and robe.

Sometimes after the kids are asleep, I change into the silky set just to read, because it feels so nice. (I stash a flannel robe nearby in case someone calls me in their sleep.) Or I'll take a post-bedtime bath—you know, the luxurious prekid kind, complete with matching scented oil, soap, candle, and moisturizer—just so I can extend the indulgence afterward by wearing the nightgown and robe as I fold laundry or pick up LEGOs. Or after a madhouse day of work and play and bedtime battles, when I'm so spent I'm sure I'll fall asleep with my toothbrush in my mouth, it's amazing how I can somehow reenergize for romance if I reach for the silks instead of my usual oversized T-shirt.

The nightgown and robe cheer me even when they're just hanging in my closet between my all-purpose denim dress and my boring navy blazer. A month or two might go by between wearings, but I know they're there, like an alternate persona I can slip into at will.

In my heart of hearts, though, I know that it's neither sex nor glamour nor comfort nor the guilty pleasure of conspicuous consumption that led me to welcome the black trousseau-wear to my wardrobe. Perception did. The nightgown and robe allow me to feel like one hot mama—because I want to, not because I'm competing with anybody else—and the mere fact that my husband picked them out for me means that's how he sees me, too. Not like a diaper-dispensing suburban mom in black stretch pants and flannel, but as the kind of beautiful woman who sometimes wears black silk.

And for someone who *is* a diaper-dispensing suburban mom in black stretch pants and flannel, that's a perfect reminder, the perfect gift.

Momfidence...

. . . is ogling *Vogue* without feeling obligated to show up at a PTA meeting looking like you do.

. . . is skipping PTA because you and Daddyo have a date and, well, first things first.

If a Birthday Falls in Suburbia and Nobody Takes a Picture, It Still Happened

20

On Memories

Once you begin a family album tradition, you'll wonder why you didn't start sooner. Before you know it, you'll have a collection of albums documenting each year and all your special memories.

—*Creative Memories, the scrapbook supplies marketer*

"**M**om?"

Another morning, another dream deferred. This time, though, it wasn't my husband, but Fitzwilliam Darcy who was right here next to me a minute ago. He was wearing a long black coat and saying something about his estate and his barouche while I lay on a chaise lounge in this filmy empire waist gown, not my usual look, but surprisingly sexy, and . . .

"MOM!"

"Mmmm?"

"What if, after you had a dream, you had a tape and you could watch your dream?"

There's no gentle warm-up to a day with kids. No "Good

230

morning," or "How you doin' Mommy?" It's *splash!* Dive right in to whatever's on their brains the instant they wake up. Henry once conked out in midtantrum, then woke up ten hours later still raging right in the same sentence where he'd left off. Who needs to set an alarm to the drone of talk radio when you have a child under five in the house?

What I say is, "Oh, good morning, Margaret. Wow, that would be really cool. What did you dream about last night that made you think of that?"

What I think is, *Wow, that would be really cool. If I could tape my dreams, I could hit "pause" on Mr. Darcy and replay our scene from the beginning after I've fixed breakfast, packed lunches, located missing socks, stuffed stray folders into their proper backpacks, and issued my usual 150 declarative sentences on the way to getting everyone to school: Put your shoes on. Comb your hair. Brush your teeth. Don't walk around with a Pop-Tart in your mouth. Put your shoes on. Stop flicking rubber bands at your sister. Get that lunch box away from the dog. Put your shoes on. Put your shoes on. Put your shoes on NOW.*

The real beauty of Margaret's would-be invention doesn't strike me until later in the day (by which time all memories of men in black frock coats have irretrievably faded). The mail brings a stack of snapshots from my sister. No detail of our families' recent visit went undocumented by her camera. See Henry and his cousin Joe sit at a picnic table. See Henry eat french fry. See Joe eat french fry. See Henry and Joe use french fries like light sabers. See french fry light sabers inserted in boys' nostrils . . .

What if the dreams a child had at night could be taped and replayed endlessly? Why then we'd accomplish nothing less than the complete and total preservation of childhood! At long last, 24/7 coverage of a child's life! Every word, thought, deed, milestone, recital, practice, game, birthday party, holiday, first day of school, unfortunate haircut, and now yes, even every middle-of-the-night dream and nightmare, could be captured for posterity.

As if posterity cared.

We're practically there already. It's not enough to live with your child the first time. You must relive each moment as well. (And then we all wonder why we feel perpetually short on time!) No occasion is too minor to record if it's happening to your precious flesh and blood.

To be sure parents have always sought mementoes of their children, whether bronzed baby shoes or black paper silhouettes. My dad used to bring out his heavy steel Ricoh at every family party and holiday. Everyone was required to freeze their increasingly unnatural smiles on their faces for so long while he focused that visiting cousins learned to run the other way at the first glimpse of his hefty black camera bag. (We, his children, had been trained from an early age to submit.)

Nowadays, though, every single moment is considered perpetuity worthy. It's a rare child who's camera-shy anymore, having been primed to say "cheese" before knowing what cheese is.

The weird parent is not the one front and center at every school event with a camcorder; it's the one who's sitting there watching with her naked eye.

Whether your family photos are in lavish acid-free scrapbooks with color coordinated borders and funny captions (like my sister's, which I admire and envy even as I wonder where she finds the time) or stuffed in a shoe box (like mine used to be) or languishing on your hard drive (like mine are now), the point is that they exist. Photographs, cell-phone-snap downloads, professional portraits, videos, albums, scrapbooks, artwork portfolios, framed essays, report card files, trophies, plaques, ribbons, certificates, hair locks, baby teeth, pregnancy belly casts (eeeww!)—there's just no excuse for leaving your child's life to the unreliable wisps of mere memory.

Never in history has a generation been so well preserved without formaldehyde.

Lest I imply that memorabilia run amok is the problem of *other* people, let me confess that Henry's first stitches now reside on a tongue depressor in his baby book. And Page's umbilical stump rests inside a beaded Sioux pouch my husband bought in South Dakota before she was born, although it's sewn shut and the turtle-shaped pouch is so lovely, so no one would ever guess there's a rotted body part inside. This is your life, Page Spencer!

Why do we do it?

To embarrass our children on their wedding day? I could trot out an array of filthy blankies and tattered Love Toys for that purpose (if not this very book).

To remind them of every step of their journey from adorable newborn cherub to gawky teen? ("Gee thanks, Mom.")

To fatten their heads in the delusional and sorely mistaken belief that anyone who warrants this much press must be the very center of the universe?

Or do we preserve their every moment as a way of hanging on to our own pride and bliss about these happy years? Never mind that they'd be a lot more blissful if we weren't worrying about whether we got that shot of the candles before they were blown out or staying up until 3 a.m. feverishly cropping the "Our Summer Vacation" album.

But for all our elaborate chronicling, I'm not sure that we're capturing the essence of a childhood. One year my sister Patti, the scrapbook Michelangelo, retrieved all the old slide boxes from under our parents' bed, blew off thirty years of dust, and had the shots featuring the two of us made into prints. Then she arranged the pictures into a sisters scrapbook—hands down one of the best presents I ever received.

The vision of our childhood that the snapshots added up to was a succession of Easter egg–dyeing sessions, birthday parties with orange cakes (my favorite color), Mom-made Halloween costumes, and impatient lineups on Christmas morning and the first day of school. It was the *camera-ready* version of childhood.

What I especially enjoyed about this trip down memory lane, however, were the bits my dad had not intentionally recorded: a Poppin' Hoppies game and a red Close'n Play record player visible under the Christmas tree behind us. A glass home-delivered Twin Pines Dairy bottle on an uncleared kitchen table. The cover of a book I'm holding, that great literary classic, *Gilligan's Island.* Hints of everyday childhood reality that had aged to dust in my overloaded memory.

If we really want to preserve our children's lives, we'd be better off taking photos of their playroom floor. The bathtub. A close-up inside the backpack. Or the places parents rarely see: the backseat, the treehouse interior, the day-care playground, their best friend's room. Daddyo once wanted to have a portrait painted of our refrigerator door. At the time I thought he was bonkers, but now I regret not going along. What other square footage in the entire house more compactly represents family central? (Our new house has one of those sleek black refrigerators on which magnets don't stick, and I'll never get used to the loss.)

Our best home video features no adorable dresses or birthday cakes; it's a dinner where we set up the tripod and let the camera roll for the eleven or twelve minutes this particular meal lasted, without telling anyone it was recording. Knock-knock jokes, complaints, reminders about not rocking in the chair, snorts, whines, uproarious giggles, even the inevitable spilled milk—a slice of our unchoreographed real life was preserved in all its fun and semidisgusting glory.

Here are a few more such memories that deserve to live forever but, alas, tend to go quite ignored by even the most preservation-minded parent:

- First time *Boohbah* mesmerizes your toddler long enough for you to go to the bathroom unaccompanied
- First time same toddler takes in the full half hour of *Boohbah* without popping up to ask "Where Boo Boo go?" the minute the blobs leave the screen. Now you can go to the bathroom and read the mail, too.
- First day-care or babysitter separation without tears from parent or child
- First thoughtful observations not directly planted by Mom or Dad: "When I sing, it makes my heart feel glad"; "God is so big you can't even see him"; "There's nothing like coming home from a long hard day and rewinding on the sofa"
- First opening of refrigerator door by hungry child to retrieve a snack without your help
- First voluntary closing of refrigerator door after opening
- Last diaper
- First self-initiated playdate
- First solo bath or shower
- First voluntary toothbrushing (Still waiting . . .)
- First family portrait in which everyone is smiling (Still waiting . . .)
- First time you hear "I hate you" (Daggers!)
- First time you hear "I love you" from child with embellishments tailor-made just for you: "In the whole universe you are the most special Mama. You can kiss me if you like."

- First time you're asked "Do kisses come off?"
- And the first time you reply "No way." Some things are forever, no camcorders necessary.

Momfidence...

. . . is asking another parent at the class program to snap a picture for you so you can just enjoy the show. They may take only one shot of your child (compared with one hundred of their own), but one is all you need.

. . . is not feeling guilty that the baby books you received as a shower present are still as blank as the growing bald spot on Daddy's head. Who really cares what date your child rolled over or sprang a left lateral incisor? As for what the "current hit movie" or "biggest world event of the year" were on the day he was born, for that we have Google.

Even the Best-Laid Plans Fall Down

On Family Traditions

> During the holidays, the house you know so well becomes a magical, welcoming place; the weeks before Christmas are a time for creating a new, surprising world indoors . . . decorations, gifts, wrapping, and the holiday menu can all be reinvented, in part or in whole.
>
> — *Martha Stewart,* Christmas with Martha Stewart Living

"**W**ow! Look at that one! Can we taste it?"

Just after Thanksgiving, Eleanor and I are viewing a display of the finalists in a gingerbread house contest. Only calling these works of art "houses" is like calling Picasso's paintings "doodles." There are castles and log cabins, snug bungalows with snowy eaves, even a perfect re-creation of the stone country inn where the judging has taken place. And every bit edible! Gumdrop gardens, pretzel fencing, Necco wafer pathways shimmering on wintry lawns of coconut flakes and sanding sugar.

We're both enchanted. Visions of sugarplum architecture dancing in my head, I instantly resolve to start a new holiday tradition: My daughter and I will make our own magical gingerbread house.

So what if my holiday baking is limited to a batch or two of slice-and-bake sugar cookie logs?

This will be different. I picture Eleanor and I in festive matching aprons, setting our finished mansion on the table for all to admire. It will be the centerpiece of our holiday decor, a sweet symbol of mother-daughter unity. We'll do it every year, trading up, each house bigger and better than the last. Maybe we'll enter the contest ourselves one day. Margaret and Page, too. Maybe we'll win. "Wasn't she a great mom?" the girls will one day reminisce, looking back on the newspaper clippings and family photos of this monument of my maternal skill.

That's the idea anyway.

The impulse to be the architect of great family traditions strikes unexpectedly, and not without a certain amount of alarm. Gradually it dawns on you that the pomp and circumstance of your own childhood holidays and special events had a planner and a doer behind them, and her name was Mom. Now you're her. From decking the halls to filling the social calendar to carrying out all the to-dos that risk turning you into a she-grinch, it's up to you. Dare leave anything to chance and your children may be left with unhappy childhoods and rotten memories.

And who wants to be responsible for that?

Eager to get some great ideas going myself, I once pitched to a magazine a story on family traditions. The plan was to canvass a zillion moms and get them to share their traditions and inspire readers (and me). But the backstory proved almost more interesting: the power of the guilt over traditions. For every mom who shared her recipe for king's cake with three beans hidden inside, there were six who were too paralyzed by the enormity of the responsibility to pass along a single idea.

"My granny made tamales cooked in corn husks [or seven kinds of fish or rock-hard fruitcake], but I don't know the recipe and I don't have time . . ."

"I don't do enough . . ."

"I should be doing more . . ."

"I'm researching it. I heard HGTV had good ideas."

"I know it's so important, but I don't know what to do!" one flat-out wailed to me. "What does everybody else say?"

The compulsion to overproduce the events isn't limited to Christmas. Although 96 percent of Americans celebrate Christmas, according to Gallup, no American magazine puts out a December issue without including the feasts of Hanukkah and Kwanzaa, and Eid-ul-Fitr. So I also interviewed moms about their traditions around these events (though I drew the line at dredging up Wiccans, who get enough attention as it is at Halloween). Whatever the occasion, the anxiety about making their celebration Memorable and Meaningful was the same. We may celebrate a diverse bunch of special events here in the United States, but we share a universal drive to make heap-big memories out of them for our kids.

Extravaganza-itis may reach its apex at the no-longer-lowly birthday party. One burned-out year I simply bought hats, balloons, bubble wands, and a candy-filled piñata, and invited a bunch of kids over to eat cake and run around. In our yard. The bash was a hit—I think because of the novelty. Most of the young guests had never been to a birthday like it before.

Soon after our outing to the gingerbread house contest, I drag Eleanor from the toy catalogs she's ogling with the promise of getting to lick some beaters. Perhaps amazed by my uncharacteristic kitchen zeal, Daddyo has bought us a "Fun & Easy" gingerbread-cottage starter kit. It consists of a heavy iron mold, a recipe, and instructions. I even bought the ingredients during my last milk run. Now here was our big moment, while her sisters are down for what I can only hope will be a long winter's nap.

We're off. We measure and mix the shortening, sugar, and molasses—I feel pretty smug about remembering to buy such an obscure ingredient as molasses. Then, whoops. One teaspoon ginger. I vainly search the jammed lazy Susan where I keep my spices, most of which are older than Eleanor, having arrived as part of a wedding gift. No ginger. Could I skip it? This house is just for looks anyway. I have no idea if it's the ginger or the baking that will turn the house brown. No. No shortcuts.

Determined to do this right, I call on my neighbor Sandy, whose spices are probably alphabetized and who would never dream of making gingerless gingerbread.

"We're making a gingerbread house!" Eleanor tells Sandy. "So we need gingerbread."

"Ginger," I clarify. "I thought I had ginger but we're out. Can we borrow some?"

"Sure. Sounds like fun," Sandy says. "How much do you need?"

I have no idea. She pours enough in a plastic Baggie to build a gingerbread subdivision.

"I didn't know your mom was a chef," she says to Eleanor with a smile at me.

"She's not cheffing. She's building. And I'm tasting the battery!"

Sandy smiles, though I'm not sure which she finds more amusing, Eleanor's words or my unlikely ambitions. I thank her and hustle Eleanor home before she gets a peek at the magnificent Bûche de Noël on Sandy's sideboard in the next room. Not that I'm getting nervous or anything.

"When can I eat it?" Eleanor wants to know when we get back home.

"We're just starting! Greatness takes time!"

Lots and lots of time, actually. The "battery," I discover, has to chill for an hour. We don't have that long, on account of the nappers, but luckily the quick-freeze shelf of the freezer lives up to its name. Then we press the rock-hard dough into the hollows of the mold, bake it, and wait for it to cool in the pan. And there is so much leftover that, to stave off Eleanor's hungry whines, I promise we can make gingerbread men, too.

"I love to eat those," she agrees.

Transferring the pieces—wall, roof, tree, chimney—from the pan to the cooling rack (is this where the word "gingerly" comes from?), I frown. Shouldn't a house have more walls? That's when I reread the instructions and realize we were supposed to bake the mold *twice.* That explains all the extra dough.

In the nick of time, I grab the gingerbread man cookie cutter from my annoyed (and now *very* hungry) helper. I unwrap a candy cane plucked from the tree to mollify her.

When at last we have the right number of walls and rooftops, fully cooled, it's time to whip up the glossy frosting "glue." "Use it like you were gluing a model," say the instructions, which would have been useful advice were I a ten-year-old boy or the mother of one in the dull pre–Game Boy era who might have been accustomed to gluing models. Eleanor perks up, though, drawn to the bowl of fluffy whiteness. Occasionally she lends a frosting-dipped finger to help prop a sagging wall. When the structure finally stands on its own, I am so amazed that I choose to ignore the fat rivulets of frosting that overflow along its seams like a bad caulking job.

"Looks great!" Eleanor enthuses. "Can we eat it?"

"Oh no, now we get to decorate it," I reply. *Surely she'll finally realize, when she sees the glorious end result, that this project had never been meant for a snack.*

I try to remember exactly how all those gumdrops and lady-fingers had embellished the prize-winning Hansel-and-Gretel numbers we had seen. Not that I had had the foresight to buy such edible decorations. I don't even have a tube press for piping even, thin lines of trim. I improvise using a plastic bag with a corner snipped off, a breakthrough moment. *I have the knack! I am unstoppable!*

Ransacking the cupboards, I find mini-marshmallows to dot the roof like so many plump shingles. Graham crackers become shutters and sugar makes the rooftop glisten. More candy canes off the tree mark a green Froot-by-the-Foot lane leading to the entrance, where miniature chocolate chips dot the door and anywhere else Eleanor flings them. In a final flourish, we smear the leftover icing around the base like new-fallen snow.

"Perfect! Beautiful!" cheers Eleanor between bites of marshmallow. "*Now* can we eat it?"

"Not yet," I put her off. "Let's wait until Daddy sees it and takes a picture." Never mind that the finished product looks more like a fixer-upper in a "before" picture than the charming Victorian cottage described on the kit. We did it! Margaret and Page will be up from their naps soon and Henry will be home from his friend's house and they'll all be astonished. Next year everybody will want in on this Mommy-and-me magic. I call to Daddyo to come and see and to bring the camera.

Eleanor and I are combing our hair for the posterity portrait when he sidles up next to me. "Uh, what happened to your ginger-bread house?" he asks in a low voice. The last time he used this tone I had just attempted to give myself blonde highlights, a process that proved neither nice nor easy. "Uh, what happened to your hair?" he had asked in a way that sent me running to a mirror. My head looked as if I had combed burnt sweet potato through it.

I race to the kitchen. Our house, the new little gingerbread cottage that we'd been so proud of just minutes earlier, looks as if the Abominable Snowman set foot on it. Our afternoon of work, collapsed! Our Christmas centerpiece! Our first-annual tradition! I'm crushed.

And what will I tell Eleanor?

I don't have to tell her anything. She'd followed us into the kitchen and now she, too, is taking in the disastrous spectacle of our gingerbread heap. My heart aches for her. I have one of those damnable lumps in my throat that you get when some mean kid has made fun of your oblivious child's uncombed hair or you have to deliver the bad news that the dog has chewed the head off a favorite doll. I search for the right motherly words of comfort.

Eleanor, however, is not a bit distressed. "Hooray!" she cries. "Now we can eat it!"

Momfidence...

. . . is the living for the process, not the results.

. . . is making Christmas cookies every single year not because you're invited to a cookie exchange but because a kitchen where jimmies and colored sugar are flying is a happy one. (Pink trees? Green snowmen? Why not!)

. . . is including some dull and dreadful traditions like early to bed on Christmas Eve and the forced writing of thank-you cards over the long school holiday.

. . . . is leaving extra dough in the bowl and on the beaters when you turn them over to be licked clean.

Stop and Smell the Crayons

22

On Downshifting

> Can you even begin to imagine what life would be like for women if they didn't have the crushing responsibility to provide most of their children's emotional and physical nurturing?
>
> —*Christiane Northrup,* Women's Bodies, Women's Wisdom

> Yes I can. It would look a lot emptier.
>
> —*Paula Spencer, tired but uncrushed mother*
> *(who thought providing most of children's emotional and*
> *physical nurturing was the whole point of motherhood)*

Shoes tied. Sunglasses located. Cap on. Children occupied. Hand on doorknob. O-kay! I'm outta here!

"Can I come with you?"

Phoo! Stopped in my tracks again by a wee small voice.

"Not this time, Sweetie."

"Pleeeze?"

"I have to go for my walk for some exercise. And you're already wearing your pajamas!"

"I can walk fast."

"Don't you want to play with Brownie?"

"No."

"Or Daddy?"

"No. I only want to be with you."

I've been looking forward to this walk all day, my sacrosanct hour to burn off some insanity and some calories around my neighborhood streets. My back gets stiff sitting in front of a computer half the day, too, and I like to stretch it before hunching over books and bunk beds at tuck-in time.

Then I notice that Page is wearing sneakers with her pj's. And they are on the correct feet.

No! No falling for the heart-rending detail! Mustn't give in!

"Look, I'll be back soon and then we can walk together a little bit," I try.

"I want to go with you now. I said 'please,'" she points out.

"Yes, that was very polite. But I really have to go and walk really fast before it gets dark."

"That's what you said yesterday."

Got me! Score, Page!

Margaret hears all this and understands I have succumbed. Before I know it, she's Velcro-ing up her shoes, too. At least they didn't suggest we also bring the dog. The last time Brownie went on a walk he just stopped midway. Planted his skinny brown dachshund behind in the street like a balking mule, a half mile from the house, and had to be carried the rest of the way. Not even Page barking encouragingly in her dog costume could cajole him to take another step. At least babies can be lugged around in Snuglis.

So off we go—me, Margaret, Love Toy, Page, Ratty (her rubber goo-toy), and a couple of blankies.

Sure enough, we don't make it past three houses when we have to stop to taste some honeysuckle. A few paces later we watch a cat climb on a roof. We chase a squirrel, pick up a ladybug, feel droplets from a neighbor's sprinkler as it arcs over the garden onto the street.

We trace letters that have been formed by cracks in the road. We read road signs. S-T-O-P.

Ratty is dropped, and we backtrack to retrieve him.

At first I am itchily impatient, even though I try not to look it. My pulse rate is barely registering above resting. I have to shorten my gait to geisha steps in order not to outpace the girl on either side. I glance at my watch and the setting sun.

We observe that pink, purple, orange, and red are sunset colors, but not green.

We watch dandelion seeds float on the breeze and try to catch them in order to make a wish.

By the time we see the hydrangea-blue fairy floating over the road—a real one, with tiny silvery wings, probably on her way to a ball, Margaret guesses—I realize that I'm having a pretty good time. A better time than usual, in fact, and my back feels fine. Instead of just pumping my lungs while working out a story or a to-do list in my head as the scenery whizzes past unseen, I am walking the way a three-year-old and a five-year-old do, with my whole body and all five senses. It seems natural to skip for a few steps and burst into a few bars of "John Jacob Jingle Heimershmitt."

It's not every day you see a fairy.

Between wiping noses, molding manners, cleaning messes, and reminding them not to run in the street, opportunities to simply *be* with my kids can seem as rare as unspilled milk. If I'm not tending to their morals or their fingernails, it's laundry and lunch boxes, playtime and discipline, homework and carpool.

Sometimes I'm too busy being a mom to enjoy being a mom. *Hurry up! We're going to be late! Stop dawdling! You're going to miss the bus! Not now. Here, let me do that for you.* Partly the rushing is an inevitable function of modern parenthood. Getting from A to B can be challenging enough with just yourself to think about. Marshaling one or two (or five) other bodies along with you can't help but bog you down sometimes. Not even the U.S. Army moves troops that fast. And they have military precision on their side, which Lord knows I do not. We also live in a world where everybody moves fast and expects faster: *overnight* shipping, *high-speed* Internet access, *thirty-minute* dry cleaning, *instant* rice.

I'd like to think my girls will always remember me as I was on our walk: patient, attentive, exploratory, loving, fun. Or will they recall only the blur of the warp-speed dervish from Most of the Time, hustling them through room pickups and playdate pickups on her way to ten thousand other tasks?

An hour with a small child can sometimes drag like a whole day, and a day can sometimes feel like a week. But the weeks melt into months just like that, and the years—well, let's just say I am still trying to figure out how they can outgrow their clothes and expand their vocabularies at such a rapid rate when Daddyo and I are just standing still.

"How old are you?" Page wanted to know on my last birthday.

"Twenty-nine!" said Daddyo, rescuing my lips from having to form the actual dread number.

"Hey! You were twenty-nine last year!" Margaret frowned.

"Yeah," chimed in Eleanor suspiciously. "You must be thirty one of these birthdays."

Henry, with higher-level math on his side, went for the jugular. "Exactly what year were you born in anyway?"

Like I said, how can they be evolving so rapidly when I'm not changing a bit? Best not to hurry things along any faster than they need be.

To move on child time is to borrow a page from the Slow Movement. That's the hot trend in the food world toward old-time dishes that are slow-cooked and then leisurely savored. Not that my clan could ever sit up straight long enough to make our usual fifteen-minute gobble-fest last three hours. But you get the idea. Slow-ites stop to smell the metaphorical roses.

If you've ever watched a three-year-old make a single Oreo last for twenty minutes, you've seen this pleasure Zen in action.

When asked why they have kids, most parents give lofty reasons: to experience the warmth of family, to perpetuate the species, to see what marvel will result from the mixing of their gene pool with their mate's. But slowing down to kid time reminds me of parenthood's other little perquisites.

When you have a child, you get to do all of the following.

- Clobber Wiffle balls with a plastic bat and become your child's sports idol, even if you were a benchwarmer in school.
- Get reacquainted with Dr. Seuss, Madeline, Curious George, and Harold and his purple crayon and realize why you never really forgot them.
- Ride the merry-go-round, swing on playground swings, build snowmen, and catch fireflies until *you* decide it's time to quit.
- Discover how bright the 3 a.m. moon is.
- Watch Bugs Bunny cartoons again, this time appreciating the classical music and references to 1940s movie stars.
- Learn the scientific names of dinosaurs from apatosaurus to zephyrosaurus.

- Discover that the bunny's name isn't Pat.
- Marvel at diggers.
- Nibble animal crackers in the middle of the grocery store (because you can't make it to checkout with a toddler without opening a box).
- See tigers in the trees and fairies right in the middle of your suburban street.

Yesterday when Margaret and Page hauled out the battered tin of crayons and some paper snuck from my printer, my first impulse was to simultaneously scan the newspaper, fix dinner, and check my e-mail while they were preoccupied. Instead, I sat down with them.

Forest Green. Robin's Egg Blue. Purple Mountain Majesty. Even the colors' names were relaxing. We drew flowers, spider webs, and countless rainbows. They were delighted, and so was I. An hour sped by before I got a crick in my back from sitting so long in a stiff, ergonomically incorrect kitchen chair. I stood up.

"C'mon guys. Let's go for a walk."

Momfidence...

. . . is hiding a sixty-four-count box of Crayolas just for your personal use (so the tips stay pointy and the black one doesn't get lost).

. . . is unconsciously holding your breath in tense impatience while an eight-year-old tells . . . a . . . story . . . in . . . all . . .

its . . . halting . . . glorious . . . detail. Or while watching a five-year-old keep trembly hold of two bunny ears while she learns to tie her laces. Or while helping a ten-year-old with math homework. And then, before you burst, slowly exhaling and congratulating yourself on your patience, if not your blood pressure.

Lost Socks Are Not Found Again

On Fate

23

> The trouble is that when many parents find themselves in difficulties, they're too emotionally involved to see the bigger picture.
>
> — *"Supernanny" Jo Frost*

"The girls I want to see most at Disney World are Cinderella, Ariel, and Snow White. The boy I want to see most is Goofy," Page announces.

She pauses. "Is Piglet a girl or a boy?"

"Neither!" Margaret interrupts triumphantly. "Piglet is a pig. And Goofy is—Mom, is Goofy a wolf or a dog?"

There's a stumper.

I am sorting and folding laundry so I can pack for our big Florida trip. Tops, bottoms, underwear, pj's, bathing suits—and, hmmm, way too many sock singletons. Laundry time always ends the same way: one neat stack for each family member and an unruly linguine of mateless socks.

A mother of thirteen once confided in an interview that one of her greatest parenting secrets was buying everyone white socks. I'd been expecting something more seismic, like a system for splicing herself into a baker's dozen of laps and eyes. Or at the very least the name of the best brand of earplugs. But no. White socks.

Though her idea sounded plausible at the time, I am here to say it doesn't work. You still have different-sized feet in the house. And manufacturers interpret "plain white socks" in a staggering variety of ways. One day you'll buy white socks with wide ribs and then the next time come home with narrower ribs. One kid likes trifolds and the other says bare ankles are much more "in style." Then, despite your vow of podiatric pallor, you'll succumb to an adorable pair designed to coordinate with a special outfit, forgetting that one always promptly goes AWOL. Or Grandmom will send seasonal cuties adorned with gingerbread men or Halloween pumpkins. Net result: You will still wind up with a dozen forlorn singletons at the end of each laundry session.

I always set them aside in a basket, hoping for happy reunions down the line. When we moved a couple of years ago, there must have been fifty such socks, still waiting for their partners, in all colors, shapes, sizes, and probably creeds. I couldn't bear to leave them behind, but Daddyo—gung-ho to lighten the moving load by leaving any underused possession behind—tossed the basket while I was out buying plastic bins at Target so I could store my favorite baby clothes for future grandchildren. Now here I am at the new house with another big basket of unmatched socks. I bet half these poor soles lost their mates back in the big move.

These things happen.

Everyone agrees that socks get lost more than any other item of clothing, but no one has ever conclusively proved where they go. The point is that they do. Things happen that can't be foreseen, can't be explained.

·········

It's popular to give Disney World a bad rap because it's so crowded, corny, and expensive. Which it is. But there are certain family-outing clichés—Ringling Brothers Barnum & Bailey Circus and *The Nutcracker* also come to mind—that give me maternal goose-bumps. They're such icons of childhood pomp. You're there and the thought strikes you: "I'm here! With a kid! My kid! My lucky kid!" You get choked up. So you might as well surrender to the magic, the madness, and the inevitable souvenirs.

Which brings us to Orlando, where pixie dust is the only plau-sible explanation for the way twenty-dollar bills fly up from our wallets. We do it all. The spinning teacups, the Astro Orbiter, the flying Dumbos, "the ride with the horses and the ride with the dolls" (aka the carousel and It's a Small World). And did I mention the spinning teacups and the flying Dumbos? Playing the mommy card, I drag everyone to my personal favorite, the Hall of Presi-dents, where Page promptly conks out in the cool dark room and the others squirm and whine, "This is just like schoooooool!" Henry craves the Xbox Live rush of roller coasters, while the girls would be happy if their entire vacation took place within Fantasy-land. So we separate along gender lines for half an hour to do boy things and girl things, and plan to meet up for ice cream cones and to watch the big parade.

I wonder if a certain strata of parent doesn't avoid Disney be-cause they know their careful provision of gender-neutral toys, books, and clothes will be exposed as the waste of time it is the minute their sheltered boy gets a chance to shoot a rifle in Fron-tierland or their little princess-at-heart gets one look at those gaudy net-ball-gowns-to-die-for in the shops of Fantasyland.

Later, after we've all reunited and the floats and songs have drifted past us, comes the opportunity for a classic Disney vacation snapshot. "Come on, guys, over here," I say, walking toward the middle of Main Street USA, where Cinderella's castle rises up as the perfect backdrop. Other families are lining up in similar formations. The kids cluster around me as Dad frames the shot. Perfect.

"Wait! Where's Margaret?"

She'd been right beside us watching Mickey and Minnie on parade only seconds before. We'd shifted maybe a hundred feet up the street for the picture. Or rather, five of us did.

"I thought she was with you," I say to Daddyo.

He shakes his head. "I thought she was with you."

Adrenaline jolts me from my mellow theme-park trance.

Whoop! Whoop! Child missing! Sharpen the radar! Look all around. Remember to breathe!

"You and Henry go back where we watched the parade. I'll stay here with the girls," Daddyo commands. At least somebody is calm.

So Henry and I plow through the crowd. "She's probably just fallen behind," I tell him, playing it cool for both our benefits.

We'll soon see her, obliviously sucking her thumb.

Please.

We don't.

Now my alarm bells clang louder. I scan the whole area—the length of the curb, the garden beyond, the tables by the ice-cream shop. I run in the parade's wake, shouting her name. Happy families stare.

Everyone seems to be in slow motion but me. I scan the crowd for police. Where are they?

Oh God. This is something that happens to other people.

"Um, let's just go up the street a little, Henry. Maybe she went the wrong way."

"Okay."

I imagine my beautiful baby being dragged to a rest room by some monster who is dyeing her hair—that lovely brown hair with the blonde highlights I'd pay a small fortune to have replicated on my own head—an unrecognizable orange. Maybe her clothes are being changed to hustle her out of the park undetected.

The distance from joy to disaster in my heart is as brief as the span in the delivery room from miserable laboring whale to smiling besotted mother. Tears prick my eyes at the thought of never seeing her again. Ever!

Where are the police? Does Disney World issue AMBER Alerts?

I'm vaguely aware of Henry struggling to keep up as I lose all ability to maintain a brave-mom face for him. "Margaret! MARGARET!"

We storm the length of Main Street, to where the parade has obliviously come to a jolly end, then double back. The listless pace of the crowd that I had fallen in step with all morning now is unbearable. It is life threatening! A few concerned moms and dads look up as if to help but now I'm so worked up that I can't stop to talk to a soul as I fly frantically down the block.

"MARRRRR-GRRRRRET! MARRR-GRRRRRRET!"

Back where we started, I see Daddyo talking to a security officer who looks reassuringly like our pediatrician back home. (Picture Santa without the beard or red suit. Comforting. Trustworthy.) Eleanor and Page are sitting on the curb, bored. Actually Page is stretched full out on the concrete if she were home in bed having a nap. At the sight of my distressed face they perk up a little.

"This is Ray and he will help us find Margaret," my husband says evenly.

Ray puts his arm around my heaving shoulders. "Don't worry, Mrs. Spencer. This happens all the time. Your husband has just described her. What was she wearing?"

I blank. Red? Blue?

Why didn't I hold on to her in a crowd? I should have been counting heads constantly. Who was I to think I could enjoy myself at Disney World? Who was I to think I could have one second of enjoyment in eighteen years?

"Um, she was wearing, uh—"

"She had my old turquoise top with the green trim and matching shorts with white socks that had lace," Eleanor supplies. *Right. Turquoise. Lace.*

"And please show me where you last saw her."

Ray and I walk the few seconds back to the spot where we'd all sat so happily licking our ice cream cones and watching the dancing brooms and Cinderella's coach glide by.

Where is my fairy godmother? Scratch that. If she showed up she'd probably zap me into a rat. Or worse, she'd send me back to my lonely single-gal New York City days where I couldn't afford the likes of Disney World and never had anything close to the love and joy of a family of six.

Family of six minus one, undeserving wretch that I am!

All of maybe five minutes have now passed. It seems as though I haven't seen my little girl in an eternity. So many strangers!

Ray says something into his walkie-talkie. It's the first time I notice that he's held the thing near his ears throughout our conversation. Then he nudges my elbow and points back toward the rest of my family. A second security guard has brought over a crying Margaret. I rush over and take her in my arms.

"I stopped to look at something and you weren't there!" she chokes out before plugging her thumb back in her mouth. She takes it out one more time: "They asked me what you look like—but I couldn't remember if your hair was black or brown!"

The guard explains that a store clerk had seen her crying and alerted security. Apparently only a minute or two had passed before these two kind people were helping her. Even though she's growing tall and gangly, I clutch her like a baby. Ray lingers to make sure we're all right. Daddyo shakes everybody's hands.

"Now where's Henry?" he asks me.

Uh-oh. I'd last seen him somewhere on Main Street in midpanic. *This can't be happening!*

Ray is instantly working his walkie-talkie. Almost before this fresh panic can register, Henry is located. Unlike Margaret, my ten-year-old thinks it's cool to be cut loose from the gang. "I knew where you were all the time," he scoffs.

"Well now that we're all here, how about that picture—would you mind?" Daddyo asks Ray, handing him our camera. Everybody alive? Accounted for? Secure? Check, check, move on.

Ray obligingly snaps the shot—the castle of dreams looming above six relieved Spencers, one of them hiding her mortification with a chipper smile and another still frowning and sucking her thumb.

Okay. I'll come clean. It wasn't even the first time I misplaced a child. When Henry was a toddler, I lost him in a Baby Gap. He'd hopped from his stroller while I pawed through 3T sweatpants on sale. I felt around deep inside the nearby racks under the clothes where kids tend to gravitate before they're old enough to care about coveting the styles. I looked under the tables. I didn't completely lose it, though, until I registered the store's vast entrance that led, ominously, to the even vaster mall beyond. That's when I began to yelp out his description to anyone in earshot.

I'm happy to report that in the mellow quiet of a Baby Gap store, your fellow moms are quicker to jump to the rescue than they are in the cacophony of Disney World, where your lunatic shouts might represent an emergency or might just be ordinary theme-park lunacy.

A dozen voices fanned out: "Henry! Henry!"

"Anybody see a blonde toddler in a denim cap and blue jeans?"

It was one of the sales clerks who found him—in the store's windowfront display alongside the child-sized mannequins, smiling adorably as he struck a pose.

And then, incredibly, it happened again.

I lost another child at Disney World.

I know, I know. What kind of mother am I? You can't be any harder on me than I've been to myself. It's one thing to misplace your glasses or your keys, but your child?

Things happen that can't be foreseen or explained.

I was helping Eleanor choose a Minnie Mouse shirt in the end-less stores-within-stores along Main Street, a year or so after Margaret's misadventure. This time it was Page who slipped beneath my radar.

She'd been right there beside me. Right exactly next to me, as she had been the whole day, as you can bet I made darn sure of on this trip. I counted heads obsessively and never had a hand free for so much as a Diet Coke, since I hung on to both Margaret and Page as much as possible.

Somehow, though, I let go. I fished out a lone size S T-shirt featuring Minnie with flowers from deep within a rack full of size S tees featuring Minnie with butterflies, and she suddenly wasn't there. Vanished, in two nanoseconds—and I am not just saying it was nanoseconds when really it was five or ten minutes, like you hear anguished parents say when their kids disappear and wind up drowned in a pool two miles away and you wonder whether they are being completely candid. It was *nanoseconds!*

Same drill: panicked loser mom, cool security guard, incredulous dad, slackjawed gawkers . . . and then a second smiling Mouse cop appearing with child in hand. Page had been mesmerized by a tower of plush Tiggers a few feet away.

"Happens every five minutes," reassured the guard.

I believe him.

There are no instant replays. You will do the wrong thing. You will say the wrong thing. You will do the right thing but get the wrong result. And there's no going back. (Although who's to say what was right or wrong until it all works out just fine? Or doesn't.)

Parenthood keeps on moving forward. All you can do is dust yourself off and keep moving with it.

Momfidence...

. . . is buying the colorful socks anyway and enjoying them as long as you can.

No Mom Is an Island
On Strength in Numbers

Oughta *put in some qualifiers about how one swat on the tush per blue moon isn't an endorsement of child abuse or anything. Shoulda added more references to how crazy I am about my kids—no matter how crazy they make me. Shoulda made it more abundantly clear that I couldn't do what I do without Daddyo (and that half the time when I'm writing "I," I'm meaning "we.")*

Coulda presented my ideas with copious footnotes so readers would Take Me Seriously—if only I'd paid attention when Henry was showing me all the cool things my computer could do, like make footnotes.

Woulda surprised the children with homemade chocolate chip cookies after school today, if I hadn't already nibbled the last of the chocolate chips straight from the sack. Coulda nipped this nervous habit of noshing chocolate every time I'm on a deadline, if only I were a Stronger Person, a Better Mother, and a More Responsible Global Citizen—or just had more willpower.

So what if I actually remembered to turn in the Scholastic book order forms to the right teachers on time this month? I forgot Preschool Snack Day again!

Finishing chocolate, −25 points. Forgetting snack, −50 points. Wasting mental energy on self-flagellation that might have been put to better use studying latest lists of boldfaced parenting tips for personal and professional edification, −1,000 points.

Realizing that I've probably already heard—and confidently ignored—the latest lists of boldfaced parenting tips but feel guilty about even this—oh, how low can this infernal internal scoreboard go?

Tilt! Tilt! Game over!

See how the pesky momologues weasel into my brain even when I'm sitting here minding my own business?

Even when I know I'm right?

I met a mother of ten—ten!—who still hears 'em.

I know another mom all the way at the finish line—which I like to think of as college graduation, not a minute later—who's still gnawing over the time she let her son quit Webelo Scouts in the fourth grade. She hears 'em, too.

Heck, I've just written a whole book about trusting your gut, not your guilt, and still the voice in my head whispers, *Really?*

Are you sure?

You left out . . .

How dare you say that!

As Page says when she needs to catch her breath from laughing too hard while playing Big Tiger and Baby Tiger with Daddyo, "Pause the game, Dad! Pause the game!"

Whether you're an old hand or a newbie, brimming with Momfidence or still working on it, the second-guessing and woulda-coulda-shouldas just keep yammering away.

As much as I'd like to report that I've discovered the cure for the common guilt, I no longer think such a thing is possible. This spigot has no shut-off valve. There's just too much in the pipeline. Like the mystery grime that collects behind the faucets, like the detritus that accumulates in the minivan, I've simply learned to live around it.

Tune out the pesky whispers. Tune in to what's real.

Recent backseat haul: Three pencils (two broken, one unsharpened), one pink left sandal (child's size 9), one blue raspberry Dum Dum wrapper, one smashed and likely stale graham cracker, one star-shaped pencil eraser, six pennies, one nickel, numerous playground pebbles, fluorescent-green swim goggles, a slightly damp and moldy towel, a paraplegic Strawberry Shortcake doll (bad dog, Brownie!), the long-lost library book I just paid the $25 library fine to replace, and—unremoveable, unmistakable—the faint aroma of french fries.

"I'm worried moms will think I'm too glib and laid-back," I say to Daddyo when he finds me slumped over my iMac with chocolate on my breath.

"You are glib and laid-back," he says.

"Oh."

"But that's good! People need to hear about Momfidence!" he bolsters. "You are Momfidence personified!"

Maybe I look dubious. Or tired. Because he adds, "You're just not very writer-fident at the moment. Go to bed."

Bed! I glance at the clock. *Nine forty-five already?*

"I've been trying to finish this book. I need to get Page in bed." In fact I should have done the former two weeks ago and the latter one hour and forty-five minutes ago. At last glance—just before the usual bedtime—Margaret had been reading *Hop on Pop* to her sister. The scene was so sweet and unexpected that I had quietly backed out of the room and let them be—though, hmmm, you'd have to go through an awful lot of Dr. Seuss Bright and Early

Books for Beginning Beginners to fill an hour and forty-five minutes . . . What *have* they been up to?

And where's everybody else? Surely Henry and Eleanor are not still playing outside now that it's dark? What's Daddyo been doing—hey, was that a cold evening beverage in his hand? How can he unwind already when I'm still so wound up myself?

I sigh, then switch on the maternal autopilot. "Where are the kids? How did it get so late? They should all be in bed!"

"Look out the window. Catching fireflies. It's Saturday," answers Mr. Momfidence, heading to the sofa, sipping. "They're fine."

Of course they are. Luckily, for every self-imposed expectation, every expert, every talking head full of answers, and every apparently perfect mom "out there" who makes me hyperventilate, there are plenty of souls closer to home who restore my normal breathing. Many of them live under this very roof, in fact. Well, okay, Daddyo and the children sometimes make me breathe faster than normal, each in their own way, but on the whole they have a relatively calming effect. I know I'm definitely happiest when I'm around them (which is not true of the company of the aforementioned negative influences).

My e-mail in-box dings. My sometime walking buddy Carol is checking if we are still on for Monday.

"Sure," I fire back, "so long as I finish this chapter this weekend and E's sore throat doesn't keep her home sick from school (tho she's outside catching fireflies so she's probably ok) and I get back from Page's teacher conference by 5:30. Something about barking at Circle Time; how long can it take?"

"LOL!" comes Carol's response. "Just call when you're ready. I plan to finish work early to take R to the

dentist and then to her practice and maybe we can walk
by UPS so I can drop off a package of stuff M forgot
when he went back to school last week.

"P.S. Wouldn't worry about the barking—it's not like
she's growling or biting anyone. And she's had all her
shots!"

"LOL back. Ok. Gotta go find children and put them
to bed. Hahahahahahahahahaha . . . [Read as frantic
loonlike sounds]"

Carol, a yoga teacher, quickly sends a final reply. "P.S.
Keep breathing! So that should be Ha. Ha. Ha. Ha. Ha."

TGFM—thank goodness for *mamaraderie*—the camaraderie among
mamas that's the unsung gift to every mother on the planet. Like
Daddyo and my kids, it's another source of bolstering I depend on.
You receive its full benefit simply by virtue of having a child. No
applications to fill out, no meetings to attend. If you're a mom,
you're in.

Mamaraderie uses a language where priorities are understood
without being spelled out. Stressors, too. You hear it on park benches
and in the school parking lot at pickup time, among kindred spirits who tip you off to toy sales, who pass along outgrown Gymboree
sweaters. We watch one another's kids when we have to run to the
doctor. We set another plate for each other's children at the dinner
table without batting an eye. We know the eating quirks, play pas-
sions, and stuffed animals' names of one another's children, as well
as one another's entire household schedules. We never clean up the
house when these moms are dropping by; we don't even have to
apologize for the mess.

Once when I was hugely pregnant, a perfect stranger crawled
up and fetched my panicked toddler from the top of a McDonald's

Play Land structure almost before I'd even recognized my daughter's cry. That's mamaraderie, too.

Put a group of moms together to plan who's bringing what to the class picnic, and if mamaraderie is there, they'll blitz through summer camp tips, favorite beaches, whether Lands' End or L.L. Bean makes better bathing suits, and which kinds of dogs make the best pets long before anyone has ever mentioned the words *potato salad*. Conversely, if the conversation devolves into color coordinating the paper goods and the dubious nutritional merits of potato salad, you must sidle out, fast. That's not mamaraderie; it's mompetition gone mad.

If this comradeship sounds obvious, that's only because it's so taken for granted. Imagine if no one understood why your child fell apart at her birthday party because their kids hadn't done exactly the same thing at their own parties. Or if no one could relate to all that's telegraphed in phrases like "sleeps through the night" and "head lice."

These fellow mamas are not always my prekid friends, or women I might have chosen for friends. We're thrown together by circumstances as random as conceiving within a few months of one another or by virtue of our sons having been seated together at school. And yet I entrust my kids to these women's care, and vice versa.

Fellow walker Carol, whose children are several years older than mine, is unusual in that I met her postkids but not through kids. We were professional acquaintances and, it turned out, neighbors. We became bona fide friends, though, soon after I told her I was writing a book about feeling like the worst mom on earth half the time even though I wrote about parenting for a living. She signed her next e-mail "fellow DMFH who can relate."

"DMFH?" I typed back.

"Dirtmotherfromhell," came the reply. "The only PTA meetings I've ever gone to are 'Back to School' night! I was never the room mother! When the teacher called for volunteers, my kids were strictly instructed to sign me up for NAPKINS!"

A kindred spirit!

"P.S.," she added. "Momfidence is a much happier way to think about it!"

After watching Henry and Eleanor fill a glowing Duke's mayo jar with fireflies, I discover that Page has put herself to bed—an event as rare and thrilling as a comet. She appears to be sleeping inside Noah's ark, surrounded by mounds of teddy bears and all breeds of stuffed animal (including a few creatures created post-ark, like Teletubbies and Olivia the Pig). Adding to the menagerie effect are the facts that she's still wearing her dog costume and holding Ratty close against her pink cheek.

Margaret is still reading on the bedroom floor, amid an impressive heap of *Fox in Socks, Hop on Pop, Green Eggs and Ham,* and the Seuss title I most identify with, *If I Ran the Circus.* Those books were for Page and now she's deep into her own, a recent library pick about her current fascination, weather. (Previous jags have included the human body and the solar system. When she gets to astrophysics— or third grade—I may have to go back to school for a PhD.)

I let her stay up if she promises to go to bed at the end of the chapter, though since it's on killer tornadoes, this is a possible nightmare risk.

Everyone thus occupied, I make a cup of decaf Constant Comment and pad back to my office. The dog pads along behind me, probably hoping for dropped chocolate bits. But counting up my baby chicks and seeing all's well has reenergized me. Maybe I can squeeze in just a tiny bit more work.

I do. For maybe six minutes.

"Mom?"

"Oh. Finished already, Margaroo?"

"Is it hard being a writer?"

"Hard? Um, no. Yes. Sometimes. Why?"

"You were just making faces at your computer."

"Was I? Well, I was just, ah, stretching my face muscles."

"Oh. It looked like the face you made when you were yelling at Henry for sticking his fingers in the birthday cake before the party."

"Really? You're very observant."

"What's 'observant' mean?"

"You're a good watcher."

"You're a good watcher, too, Mom."

"Gee, thanks, Margaret."

"You watch us all the time."

"I sure do."

She frowns thoughtfully. "Is it hard being a mom?"

"Uh, no. Yes. Sometimes. Not really."

How to explain that all four are true at once? That mothering is not as hard as it sometimes looks, not as hard as we make it out to be—though neither is it always a piece of cake. Fruitcake, maybe. Realizing that explaining such distinctions would require many sentences—a whole book of sentences, come to think of it—I offer a hug instead.

"Mom?"

"Hmm?"

"Do you like being a mom?"

Finally an easy one.

"Oh yes!"

Feel warm and fuzzy maternal glow. Hit SAVE on computer and prepare to rise for child bonding. Should we join the firefly catchers? Cuddle and read a chapter together on the aurora borealis? Continue meaningful conversations that offer amazing insights into the wisdom of children and which I will treasure forever?

"Mom?"

"Hmmm?"

"I just remembered why I came down. Can you change my sheets? I think Brownie or Page peed on them."

Oh yes.

Acknowledgments

I've been meaning to write this book for ten years. I used to blame not getting around to it on naps that were too short, but now I see the truth: that I could only write these things by living them. There's nothing like a nonstop decade of diapering to provide a realistic perspective on the whole business.

Deep thanks are due to many friends and loved ones along that way.

My Main Characters
Whom, with the exception of my dear husband, I have capped here at age ten in order to preserve their privacy.

My Starter Family
Sylvester and Eleanore Patyk (aka Mom and Dad, but they like to see their names in print) and my siblings, Pamela, John, Patti, and Paul (who don't always like to see their names in print, especially when I am dredging up old stories about them, but who humor me anyway).

The Editors Who "Got" It
And who encouraged my evolving ideas about Momfidence even before I put a name to it: Janet Chan, Jane Chesnutt, Susan Kane, Lisa Bain, Maura Rhodes, Ellen Breslau, Susan Hayes, Linda Rodgers, Anne Krueger, and Bruce Raskin.

The Midwives
Mark Reiter, Katie McHugh, Shana Drehs, Carol Krucoff, and Patti Anderson.

And the Real Experts
All the wise and generous moms (some dads, too) whom I've interviewed over the years, traded e-mail messages with, or hung out with at birthday parties and on soccer field sidelines.

About the Author

·····························

PAULA SPENCER lives with her husband George and their four children in Chapel Hill, North Carolina. She's the "Momfidence!" columnist (formerly "The Mom Next Door") in *Woman's Day* magazine and a longtime contributing editor of *Parenting* and *Baby Talk*. Her articles have also appeared in many other national magazines and at BabyCenter.com and ParentCenter.com. She's written four books for *Parenting* and coauthored *The Happiest Toddler on the Block* with Harvey Karp, MD. Not least, she's faithfully kept a daily diary since she was nine years old.

Everybody can use more *Momfidence!* Read a bonus chapter and rate your own Momfidence at www.momfidence.com.